T0239298

Docker Management Design Patterns

Swarm Mode on Amazon Web Services

Deepak Vohra

Apress®

Docker Management Design Patterns: Swarm Mode on Amazon Web Services

Deepak Vohra
White Rock, British Columbia, Canada

ISBN-13 (pbk): 978-1-4842-2972-9   ISBN-13 (electronic): 978-1-4842-2973-6
https://doi.org/10.1007/978-1-4842-2973-6

Library of Congress Control Number: 2017955383

Copyright © 2017 by Deepak Vohra

This work is subject to copyright. All rights are reserved by the Publisher, whether the whole or part of the material is concerned, specifically the rights of translation, reprinting, reuse of illustrations, recitation, broadcasting, reproduction on microfilms or in any other physical way, and transmission or information storage and retrieval, electronic adaptation, computer software, or by similar or dissimilar methodology now known or hereafter developed.

Trademarked names, logos, and images may appear in this book. Rather than use a trademark symbol with every occurrence of a trademarked name, logo, or image we use the names, logos, and images only in an editorial fashion and to the benefit of the trademark owner, with no intention of infringement of the trademark.

The use in this publication of trade names, trademarks, service marks, and similar terms, even if they are not identified as such, is not to be taken as an expression of opinion as to whether or not they are subject to proprietary rights.

While the advice and information in this book are believed to be true and accurate at the date of publication, neither the authors nor the editors nor the publisher can accept any legal responsibility for any errors or omissions that may be made. The publisher makes no warranty, express or implied, with respect to the material contained herein.

Cover image by Freepik (`www.freepik.com`)

Managing Director: Welmoed Spahr
Editorial Director: Todd Green
Acquisitions Editor: Steve Anglin
Development Editor: Matthew Moodie
Technical Reviewers: Michael Irwin and Massimo Nardone
Coordinating Editor: Mark Powers
Copy Editor: Kezia Endsley

Distributed to the book trade worldwide by Springer Science+Business Media New York, 233 Spring Street, 6th Floor, New York, NY 10013. Phone 1-800-SPRINGER, fax (201) 348-4505, e-mail orders-ny@springer-sbm.com, or visit `www.springeronline.com`. Apress Media, LLC is a California LLC and the sole member (owner) is Springer Science + Business Media Finance Inc (SSBM Finance Inc). SSBM Finance Inc is a **Delaware** corporation.

For information on translations, please e-mail rights@apress.com, or visit `http://www.apress.com/rights-permissions`.

Apress titles may be purchased in bulk for academic, corporate, or promotional use. eBook versions and licenses are also available for most titles. For more information, reference our Print and eBook Bulk Sales web page at `http://www.apress.com/bulk-sales`.

Any source code or other supplementary material referenced by the author in this book is available to readers on GitHub via the book's product page, located at `www.apress.com/9781484229729`. For more detailed information, please visit `http://www.apress.com/source-code`.

Printed on acid-free paper

Contents at a Glance

Contents

About the Author

Deepak Vohra is an Oracle certified Java programmer and web component developer. Deepak has published in several journals, including *Oracle Magazine, OTN, IBM developerWorks, ONJava, DevSource, WebLogic Developer's Journal, XML Journal, Java Developer's Journal, FTPOnline*, and *devx*. Deepak has published three other books on Docker, and a dozen other books on other topics. Deepak is also a Docker Mentor.

About the Technical Reviewers

Michael Irwin is an Application Architect at Virginia Tech (Go Hokies!) where he's both a developer and evangelist for cutting-edge technologies. He is helping Virginia Tech adopt Docker, cloud services, single-page applications, CI/CD pipelines, and other current development practices. As a Docker Captain and a local meetup organizer, he is very active in the Docker community giving presentations and trainings to help others learn how to best utilize Docker in their organizations. Find him on Twitter at @mikesir87.

Massimo Nardone has more than 23 years of experience in security, web/mobile development, and cloud and IT architecture. His true IT passions are security and Android systems.

He has been programming and teaching people how to program with Android, Perl, PHP, Java, VB, Python, C/C++, and MySQL for more than 20 years.

He holds a Master's of Science degree in Computing Science from the University of Salerno, Italy.

He worked as a project manager, software engineer, research engineer, chief security architect, information security manager, PCI/SCADA auditor, and senior lead IT security/cloud/SCADA architect for many years.

His technical skills include security, Android, cloud, Java, MySQL, Drupal, Cobol, Perl, web and mobile development, MongoDB, D3, Joomla, Couchbase, C/C++, WebGL, Python, Pro Rails, Django CMS, Jekyll, Scratch, and more.

He worked as a visiting lecturer and supervisor for exercises at the Networking Laboratory of the Helsinki University of Technology (Aalto University). He holds four international patents (in the PKI, SIP, SAML, and Proxy areas).

He currently works as the Chief Information Security Office (CISO) for Cargotec Oyj and is a member of ISACA, Finland Chapter Board.

Massimo has reviewed more than 40 IT books for different publishers and he is the coauthor of *Pro Android Games* (Apress, 2015).

Introduction

Docker, made available as open source in March 2013, has become the de facto containerization platform. The Docker Engine by itself does not provide functionality to create a distributed Docker container cluster or the ability to scale a cluster of containers, schedule containers on specific nodes, or mount a volume. The book is about orchestrating Docker containers with the Docker-native Swarm mode, which was introduced July 2016 with Docker 1.12. Docker Swarm mode should not be confused with the legacy standalone Docker Swarm, which is not discussed in the book. The book discusses all aspects of orchestrating/managing Docker, including creating a Swarm, using mounts, scheduling, scaling, resource management, rolling updates, load balancing, high availability, logging and monitoring, using multiple zones, and networking. The book also discusses the managed services for Docker Swarm: Docker for AWS and Docker Cloud Swarm mode.

Docker Swarm Design Patterns

"A software design pattern is a general reusable solution to a commonly occurring problem within a given context in software design." (Wikipedia)

Docker Swarm mode provides several features that are general-purpose solutions to issues inherent in a single Docker Engine. Each chapter starting with Chapter 2 introduces a problem and discusses a design pattern as a solution to the problem.

Why Docker Swarm Mode?

Why use the Docker Swarm mode when several container cluster managers are available? Docker Swarm mode is Docker-native and does not require the complex installation that some of the other orchestration frameworks do. A managed service Docker for AWS is available for Docker Swarm to provision a Swarm on production-ready AWS EC2 nodes. Docker Cloud may be linked to Docker for AWS to provision a new Swarm or connect to an existing Swarm. Docker 1.13 includes support for deploying a Docker Stack (collection of services) on Docker Swarm with Docker Compose.

What the Book Covers

Chapter 1 introduces running a Docker standalone container on CoreOS Linux. The chapter establishes the basis of the book and subsequent chapters discuss how the management design patterns provided by the Swarm mode solve problems inherent in a standalone Docker Engine.

Chapter 2 introduces the Swarm mode, including initializing a Swarm and joining worker nodes to the Swarm. Chapter 2 includes promoting/demoting a node, making a node (manager or worker) leave a Swarm, reinitializing a Swarm, and modifying node availability.

Chapter 3 discusses the managed service Docker for AWS, which provisions a Docker Swarm by supplying the Swarm parameters, including the number of managers and workers and the type of EC2 instances to use. AWS uses an AWS CloudFormation to create the resources for a Swarm. Docker for AWS makes it feasible to create a Swarm across multiple AWS zones.

Chapter 4 is about Docker services. Two types of services are defined—replicated and global. Chapter 4 discusses creating a service (replicated and global), scaling a replicated service, listing service tasks, and updating a service.

Chapter 5 discusses scaling replicated services in more detail, including scaling multiple services simultaneously. Global services are not scalable.

In Chapter 6, two types of mounts are defined: a *bind* mount and *volume* mount. This chapter discusses creating and using each type of mount.

Chapter 7 is about configuring and using resources in a Swarm. Two types of resources are supported for configuration: memory and CPU. Two types of resource configurations are defined: *reserves* and *limits*. It discusses creating a service with and without resources specification.

Chapter 8 discusses scheduling service tasks with the default and custom scheduling. Scheduling constraints are also discussed.

Chapter 9 discusses rolling updates, including setting a rolling update policy. Different types of rolling updates are provisioned, including updating to a different Docker image tag, adding/removing environment variables, updating resource limits/reserves, and updating to a different Docker image.

Chapter 10 is about networking in Swarm mode, including the built-in overlay networking called *ingress* and support for creating a custom overlay network.

Chapter 11 is about logging and monitoring in a Swarm, which does not provide a built-in support for logging and monitoring. Logging and monitoring is provided in a Swarm with a Sematext Docker agent, which sends metrics to a SPM dashboard and logs to a Logsene user interface and Kibana.

Chapter 12 discusses load balancing across service tasks with *ingress* load balancing. An external AWS elastic load balancer may also be added for distributing client requests across the EC2 instances on which a Swarm is based.

Chapter 13 discusses developing a highly available website that uses an Amazon Route 53 to create a hosted zone with resource record sets configured in a Primary/Secondary failover mode.

Chapter 14 discusses another managed service, Docker Cloud, which may be used to provision a Docker Swarm or connect to an existing Swarm.

Chapter 15 discusses Docker service stacks. A *stack* is a collection of services that have dependencies among them and are defined in a single configuration file for deployment.

Who this Book Is For

The primary audience of this book includes Docker admins, Docker application developers, and Container as a Service (CaaS) admins and developers. Some knowledge of Linux and introductory knowledge of Docker—such as using a Docker image to run a Docker container, connecting to a container using a bash shell, and stopping and removing a Docker container—is required.

CHAPTER 1

Getting Started with Docker

Docker has become the de facto containerization platform. The main appeal of Docker over virtual machines is that it is lightweight. Whereas a virtual machine packages a complete OS in addition to the application binaries, a Docker container is a lightweight abstraction at the application layer, packaging only the code and dependencies required to run an application. Multiple Docker containers run as isolated processes on the same underlying OS kernel. Docker is supported on most commonly used OSes, including several Linux distributions, Windows, and MacOS. Installing Docker on any of these platforms involves running several commands and also setting a few parameters. CoreOS Linux has Docker installed out-of-the-box. We will get started with using Docker Engine on CoreOS in this chapter. This chapter sets the context of the subsequent chapters, which discuss design patterns for managing Docker Engine using the Swarm mode. This chapter does not use Swarm mode and provides a contrast to using the Swarm mode. This chapter includes the following sections:

- Setting the environment
- Running a Docker application

Setting the Environment

We will be using CoreOS on Amazon Web Services (AWS) EC2, which you can access at `https://console.aws.amazon.com/ec2/v2/home?region=us-east-1#`. Click on Launch Instance to lauch an EC2 instance. Next, choose an Amazon Machine Image (AMI) for CoreOS. Click on AWS Marketplace to find a CoreOS AMI. Type CoreOS in the search field to find a CoreOS AMI. Select the Container Linux by CoreOS (Stable), as shown in the EC2 wizard in Figure 1-1, to launch an instance.

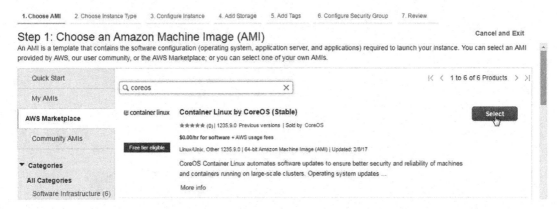

Figure 1-1. *Selecting an AMI for CoreOS Linux*

© Deepak Vohra 2017

D. Vohra, *Docker Management Design Patterns*, https://doi.org/10.1007/978-1-4842-2973-6_1

From Choose an Instance Type, choose the t2.micro Type and click on Next. In Configure Instance Details, specify the number of instances as 1. Select a network or click on Create New VPC to create a new VPC. Select a subnet or click on Create New Subnet to create a new subnet. Select Enable for Auto-Assign Public IP. Click on Next.

From Add Storage, select the default settings and click on Next. In Add Tags, no tags need to be added. Click on Next. From Configure Security Group, add a security group to allow all traffic of any protocol in all port ranges from any source (0.0.0.0/0). Click on Review and Launch and subsequently click on Launch.

Select a key pair and click on Launch Instances in the Select an Existing Key Pair or Create a New Key Pair dialog, as shown in Figure 1-2.

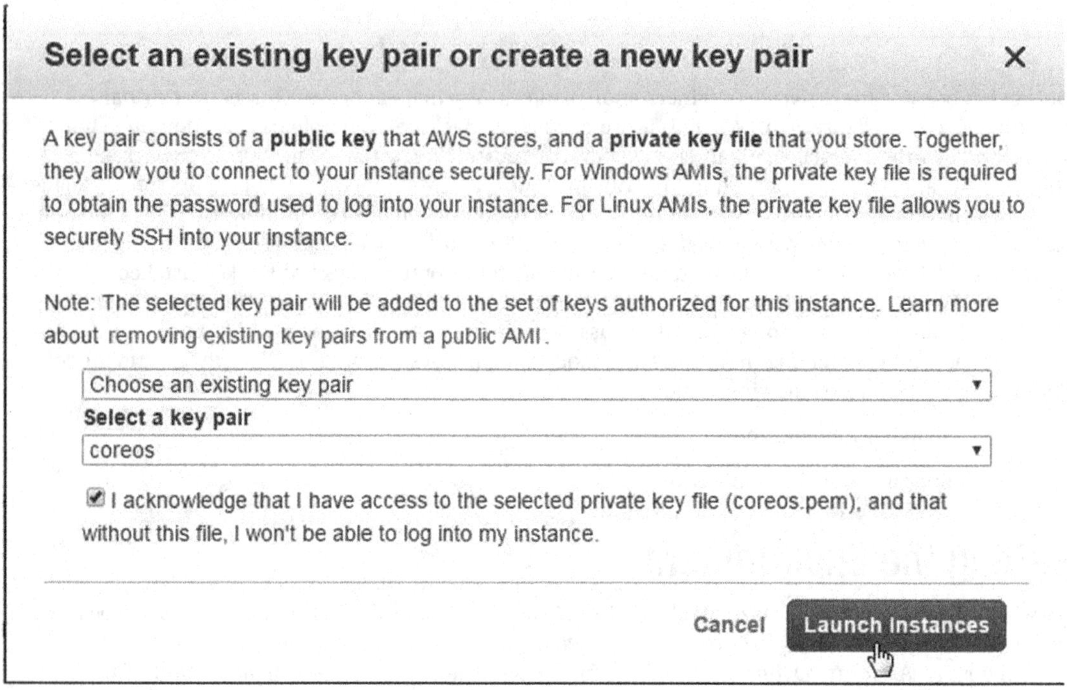

Figure 1-2. *Launch instances*

An EC2 instance with CoreOS is launched. Obtain the public DNS or IPv4 public IP address of the EC2 instance from the EC2 Console, as shown in Figure 1-3, to SSH login into the instance.

Figure 1-3. *Public DNS and public IPv4*

SSH login into the EC2 instance as user "core".

```
ssh -i "coreos.pem"  core@<public ip>
```

Running a Docker Application

As mentioned earlier, Docker is pre-installed on CoreOS. Run the docker command to list its usage, as shown in the following bash shell:

```
core@ip-172-30-4-75 ~ $ docker
Usage: docker [OPTIONS] COMMAND [arg...]
       docker [ --help | -v | --version ]
A self-sufficient runtime for containers.
Options:
  --config=~/.docker          Location of client config files
  -D, --debug                 Enable debug mode
  -H, --host=[]               Daemon socket(s) to connect to
  -h, --help                  Print usage
  -l, --log-level=info        Set the logging level
  --tls                       Use TLS; implied by --tlsverify
  --tlscacert=~/.docker/ca.pem    Trust certs signed only by this CA
  --tlscert=~/.docker/cert.pem    Path to TLS certificate file
  --tlskey=~/.docker/key.pem      Path to TLS key file
  --tlsverify                 Use TLS and verify the remote
  -v, --version               Print version information and quit

Commands:
    attach    Attach to a running container
    build     Build an image from a Dockerfile
    commit    Create a new image from a container's changes
```

3

```
cp          Copy files/folders between a container and the local filesystem
create      Create a new container
diff        Inspect changes on a container's filesystem
```

Output the Docker version using the docker version command. For native Docker Swarm support, the Docker version must be 1.12 or later as listed in the bash shell output.

```
core@ip-172-30-4-75 ~ $ docker version
Client:
 Version:      1.12.6
 API version:  1.24
 Go version:   go1.7.5
 Git commit:   a82d35e
 Built:        Mon Jun 19 23:04:34 2017
 OS/Arch:      linux/amd64

Server:
 Version:      1.12.6
 API version:  1.24
 Go version:   go1.7.5
 Git commit:   a82d35e
 Built:        Mon Jun 19 23:04:34 2017
 OS/Arch:      linux/amd64
```

Run a Hello World app with the tutum/hello-world Docker image.

```
docker run -d -p 8080:80 --name helloapp tutum/hello-world
```

The Docker image is pulled and a Docker container is created, as shown in the following listing.

```
core@ip-172-30-4-75 ~ $ docker run -d -p 8080:80 --name helloapp tutum/hello-world
Unable to find image 'tutum/hello-world:latest' locally
latest: Pulling from tutum/hello-world
658bc4dc7069: Pull complete
a3ed95caeb02: Pull complete
af3cc4b92fa1: Pull complete
d0034177ece9: Pull complete
983d35417974: Pull complete
Digest: sha256:0d57def8055178aafb4c7669cbc25ec17f0acdab97cc587f30150802da8f8d85
Status: Downloaded newer image for tutum/hello-world:latest
1b7a85df6006b41ea1260b5ab957113c9505521cc8732010d663a5e236097502
```

List the Docker container using the docker ps command.

```
core@ip-172-30-4-75 ~ $ docker ps
CONTAINER ID    IMAGE               COMMAND             CREATED         STATUS
PORTS                   NAMES
1b7a85df6006    tutum/hello-world   "/bin/sh -c 'php-fpm "   19 minutes ago  Up 19 minutes
0.0.0.0:8080->80/tcp    helloapp
```

The port mapping for the Docker container is also listed using the docker ps command, but it may also be obtained using the docker port <container> command.

```
core@ip-172-30-4-75 ~ $ docker port helloapp
80/tcp -> 0.0.0.0:8080
```

Using the 8080 port and localhost, invoke the Hello World application with curl.

```
curl localhost:8080
```

The HTML markup for the Hello World application is output, as listed shown here.

```
core@ip-172-30-4-75 ~ $ curl localhost:8080
<html>
<head>
        <title>Hello world!</title>
        <link href='http://fonts.googleapis.com/css?family=Open+Sans:400,700'
         rel='stylesheet' type='text/css'>
        <style>
        body {
                background-color: white;
                text-align: center;
                padding: 50px;
                font-family: "Open Sans","Helvetica Neue",Helvetica,Arial,sans-serif;
        }
        #logo {
                margin-bottom: 40px;
        }
        </style>
</head>
<body>
        <img id="logo" src="logo.png" />
        <h1>Hello world!</h1>
        <h3>My hostname is 1b7a85df6006</h3>
</body>
</html>
```

Using the public DNS for the EC2 instance, the Hello World application may also be invoked in a browser. This is shown in the web browser in Figure 1-4.

5

Figure 1-4. Invoking the Hello World application in a web browser

The docker stop <container> command stops a Docker container. The docker rm <container> command removes a Docker container. You can list Docker images using the docker images command. A Docker image may be removed using the docker rmi <image> command.

```
core@ip-172-30-4-75 ~ $ docker stop helloapp
helloapp
core@ip-172-30-4-75 ~ $ docker rm helloapp
helloapp
core@ip-172-30-4-75 ~ $ docker images
REPOSITORY          TAG             IMAGE ID           CREATED          SIZE
tutum/hello-world   latest          31e17b0746e4       19 months ago    17.79 MB
core@ip-172-30-4-75 ~ $ docker rmi tutum/hello-world
Untagged: tutum/hello-world:latest
Untagged: tutum/hello-world@sha256:0d57def8055178aafb4c7669cbc25ec17f0acdab97cc587f30150802da8f8d85
Deleted: sha256:31e17b0746e48958b27f1d3dd4fe179fbba7e8efe14ad7a51e964181a92847a6
Deleted: sha256:e1bc9d364d30cd2530cb673004dbcdf1eae0286e41a0fb217dd14397bf9debc8
Deleted: sha256:a1f3077d3071bd3eed5bbe5c9c036f15ce3f6b4b36bdd77601f8b8f03c6f874f
Deleted: sha256:ff7802c271f507dd79ad5661ef0e8c7321947c145f1e3cd434621fa869fa648d
Deleted: sha256:e38b71a2478cad712590a0eace1e08f100a293ee19a181d5f5d5a3cdb0663646
Deleted: sha256:5f27c27ccc6daedbc6ee05562f96f719d7f0bb38d8e95b1c1f23bb9696d39916
Deleted: sha256:fab20b60d8503ff0bc94ac3d25910d4a10f366d6da1f69ea53a05bdef469426b
Deleted: sha256:a58990fe25749e088fd9a9d2999c9a17b51921eb3f7df925a00205207a172b08
core@ip-172-30-4-75 ~ $
```

Summary

This chapter sets the basis for subsequent chapters by using a single Docker Engine on CoreOS. Subsequent chapters explore the different design patterns for managing distributed Docker applications in a cluster. The next chapter introduces the Docker Swarm mode.

■ ■ ■

CHAPTER 2

Using Docker in Swarm Mode

The Docker Engine is a containerization platform for running Docker containers. Multiple Docker containers run in isolation on the same underlying operating system kernel, with each container having its own network and filesystem. Each Docker container is an encapsulation of the software and dependencies required for an application and does not incur the overhead of packaging a complete OS, which could be several GB. Docker applications are run from Docker images in Docker containers, with each Docker image being specific to a particular application or software. A Docker image is built from a *Dockerfile*, with a Dockerfile defining the instruction set to be used to download and install software, set environment variables, and run commands.

The Problem

While the Docker Engine pre-1.12 (without native Swarm mode) is well designed for running applications in lightweight containers, it lacks some features, the following being the main ones.

- *No distributed computing*—No distributed computing is provided, as a Docker Engine is installed and runs on a single node or OS instance.

- *No fault tolerance*—As shown in the diagram in Figure 2-1, if the single node on which a Docker Engine is running fails, the Docker applications running on the Docker Engine fail as well.

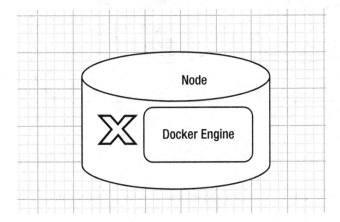

Figure 2-1. *Single node Docker cluster*

© Deepak Vohra 2017

D. Vohra, *Docker Management Design Patterns*, https://doi.org/10.1007/978-1-4842-2973-6_2

The Solution

With Docker Engine version 1.12 onward, Docker container orchestration is built into the Docker Engine in *Swarm mode* and is native to the Docker Engine. Using the Swarm mode, a swarm (or cluster) of nodes distributed across multiple machines (OS instances) may be run in a master/worker/ pattern. Docker Swarm mode is not enabled in the Docker Engine by default and has to be initialized using a docker command. Next, as an introduction to the Docker Swarm mode, we introduce some terminology.

Docker Swarm Mode

Docker Swarm is a cluster of Docker hosts connected by an overlay networking for service discovery. A Docker Swarm includes one or more *manager nodes* and one or more *worker nodes,* as shown in Figure 2-2. In the Swarm mode, a Docker service is the unit of Docker containerization. Docker containers for a service created from a Manager node are deployed or scheduled across the cluster and the Swarm includes a built-in load balancing for scaling the services. The expected state for a service is declared on the manager, which then schedules the task to be run on a node. However, the worker node itself still pulls the image and starts the container.

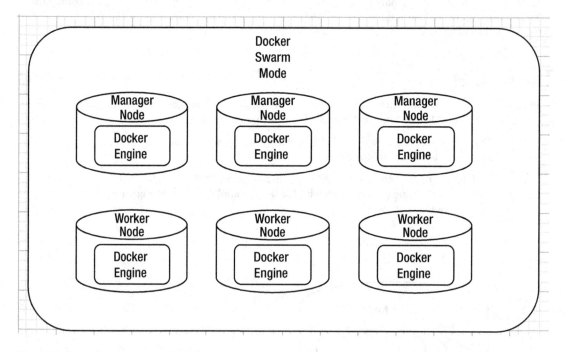

Figure 2-2. *Docker Swarm mode cluster*

Nodes

An instance of a Docker host (a Docker Engine) is called a *node*. Two types of node roles are provided: *manager nodes* and *worker nodes*.

Service

A *service* is an abstraction for a collection of tasks (also called replicas or replica tasks) distributed across a Swarm. As an example, a service could be running three replicas of an Nginx server. Default scheduling, which is discussed in Chapter 7, uses the "spread" scheduling strategy, which spreads the tasks across the nodes of the cluster based on a computed node rank. A service consists of one or more tasks that run independent of each other, implying that stopping a task or starting a new task does not affect running other tasks. The Nginx service running on three nodes could consist of three replica tasks. Each task runs a Docker container for the service. One node could be running multiple tasks for a service. A task is an abstraction for the atomic unit of scheduling, a "slot" for the scheduler to run a Docker container.

Desired State of a Service

The "desired state" of a service refers to the service state as defined in the service definition when creating the service. As an example, a service definition could define a service as consisting of three replicas of an Nginx server.

Manager Node and Raft Consensus

When the Swarm is first created, the current node becomes the first manager node. By default, all manager nodes are also workers. The manager node performs the cluster orchestration and manages the Swarm, including the initial scheduling of service tasks and subsequent reconciliation, if any, between the desired state and the actual state of services. As an example, for a service definition consisting of three replicas of an Nginx server, the manager node would create three tasks and schedule the tasks on Swarm worker nodes in the Swarm. Subsequently, if a node running a task were to fail, the Swarm manager would start a new replacement task on the worker nodes still in the Swarm. The Swarm manager accepts the service definition when a service is created and schedules the service on one or more worker nodes as service tasks. The Swarm manager node also manages the scaling of service by adding/removing service tasks. The Swarm manager assigns each service a unique DNS name and starts Docker containers via service replica tasks. The manager node monitors the cluster state. The Swarm manager is also a worker node by default, which is discussed in the next section.

To refer to "the manager node" is actually a simplification of the Swarm Manager, as a Swarm may consist of one or more manager nodes. Each manager node keeps the complete cluster state data, including which service replica tasks are running on which node and the node roles, and participates in Swarm management for the *Raft consensus*. The Raft consensus is merely an algorithm to create decisions/agreements (consensus) within a group in a distributed fashion. Swarm uses it to make decisions such as leader elections, cluster membership, service changes, etc. In the Swarm mode, Raft consensus is an agreement among the manager nodes for a global cluster state parameter such as about the state of data value stored in a database. Swarm managers share data using Raft. Raft consensus is a protocol for implementing distributed consensus among all the reachable manager nodes in a Swarm. The Raft Consensus Algorithm has several implementations and its implementation in the Swarm mode has the properties typically found in distributed systems, such as the following:

- Agreement of values for fault tolerance

- Cluster membership management

- Leader election using mutual exclusion

Only one manager node, called the *leader,* performs all the cluster orchestration and management. Only the leader node performs the service scheduling, scaling, and restarting of service tasks. The other manager nodes are for the fault tolerance of Swarm manager, which implies that if the leader node were to fail, one of the other manager nodes would be elected as the new leader and take over the cluster management. Leader election is performed by a consensus from the majority of the manager nodes.

Worker Nodes

A worker node actually runs the service replica tasks and the associated Docker containers. The differentiation between node roles as manager nodes and worker nodes is not handled at service deployment time but is handled at runtime, as node roles may be promoted/demoted. Promoting/demoting a node is discussed in a later section. Worker nodes do not affect the manager Raft consensus. Worker nodes only increase the capacity of the Swarm to run service replica tasks. The worker nodes themselves do not contribute to the voting and state held in the raft, but the fact that they are worker nodes is held within the raft. As running a service task requires resources (CPU and memory) and a node has a certain fixed allocatable resources, the capacity of a Swarm is limited by the number of worker nodes in the Swarm.

Quorum

A *quorum* refers to agreement among the majority of Swarm manager nodes or managers. If a Swarm loses quorum it cannot perform any management or orchestration functions. The service tasks already scheduled are not affected and continue to run. The new service tasks are not scheduled and other management decisions requiring a consensus, such as adding or removing a node, are not performed. All Swarm managers are counted toward determining majority consensus for fault tolerance. For leader election only the reachable manager nodes are included for Raft consensus. Any Swarm update, such as the addition or removal of a node or the election of a new leader, requires a quorum. *Raft consensus* and *quorum* are the same. For high availability, three to five Swarm managers are recommended in production. An odd number of Swarm managers is recommended in general. *Fault tolerance* refers to the tolerance for failure of Swarm manager nodes or the number of Swarm managers that may fail without making a Swarm unavailable. Mathematically, "majority" refers to more than half, but for the Swarm mode Raft consensus algorithm, Raft tolerates $(N-1)/2$ failures and a majority for Raft consensus is determined by $(N/2)+1$. N refers to the Swarm size or the number of manager nodes in the Swarm.

```
Swarm Size  = Majority + Fault Tolerance
```

As an example, Swarm sizes of 1 and 2 each have a fault tolerance of 0, as Raft consensus cannot be reached for the Swarm size if any of the Swarm managers were to fail. More manager nodes increase fault tolerance. For an odd number N, the fault tolerance is the same for a Swarm size N and N+1.

As an example, a Swarm with three managers has a fault tolerance of 1, as shown in Figure 2-3. Fault tolerance and Raft consensus do not apply to worker nodes, as Swarm capacity is based only on the worker nodes. Even if two of the three worker nodes were to fail, one Worker node, even if the manager nodes are manager-only nodes, would keep the Swarm available though a reduction in Swarm capacity and could transition some of the running tasks to non-running state.

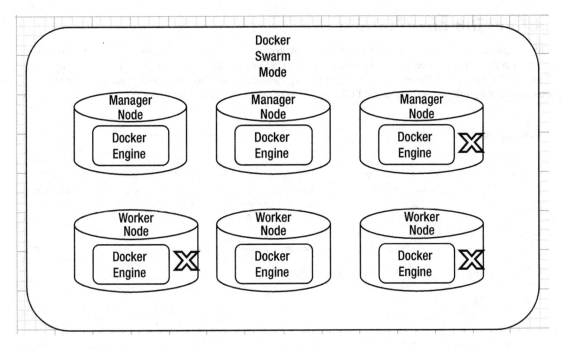

Figure 2-3. *Fault tolerance for a Swarm*

This section covers the following topics:

- Setting the environment
- Initializing the Docker Swarm mode
- Joining nodes to the Swarm cluster
- Testing the Swarm cluster
- Promoting a worker node to manager
- Demoting a manager node to worker
- Making a worker node leave the Swarm cluster
- Making A worker node rejoin the Swarm cluster
- Making a manager node leave the Swarm cluster
- Reinitializing a Swarm
- Modifying node availability
- Removing a node

Setting the Environment

This chapter shows you how to create a three-node Swarm consisting of one manager node and two worker nodes. Create three Amazon EC2 instances using CoreOS Stable AMI, as shown in the EC2 console in Figure 2-4. Enable all traffic between the EC2 instances when configuring the security group for the EC2 instances. Obtain the IP address of the EC2 instance started for the Swarm manager.

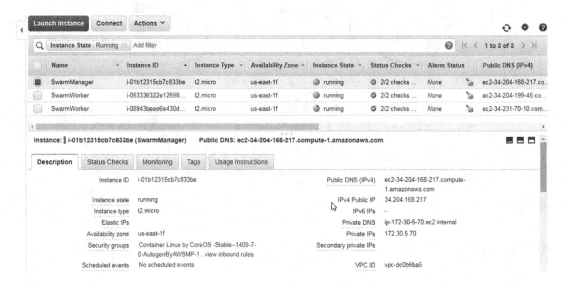

Figure 2-4. *EC2 instances*

Initializing the Docker Swarm Mode

Docker Swarm mode is not enabled by default and needs to be enabled. SSH login to the EC2 instance started for the Swarm manager using the public IP address.

```
ssh -i "coreos.pem" core@34.204.168.217
```

Docker Swarm mode is available starting with Docker version 1.12. Verify that the Docker version is at least 1.12 using the docker --version command.

```
[root@localhost ~]# ssh -i "coreos.pem" core@34.204.168.217
Container Linux by CoreOS stable (1409.7.0)
core@ip-172-30-5-70 ~ $ docker --version
Docker version 1.12.6, build a82d35e
```

To initialize the Swarm, use the docker swarm init options command. Some of the options the command supports are listed in Table 2-1.

Table 2-1. *Command Swarm init Options*

Option	Description	Default Value
--advertise-addr	Advertised address in the format <ip|interface>[:port]. The advertised address is the IP address at which other nodes may access the Swarm. If an IP address is not specified, the Docker ascertains if the system has a single IP address and, if it does, the IP address and port 2337 is used. If the system has multiple IP addresses, the --advertise-addr must be specified for inter-manager communication and overlay networking.	
--availability	Availability of the node. Should be one of active/pause/drain.	active
--force-new-cluster	Whether to force create a new cluster from the current state. We discuss why it may be required to force create and use the option in this chapter.	false
--listen-addr	Listen address in the format <ip|interface>[:port].	0.0.0.0:2377

Use the default values for all options except the --advertise-addr for which a default value is not provided. Use the private address for the advertised address, which may be obtained from the EC2 console, as shown in Figure 2-5. If the EC2 instances on AWS were in different regions, the external public IP address should be used to access the manager node, which may also be obtained from the EC2 console.

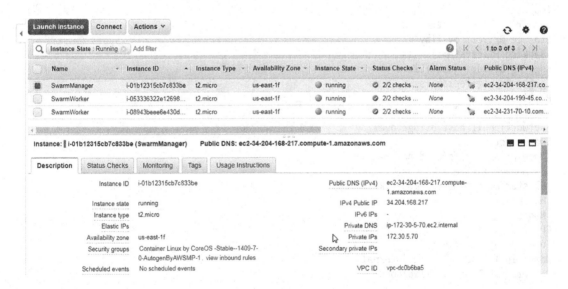

Figure 2-5. *Private IP*

Run the following command to initialize Docker Swarm mode.

```
docker swarm init --advertise-addr 172.30.5.70
```

As the output in the following listing indicates, Swarm is initialized and the current node is a manager node. The command to add a worker node is also included in the output. The command to obtain the command to add a manager node is also output. Copy the docker swarm join command to add a worker node to the Swarm.

```
core@ip-172-30-5-70 ~ $ docker swarm init --advertise-addr 172.30.5.70
Swarm initialized: current node (bgzqx2cfsf05qdradxytmdcp3) is now a manager.

To add a worker to this swarm, run the following command:
    docker swarm join \
    --token SWMTKN-1-3o3zi1rxgkzy5gq5itr580yp9pbagxnkelinzh42ovrb7znt6f-
    dmgeg3veppor942vsavma3s47 \
    172.30.5.70:2377
To add a manager to this swarm, run 'docker swarm join-token manager' and follow the
instructions.
```

Run the docker info command to get system-wide information about the Docker Engine. The command outputs the total number of Docker containers that are running, paused, or stopped; partial output is listed.

```
core@ip-172-30-5-70 ~ $ docker info
Containers: 0
 Running: 0
 Paused: 0
 Stopped: 0
Images: 0
Server Version: 1.12.6
Storage Driver: overlay
 Backing Filesystem: extfs
Logging Driver: json-file
Cgroup Driver: cgroupfs
Plugins:
 Volume: local
 Network: null host bridge overlay
Swarm: active
 NodeID: bgzqx2cfsf05qdradxytmdcp3
 Is Manager: true
 ClusterID: 056zm05kk6em6u7vlki8pbhc9
 Managers: 1
 Nodes: 1
CPUs: 1
Total Memory: 994.6 MiB
Name: ip-172-30-5-70.ec2.internal
Docker Root Dir: /var/lib/docker
```

The Storage Driver is overlay and the backing filesystem is extfs. The logging driver is json-file, which is covered in Chapter 11 on logging. The Swarm is shown to be active. Information about the node such as NodeID, whether the node is a manager, the number of managers in the Swarm, and the number of nodes in the Swarm, is also listed.

The resource capacity (CPU and memory) of the node is also listed. Chapter 7 discusses more about resource usage. The node name is the private DNS of the EC2 instance on which the Swarm is initialized. List the nodes in the Swarm with the following command:

```
docker node ls
```

A single node gets listed including the node ID, which is the only unique parameter for a node. The hostname is also unique if a node has not been made to leave the Swarm and rejoined.

```
core@ip-172-30-5-70 ~ $ docker node ls
ID                              HOSTNAME                      STATUS  AVAILABILITY  MANAGER STATUS
bgzqx2cfsf05qdradxytmdcp3 *  ip-172-30-5-70.ec2.internal  Ready   Active        Leader
```

The * after the node ID indicates that this is the current node. The nodes in the Swarm also have a STATUS, AVAILABILITY, and MANAGER STATUS columns. STATUS can be one of the values listed in Table 2-2.

Table 2-2. *Node Status*

Status	Description
Ready	Ready for use
Down	Not ready for use
Unknown	Not known

AVAILABILITY can be one of the values listed in Table 2-3.

Table 2-3. *AVAILABILITY Column*

Availability	Description
Active	Scheduler may assign tasks to the node.
Pause	Scheduler does not assign new tasks to the node but existing tasks keep running.
Drain	Scheduler does not assign new tasks to the node and existing tasks are shut down. Replacement tasks are started on other nodes.

MANAGER STATUS can be one of the values listed in Table 2-4. If the MANAGER STATUS column has no value, it indicates a worker node.

Table 2-4. *Manager Status*

Manager Status	Description
Reachable	The node participates in the Raft consensus quorum and, if the leader becomes unavailable, the node is eligible to be made the leader node.
Unreachable	The node was a manager node that was reachable but has become unreachable and is not able to communicate with the other manager nodes in the Swarm. An unreachable manager node could be made reachable though not guaranteed to be restored by doing one of the following: -Restart the machine -Restart the daemon If neither of the preceding restores a unreachable manager node, the following should be implemented. Demote and remove the failed node. `docker node demote <NODE>` and `docker node rm <id-node>` Add another manager node with `docker swarm join`. Or Promote a worker node to manager node with `docker node promote`
Leader	Primary manager node that performs all the Swarm management and orchestration.

Joining Nodes to the Swarm

Additional nodes, manager or worker, may be added or joined to the Swarm as required. By default, manager nodes are also worker nodes but not vice versa. The manager nodes are added for a different reason than the worker nodes. The manager nodes are added to make the Swarm more fault tolerant and the worker nodes are added to add capacity to the Swarm. The commands to add manager and worker nodes are also different. The command to add a worker node is output when the Swarm is initialized. The command to add a worker node may also be found using the following command.

```
docker swarm join-token worker
```

The command to add a manager node may be found using the following command.

```
docker swarm join-token manager
```

A reason for adding a worker node is that the service tasks scheduled on some of the nodes are not running and are in `Allocated` state. A reason for adding a manager node is that another manager node has become unreachable.

The node to join, manager or worker, must have Docker Engine version at least 1.12 installed. Next, you add two worker nodes. Obtain the public IP address of an EC2 instance started for a worker node. SSH login to the worker instance.

```
ssh -i "coreos.pem" core@34.204.199.
```

Run the docker swarm join command, which has the following syntax, to join the node to the Swarm as a worker node.

```
docker swarm join [OPTIONS] HOST:PORT
```

The options supported by the docker swarm join command are listed in Table 2-5.

Table 2-5. *Options for docker swarm join Command*

Option	Description	Default Value
--advertise-addr	Advertised address in format <ip|interface>[:port].	
--availability	Availability of the node. One of active/pause/drain.	active
--listen-addr	Listen address in format <ip|interface>[:port].	0.0.0.0:2377
--token	Token for entry into the Swarm.	

Run the docker swarm join command output during the initialization of the Swarm mode to join the worker instance with the Swarm. As the output message indicates, "The node joined the Swarm as a worker."

```
[root@localhost ~]# ssh -i "coreos.pem" core@34.204.199.45
Container Linux by CoreOS stable (1409.7.0)
core@ip-172-30-5-31 ~ $       docker swarm join \
>      --token SWMTKN-1-3o3zi1rxgkzy5gq5itr58oyp9pbagxnkelinzh42ovrb7znt6f-
       dmgeg3veppor942vsavma3s47 \
>      172.30.5.70:2377
This node joined a swarm as a worker.
```

Similarly, SSH login to the other worker instance.

```
ssh -i "coreos.pem" core@34.231.70.10
```

Run the same docker swarm join command and the second nodes joins the Swarm as a worker node.

```
[root@localhost ~]# ssh -i "coreos.pem" core@34.231.70.10
Container Linux by CoreOS stable (1409.7.0)
core@ip-172-30-5-108 ~ $ docker swarm join \
>      --token SWMTKN-1-3o3zi1rxgkzy5gq5itr58oyp9pbagxnkelinzh42ovrb7znt6f-
       dmgeg3veppor942vsavma3s47 \
>      172.30.5.70:2377
This node joined a swarm as a worker.
```

The following sequence of events takes place when the docker swarm join command runs to join a worker node to the Swarm.

1.   The Swarm mode for the Docker Engine on the node is enabled.

2.   A request for a TLS certificate is sent to the manager.

3.   The node is named with the machine hostname.

4.   The current node joins the Swarm at the manager listen address. Based on the token, the node is joined as a worker node or a manager node.

5.   Sets the current node to `Active` availability.

6.   The ingress overlay network is extended to the current node.

When a node is joined to the Swarm using the manager token, the node joins as a manager node. The new manager nodes should be Reachable and only the first manager node is the leader. Leader election to a different manager node occurs only if the initial leader node were to fail or be demoted.

The worker nodes differ from the manager nodes in another regard. A worker node cannot be used to view or modify the cluster state. Only the manager node can be used to view the cluster state such as the nodes in the Swarm. Only the manager node can be used to modify a cluster state such as remove a node. If the `docker node ls` command is run on a worker node, the following error message is generated.

```
core@ip-172-30-5-31 ~ $ docker node ls
Error response from daemon: This node is not a swarm manager. Worker nodes can't be used
to view or modify cluster state. Please run this command on a manager node or promote the
current node to a manager.
```

Testing the Swarm

Next, you deploy a simple Hello World service to the Swarm to test the cluster. List the nodes in the Swarm from the manager node with the following command.

```
docker node ls
```

The three nodes should be listed.

```
core@ip-172-30-5-70 ~ $ docker node ls
ID                          HOSTNAME                        STATUS  AVAILABILITY  MANAGER STATUS
9n5qmj4pp91f0n3s0n2jwjdv8   ip-172-30-5-108.ec2.internal    Ready   Active
bgzqx2cfsf05qdradxytmdcp3 * ip-172-30-5-70.ec2.internal     Ready   Active        Leader
bqq4bryuobylu0glm4p19tko4   ip-172-30-5-31.ec2.internal     Ready   Active
```

How do you tell if a node is a manager node or a worker node? From the Manager Status column. If the Manager Status is empty, the node is a worker node and if the Manager Status has a value, which would be one of the values discussed in Table 2-4, the node is a manager node. Two worker nodes and one manager node are listed.

We already discussed that worker nodes can't be used to view or modify cluster state. Next, create a Docker service using the `docker service create` command, which becomes available only if the Swarm mode is enabled. Using Docker image `alpine`, which is a Linux distribution, create two replicas and ping the `docker.com` domain from the service containers.

```
docker service create --replicas 2 --name helloworld alpine ping docker.com
```

If the preceding command runs without an error, the Docker Swarm installed fine. The command returns the service ID.

```
core@ip-172-30-5-70 ~ $ docker service create --replicas 2 --name helloworld alpine ping
docker.com
bkwskfzqa173dp55j54erg5cg
```

Services may be listed with the following command.

```
docker service ls
```

The service helloworld is listed and the number of replicas is listed as 2/2, which implies that two replicas exist and meet the desired state of two replicas. The REPLICAS column output is ordered "actual/desired". The Docker image is alpine and the command to run the service is ping docker.com.

```
core@ip-172-30-5-70 ~ $ docker service ls
ID                NAME          REPLICAS    IMAGE      COMMAND
bkwskfzqa173      helloworld    2/2         alpine     ping docker.com
```

The docker service inspect command is used to find more information about the service.

```
docker service inspect  helloworld
```

The detailed information about the helloworld service—including the container spec, resources, restart policy, placement, mode, update config, and update status—is listed.

```
core@ip-172-30-5-70 ~ $ docker service inspect  helloworld
[
    {
        "ID": "bkwskfzqa173dp55j54erg5cg",
        "Version": {
            "Index": 22
        },
        "CreatedAt": "2017-07-22T19:11:50.345823466Z",
        "UpdatedAt": "2017-07-22T19:11:50.345823466Z",
        "Spec": {
            "Name": "helloworld",
            "TaskTemplate": {
                "ContainerSpec": {
                    "Image": "alpine",
                    "Args": [
                        "ping",
                        "docker.com"
                    ]
                },
                "Resources": {
                    "Limits": {},
                    "Reservations": {}
                },
                "RestartPolicy": {
                    "Condition": "any",
                    "MaxAttempts": 0
                },
                "Placement": {}
            },
            "Mode": {
                "Replicated": {
                    "Replicas": 2
                }
            },
```

```
            "UpdateConfig": {
                "Parallelism": 1,
                "FailureAction": "pause"
            },
            "EndpointSpec": {
                "Mode": "vip"
            }
        },
        "Endpoint": {
            "Spec": {}
        },
        "UpdateStatus": {
            "StartedAt": "0001-01-01T00:00:00Z",
            "CompletedAt": "0001-01-01T00:00:00Z"
        }
    }
]
```

The replicas and the nodes on which the replicas are placed may be listed with the following command syntax.

```
docker service ps <SERVICE
```

The `<SERVICE>` placeholder is either a service name (like helloworld) or the actual service ID (like bkwskfzqa173 for this example). For the helloworld service, the command becomes:

```
docker service ps helloworld
```

The preceding command also lists the node on which a replica is running. The Docker containers started for a service are listed with same command as before, the docker ps command.

```
core@ip-172-30-5-70 ~ $ docker service ps helloworld
ID                           NAME           IMAGE   NODE                          DESIRED STATE
CURRENT STATE                ERROR
2x8gqd2qbylpkug1kg0pxi1c2    helloworld.1   alpine  ip-172-30-5-70.ec2.internal   Running
Running 34 seconds ago
6twq1v0lr2gflnb6ae19hrpx9    helloworld.2   alpine  ip-172-30-5-108.ec2.internal  Running
Running 34 seconds ago
core@ip-172-30-5-70 ~ $ docker ps
CONTAINER ID        IMAGE           COMMAND             CREATED          STATUS
PORTS               NAMES
acbdaccad6ea        alpine:latest   "ping docker.com"   47 seconds ago   Up 46 seconds
helloworld.1.2x8gqd2qbylpkug1kg0pxi1c2
```

The docker ps command is not a Swarm mode command, but may be run on the worker nodes to find the service containers running on a worker node. The docker ps command gives you all containers running on a node, even if they are not service containers.

```
core@ip-172-30-5-108 ~ $ docker ps
CONTAINER ID        IMAGE               COMMAND             CREATED             STATUS
PORTS               NAMES
74ea31054fb4        alpine:latest       "ping docker.com"   About a minute ago  Up About a minute
helloworld.2.6twq1v0lr2gflnb6ae19hrpx9
```

Only two nodes are listed by the docker service ps helloworld command on which replicas are scheduled, the manager node and one of the worker nodes. The docker ps command on the other worker node does not list any Docker containers.

```
core@ip-172-30-5-31 ~ $ docker ps
CONTAINER ID    IMAGE      COMMAND     CREATED     STATUS      PORTS       NAMES
```

The docker node inspect <node> command is used to get detailed information about a node, such as the node role, availability, hostname, resources capacity, plugins, and status.

```
core@ip-172-30-5-70 ~ $ docker node inspect  ip-172-30-5-70.ec2.internal
[
    {
        "ID": "bgzqx2cfsf05qdradxytmdcp3",
        "Version": {
            "Index": 10
        },
        "CreatedAt": "2017-07-22T19:09:45.647701768Z",
        "UpdatedAt": "2017-07-22T19:09:45.68030039Z",
        "Spec": {
            "Role": "manager",
            "Availability": "active"
        },
        "Description": {
            "Hostname": "ip-172-30-5-70.ec2.internal",
            "Platform": {
                "Architecture": "x86_64",
                "OS": "linux"
            },
            "Resources": {
                "NanoCPUs": 1000000000,
                "MemoryBytes": 1042935808
            },
            "Engine": {
                "EngineVersion": "1.12.6",
                "Plugins": [
                    {
                        "Type": "Network",
                        "Name": "bridge"
                    },
                    {
                        "Type": "Network",
                        "Name": "host"
                    },
```

```
                    {
                        "Type": "Network",
                        "Name": "null"
                    },
                    {
                        "Type": "Network",
                        "Name": "overlay"
                    },
                    {
                        "Type": "Volume",
                        "Name": "local"
                    }
                ]
            }
        },
        "Status": {
            "State": "ready"
        },
        "ManagerStatus": {
            "Leader": true,
            "Reachability": "reachable",
            "Addr": "172.30.5.70:2377"
        }
    }
]
```

A service may be removed with the docker service rm <service> command. Subsequently, the docker service inspect <service> command should not list any replicas and running docker ps will show no more running Docker containers.

```
core@ip-172-30-5-70 ~ $ docker service rm helloworld
helloworld
core@ip-172-30-5-70 ~ $ docker service inspect helloworld
[]
Error: no such service: helloworld
```

Chapter 4 discusses more about services.

Promoting a Worker Node to Manager

As mentioned before, a manager node is also a worker node by default, but a worker node is only a worker node. But a worker node may be promoted to a manager node. The Docker command to promote one or more worker nodes to a manager node has the following syntax.

```
docker node promote NODE [NODE...]
```

The command must be run from the leader node. As an example, promote the node ip-172-30-5-108. ec2.internal. As the output indicates, the node gets promoted to a manager node. Subsequently list the nodes in the Swarm and the node promoted should have manager status as Reachable.

A worker node should preferably be promoted using the node ID; the reason for which is discussed subsequently. Promote another worker node using the node ID. Subsequently, both the worker nodes are listed as Reachable in the Manager Status column.

```
core@ip-172-30-5-70 ~ $ docker node promote  ip-172-30-5-108.ec2.internal
Node ip-172-30-5-108.ec2.internal promoted to a manager in the swarm.
core@ip-172-30-5-70 ~ $ docker node ls
ID                          HOSTNAME                      STATUS  AVAILABILITY  MANAGER STATUS
9n5qmj4pp91f0n3s0n2jwjdv8   ip-172-30-5-108.ec2.internal  Ready   Active        Reachable
bgzqx2cfsf05qdradxytmdcp3 * ip-172-30-5-70.ec2.internal   Ready   Active        Leader
bqq4bryuobylu0glm4p19tko4   ip-172-30-5-31.ec2.internal   Ready   Active
```

Demoting a Manager Node to Worker

A manager node may be demoted to a worker node with the following Docker command.

```
docker node demote NODE [NODE...]
```

Any manager node, including the leader node, may be demoted. As an example, demote the manager node ip-172-30-5-108.ec2.internal.

```
core@ip-172-30-5-70 ~ $ docker node demote  ip-172-30-5-108.ec2.internal
Manager ip-172-30-5-108.ec2.internal demoted in the swarm.
```

Once demoted, the commands such as docker node ls that can be run only from a manager node cannot be run any more on the node. The docker node ls command lists the demoted node as a worker node; no MANAGER STATUS is listed for a worker node.

```
core@ip-172-30-5-70 ~ $ docker node ls
ID                          HOSTNAME                      STATUS  AVAILABILITY  MANAGER STATUS
9n5qmj4pp91f0n3s0n2jwjdv8   ip-172-30-5-108.ec2.internal  Ready   Active
bgzqx2cfsf05qdradxytmdcp3 * ip-172-30-5-70.ec2.internal   Ready   Active        Leader
bqq4bryuobylu0glm4p19tko4   ip-172-30-5-31.ec2.internal   Ready   Active
```

A node should be preferably promoted/demoted and otherwise referred to in any command that is directed at the node using the node ID, which is unique to a node. The reason being that a demoted node, if promoted back, could be added with a different node ID and the docker node ls command could list two node IDs for the same hostname. If the hostname is used to refer to a node, it could result in the node is ambiguous error message.

Making a Worker Node Leave the Swarm

Earlier you joined a node to the Swarm as a worker node. A worker node may also be made to leave the Swarm. As an example, make one of the worker nodes leave with the following command, which must be run from the node you want to remove from the Swarm.

```
docker swarm leave
```

As the message output indicates, the node has left the Swarm.

```
core@ip-172-30-5-31 ~ $ docker swarm leave
Node left the swarm.
```

Similarly, make the other worker node leave the Swarm.

```
core@ip-172-30-5-108 ~ $ docker swarm leave
Node left the swarm.
```

After a worker node has left the Swarm, the node itself is not removed and continues to be listed with the docker node ls command with a Down status.

```
core@ip-172-30-5-70 ~ $ docker node ls
ID                          HOSTNAME                      STATUS  AVAILABILITY  MANAGER STATUS
9n5qmj4pp91f0n3s0n2jwjdv8   ip-172-30-5-108.ec2.internal  Down    Active
bgzqx2cfsf05qdradxytmdcp3 * ip-172-30-5-70.ec2.internal   Ready   Active        Leader
bqq4bryuobylu0glm4p19tko4   ip-172-30-5-31.ec2.internal   Down    Active
```

Making a Manager Node Leave the Swarm

While it is easier to make a worker node leave the Swarm, it is different when a manager node must leave the Swarm. Making a worker node leave the Swarm only lowers the Swarm capacity in terms of the service tasks that may be scheduled in the Swarm. But making a manager node leave the Swarm makes the Swarm less available. If the fault tolerance does not allow for a manager node to fail or be removed from the Swarm, the same docker swarm leave command that made a worker node leave the Swarm cannot be used to make a manager node leave the Swarm. If a Swarm has only one manager node, the docker swarm leave command generates the following error message.

```
core@ip-172-30-5-70 ~ $ docker swarm leave
Error response from daemon: You are attempting to leave the swarm on a node that is
participating as a manager. Removing the last manager erases all current state of the
swarm. Use `--force` to ignore this message.
```

Add the --force option to the docker swarm leave command on the manager node to cause the manager node to leave the Swarm.

```
core@ip-172-30-5-70 ~ $ docker swarm leave --force
Node left the swarm.
```

If the only manager node is removed, the Swarm no longer exists. The Swarm must be initialized again if the Swarm mode is to be used.

```
core@ip-172-30-5-70 ~ $ docker swarm init --advertise-addr 172.30.5.70
Swarm initialized: current node (cnyc2w3n8q8zuxjujcd2s729k) is now a manager.
To add a worker to this swarm, run the following command:
    docker swarm join \
    --token SWMTKN-1-4lxmisvlszjgck4ly0swsxubejfx0phlne1xegho2fiq99amqf-
    11mpscd8gs6bsayzren8fa2ki \
    172.30.5.70:2377
To add a manager to this swarm, run 'docker swarm join-token manager' and follow the
instructions.
```

A new Swarm is created with only the manager node and the Swarm has only one node initially.

```
core@ip-172-30-5-70 ~ $ docker node ls
ID                          HOSTNAME                    STATUS  AVAILABILITY  MANAGER STATUS
cnyc2w3n8q8zuxjujcd2s729k * ip-172-30-5-70.ec2.internal Ready   Active        Leader
```

If a Swarm has two manager nodes, making one of the manager nodes leave the Swarm has a different effect. With two managers, the fault tolerance is 0, as discussed earlier. To create a Swarm with two manager nodes, start with a Swarm that has one manager node and two worker nodes.

```
core@ip-172-30-5-70 ~ $ docker node ls
ID                          HOSTNAME                     STATUS  AVAILABILITY  MANAGER STATUS
4z03hudbo3fz17q94leo24pvh   ip-172-30-5-108.ec2.internal Ready   Active
cnyc2w3n8q8zuxjujcd2s729k * ip-172-30-5-70.ec2.internal  Ready   Active        Leader
efsxwt43iskasa6poh2stkjeb   ip-172-30-5-31.ec2.internal  Ready   Active
```

Promote one of the worker nodes to a manager node.

```
core@ip-172-30-5-70 ~ $ docker node promote ip-172-30-5-108.ec2.internal
Node ip-172-30-5-108.ec2.internal promoted to a manager in the swarm.
```

The Swarm will then have two manager nodes.

```
core@ip-172-30-5-70 ~ $ docker node ls
ID                          HOSTNAME                     STATUS  AVAILABILITY  MANAGER STATUS
4z03hudbo3fz17q94leo24pvh   ip-172-30-5-108.ec2.internal Ready   Active        Reachable
cnyc2w3n8q8zuxjujcd2s729k * ip-172-30-5-70.ec2.internal  Ready   Active        Leader
efsxwt43iskasa6poh2stkjeb   ip-172-30-5-31.ec2.internal  Ready   Active
```

Run the docker swarm leave command from a manager node that's not the leader node. The following message is generated.

```
core@ip-172-30-5-108 ~ $ docker swarm leave
```

The error response from the daemon is as follows:

```
You are attempting to leave the swarm on a node that is participating as a manager.
```

Removing this node leaves one manager out of two. Without a Raft quorum, your Swarm will be inaccessible. The only way to restore a Swarm that has lost consensus is to reinitialize it with --force-new-cluster. Use --force to suppress this message.

To make the manager node leave, you must add the --force option to the command.

```
core@ip-172-30-5-108 ~ $ docker swarm leave --force
Node left the swarm.
```

When one of the two managers has left the Swarm, the Raft quorum is lost and the Swarm becomes inaccessible. As indicated, the Swarm must be reinitialized using the `--force-new-cluster` option.

Reinitializing a Cluster

A Swarm that has lost quorum cannot be reinitialized using the command used to initialize a Swarm. If the same command runs on a Swarm that has lost quorum, a message indicates that the node is already in the Swarm and first must be made to leave the Swarm:

```
core@ip-172-30-5-70 ~ $ docker swarm init --advertise-addr 172.30.5.70
Error response from daemon: This node is already part of a swarm. Use "docker swarm leave"
to leave this swarm and join another one.
```

To reinitialize the Swarm the `--force-new-cluster` option must be added to the docker swarm

```
init command. core@ip-172-30-5-70 ~ $ docker swarm init --advertise-addr 172.30.5.70
--force-new-cluster
Swarm initialized: current node (cnyc2w3n8q8zuxjujcd2s729k) is now a manager.
To add a worker to this swarm, run the following command:
    docker swarm join \
    --token SWMTKN-1-4lxmisvlszjgck4ly0swsxubejfx0phlne1xegho2fiq99amqf-
    11mpscd8gs6bsayzren8fa2ki \
    172.30.5.70:2377
To add a manager to this swarm, run 'docker swarm join-token manager' and follow the
instructions.
```

The Swarm is reinitialized and the `docker swarm join` command to add a worker node is output.

Modifying Node Availability

The availability of a node may be modified with the D command with the `--availability` option. One of the `--availability` options shown in Table 2-6 may be set.

Table 2-6. *Availability Options*

Availability Option	Description
active	Restores a paused or drained node to active.
pause	Pauses a node so that it is not available to receive new tasks.
drain	With a worker node, the node becomes down and unavailable for scheduling new tasks. A manager node also becomes unavailable for scheduling new tasks but continues to perform Swarm management.

As an example, you can drain a worker node as follows.

```
core@ip-172-30-5-70 ~ $ docker node update --availability drain ip-172-30-5-108.ec2.internal
ip-172-30-5-108.ec2.internal
```

The worker node is drained. All service tasks on the drained node are shut down and started on other nodes that are available. The output from the docker node ls command lists the node with the status set to Drain.

```
core@ip-172-30-5-70 ~ $ docker node ls
ID                              HOSTNAME                      STATUS  AVAILABILITY  MANAGER STATUS
bhuzgyqvb83dx0zvms54o0a58       ip-172-30-5-108.ec2.internal  Ready   Drain
cnyc2w3n8q8zuxjujcd2s729k *     ip-172-30-5-70.ec2.internal   Ready   Active        Leader
efsxwt43iskasa6poh2stkjeb       ip-172-30-5-31.ec2.internal   Ready   Active
```

The node detail (partial output is listed) for the drained worker node lists the node availability as "drain".core@ip-172-30-5-70 ~ $ docker node inspect ip-172-30-5-108.ec2.internal

```
[
    {
        "ID": "bhuzgyqvb83dx0zvms54o0a58",
        "Version": {
            "Index": 49
        },
        "CreatedAt": "2017-07-22T19:30:31.544403951Z",
        "UpdatedAt": "2017-07-22T19:33:37.45659544Z",
        "Spec": {
            "Role": "worker",
            "Availability": "drain"
        },
        "Description": {
            "Hostname": "ip-172-30-5-108.ec2.internal",
```

All service tasks on the drained node are shut down and started on other nodes that are available. The node availability with the docker node ls is listed as Drain.

A drained node can be made active again using the docker node update command with --availability set to Active.

```
core@ip-172-30-5-70 ~ $ docker node update --availability active ip-172-30-5-108.ec2.internal
ip-172-30-5-108.ec2.internal
```

The drained node becomes active and is listed with the status set to Active.

```
core@ip-172-30-5-70 ~ $ docker node ls
ID                              HOSTNAME                      STATUS  AVAILABILITY  MANAGER STATUS
bhuzgyqvb83dx0zvms54o0a58       ip-172-30-5-108.ec2.internal  Ready   Active
cnyc2w3n8q8zuxjujcd2s729k *     ip-172-30-5-70.ec2.internal   Ready   Active        Leader
efsxwt43iskasa6poh2stkjeb       ip-172-30-5-31.ec2.internal   Ready   Active
```

Removing a Node

One or more nodes may be removed from the Swarm using the docker node rm command, which is run from any manager node.

```
docker node rm [OPTIONS] NODE [NODE...]
```

The difference between docker swarm leave and docker node rm is that the docker node rm may be run only from a manager node. A demoted node can only be removed from the Swarm with the docker node rm command. The sequence to remove a manager node without using the --force option is the following.

1. Demote the manager node, which makes it a worker node.

2. Drain the worker node.

3. Make the worker node leave the Swarm.

4. Remove the node.

Summary

This chapter discussed using Docker in Swarm mode. First, you initialized the Swarm mode with the docker swarm init command to make the current node the manager node in the Swarm. Subsequently, you joined worker nodes to the Swarm with the docker swarm join command. The chapter also discussed promoting a worker node to a manager node/demoting a manager node to a worker node, making a worker node leave a Swarm and then rejoin the Swarm, making a manager node leave a Swarm, reinitializing a Swarm, and modifying node availability and removing a node. The next chapter introduces Docker for AWS, which is a managed service for Docker Swarm mode.

CHAPTER 3

■ ■ ■

Using Docker for AWS to Create a Multi-Zone Swarm

Docker Swarm is provisioned by first initiating a Swarm to create a manager node and subsequently joining worker nodes to that manager node. Docker Swarm provides distributed service deployment for Docker applications.

The Problem

By default, a Docker Swarm is provisioned on a single zone on AWS, as illustrated in Figure 3-1. With the manager nodes and all the worker nodes in the same AWS zone, failure of the zone would make the zone unavailable. A single-zone Swarm is not a highly available Swarm and has no fault tolerance.

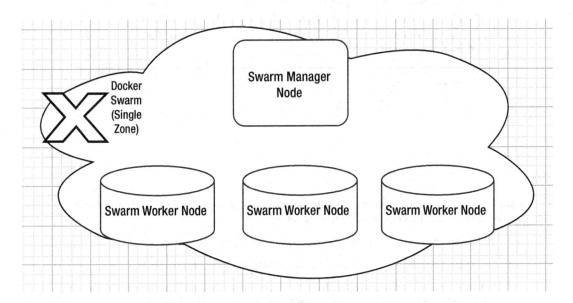

Figure 3-1. *A single-zone Swarm*

© Deepak Vohra 2017

D. Vohra, *Docker Management Design Patterns*, https://doi.org/10.1007/978-1-4842-2973-6_3

The Solution

Docker and AWS have partnered to create a Docker for AWS deployment platform that provisions a Docker Swarm across multiple zones on AWS. Docker for AWS does not require users to run any commands on a command line and is graphical user interface (GUI) based. With manager and worker nodes in multiple zones, failure of a single AWS zone does not make the Swarm unavailable, as illustrated in Figure 3-2. Docker for AWS provides fault tolerance to a Swarm.

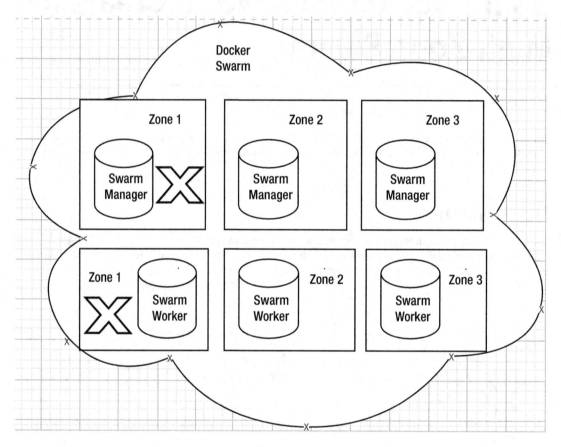

Figure 3-2. *A Multi-zone Swarm*

Docker for AWS is a managed service for Docker Swarm on the AWS cloud platform. In addition to multiple zones, Docker for AWS has several other benefits:

- All the required infrastructure is provisioned automatically.

- Automatic upgrade to new software versions without service interruption.

- A custom Linux distribution optimized for Docker. The custom Linux distribution is not available separately on AWS and uses the overlay2 storage driver.

- Unused Docker resources are pruned automatically.

- Auto-scaling groups for managing nodes.

- Log rotation native to the host to avoid chatty logs consuming all the disk space.

- Centralized logging with AWS CloudWatch.

- A bug-reporting tool based on a docker-diagnose script.

Two editions of Docker for Swarm are available:

- Docker Enterprise Edition (EE) for AWS

- Docker Community Edition (CE) for AWS

We use the Docker Community Edition (CE) for AWS in this chapter to create a multi-zone Swarm. This chapter includes the following topics:

- Setting the environment

- Creating a AWS CloudFormation stack for the Docker Swarm

- Connecting with the Swarm manager

- Using the Swarm

- Deleting the Swarm

Setting the Environment

Two deployment options are available with Docker for AWS.

- Use a pre-existing VPC

- Use a new VPC created by Docker

Letting Docker create the VPC, subnets, and gateways is the easier option and the one used in this chapter.

Create an AWS account if you don't already have one at https://aws.amazon.com/resources/create-account/. The AWS account must support EC2-VPC. Even though AWS services such as VPC are created automatically, the account must have permissions to create EC2 instances, including auto-scaling groups, IAM profiles, DynamoDB tables, SQS Queue, VPC (including subnets, gateways, and security groups), Elastic Load Balancer, and CloudWatch Log Group. The only user input other than creating an account with the required permissions is to create a SSH key pair in the AWS region in the Docker Swarm.

Select the EC2 AWS service and click on the Key Pairs link in the EC2 dashboard. Click on Create Key Pair to create and download a key pair. Specify a key pair name (docker for example) in the Create Key Pair dialog and click on Create. A key pair gets created, as shown in Figure 3-3. Copy the key pair file (docker.pem) to a local Linux machine.

Figure 3-3. *A key pair*

Set the permissions on the docker.pem to 400, which gives only read permissions and removes all other permissions.

```
chmod 400 docker.pem
```

Creating a AWS CloudFormation Stack for Docker Swarm

Navigate to https://docs.docker.com/docker-for-aws/ in a web browser and click on the Deploy Docker for AWS option, as as shown in Figure 3-4. The label could be different, such as Deploy Docker Community Edition [CE] for AWS [stable].

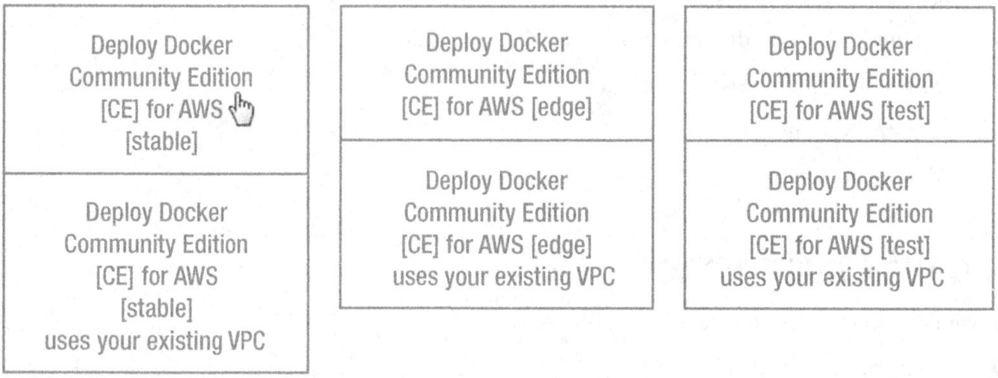

Figure 3-4. *Deploy Docker for AWS*

The Create Stack wizard is started with the provision to either design a new template or choose the default CloudFormation template for Docker on AWS. Select the Specify an Amazon S3 Template URL option for which a URL is pre-specified, as shown in Figure 3-5. Click on Next.

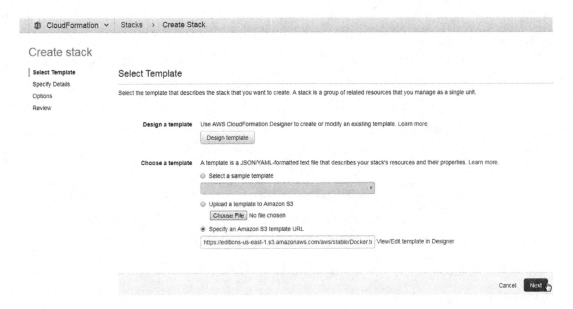

Figure 3-5. *Selecting a template*

In Specify Details, specify a stack name (DockerSwarm). The Swarm Parameters section has the fields listed in Table 3-1.

Table 3-1. *Swarm Parameters*

Parameter	Description
Number of Swarm managers?	Number of Swarm manager nodes. Valid values are 1, 3, and 5.
Number of Swarm worker nodes?	Number of worker nodes in the Swarm (0-1000).

Keep the default settings of 3 for Number of Swarm Managers and 5 for Number of Swarm Worker nodes, as shown in Figure 3-6.

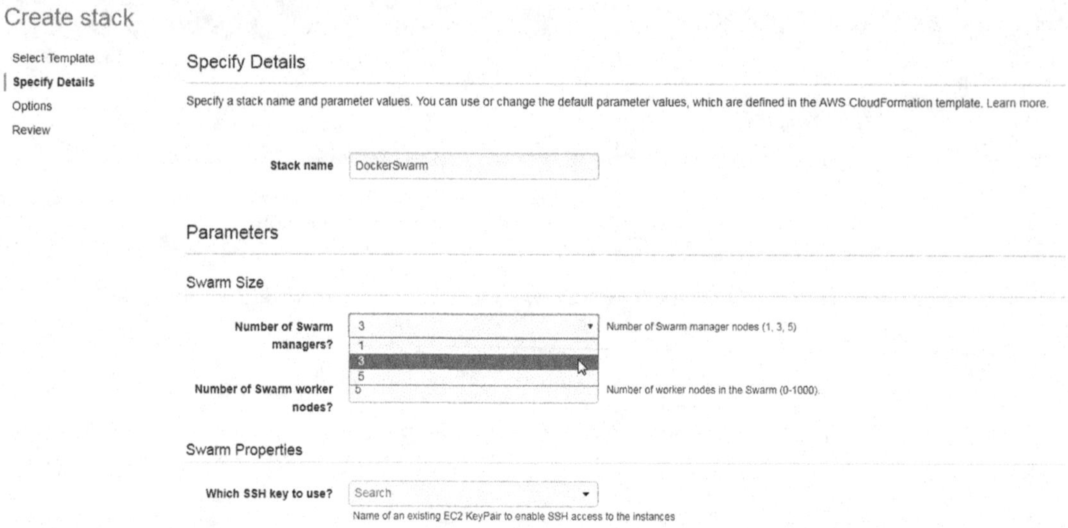

Create stack

Select Template
Specify Details
Options
Review

Specify Details

Specify a stack name and parameter values. You can use or change the default parameter values, which are defined in the AWS CloudFormation template. Learn more.

Stack name   DockerSwarm

Parameters

Swarm Size

Number of Swarm   3   ▼   Number of Swarm manager nodes (1, 3, 5)
managers?   1
3
5
Number of Swarm worker   0   Number of worker nodes in the Swarm (0-1000).
nodes?

Swarm Properties

Which SSH key to use?   Search   ▼
Name of an existing EC2 KeyPair to enable SSH access to the instances

Figure 3-6. *Specifying a stack name*

Next, specify the Swarm properties, as discussed in Table 3-2.

Table 3-2. *Swarm Properties*

Swarm Property	Description	Value Set
Which SSH key to use?	Name of an existing EC2 key pair to enable SSH access to the instances.	docker
Enable daily resource cleanup?	Cleans up unused images, containers, networks, and volumes.	no
Use CloudWatch for container logging?	Send all container logs to CloudWatch.	yes

In the Which SSH key to use? property, select the docker SSH key. The Swarm properties are shown in Figure 3-7.

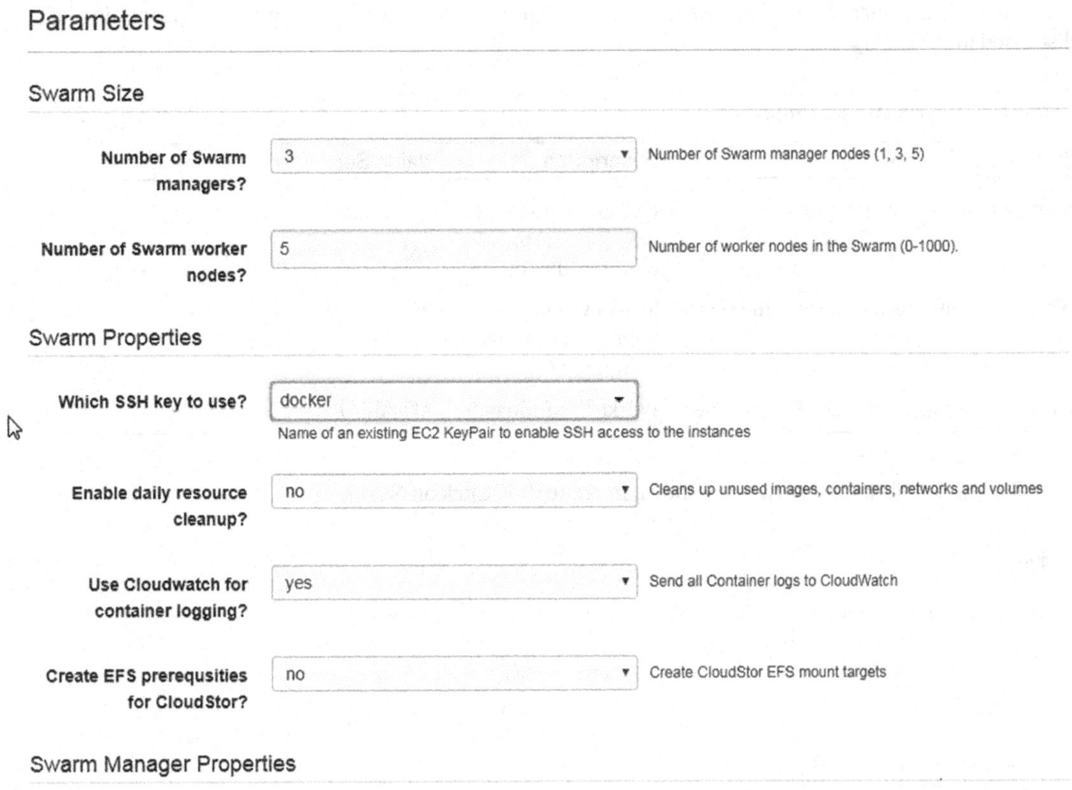

Parameters

Swarm Size

Number of Swarm managers?	3 ▼	Number of Swarm manager nodes (1, 3, 5)
Number of Swarm worker nodes?	5	Number of worker nodes in the Swarm (0-1000).

Swarm Properties

Which SSH key to use?	docker ▼	
	Name of an existing EC2 KeyPair to enable SSH access to the instances	
Enable daily resource cleanup?	no ▼	Cleans up unused images, containers, networks and volumes
Use Cloudwatch for container logging?	yes ▼	Send all Container logs to CloudWatch
Create EFS prerequsities for CloudStor?	no ▼	Create CloudStor EFS mount targets

Swarm Manager Properties

Figure 3-7. Swarm properties

Specify the Swarm Manager properties, as discussed in Table 3-3.

Table 3-3. Swarm Manager Properties

Swarm Property	Description	Value Set
Swarm manager instance type?	EC2 HVM instance type (t2.micro, m3.medium, etc.)	t2.micro
Manager ephemeral storage volume size?	Size of manager's ephemeral storage volume in GB	20
Manager ephemeral storage volume type?	Manager volume type	standard

The Swarm Manager properties are as shown in Figure 3-8. Specify the Swarm Worker properties, as discussed in Table 3-4.

Table 3-4. *Swarm Worker Properties*

Swarm Worker Property	Description	Value Set
Agent worker instance type?	EC2 HVM instance type (t2.micro, m3.medium, etc.)	`t2.micro`
Worker ephemeral storage volume size?	Size of worker's ephemeral storage volume in GB	20
Worker ephemeral storage volume type?	Worker volume type	`standard`

The Swarm Worker properties are shown in Figure 3-8. Click on Next.

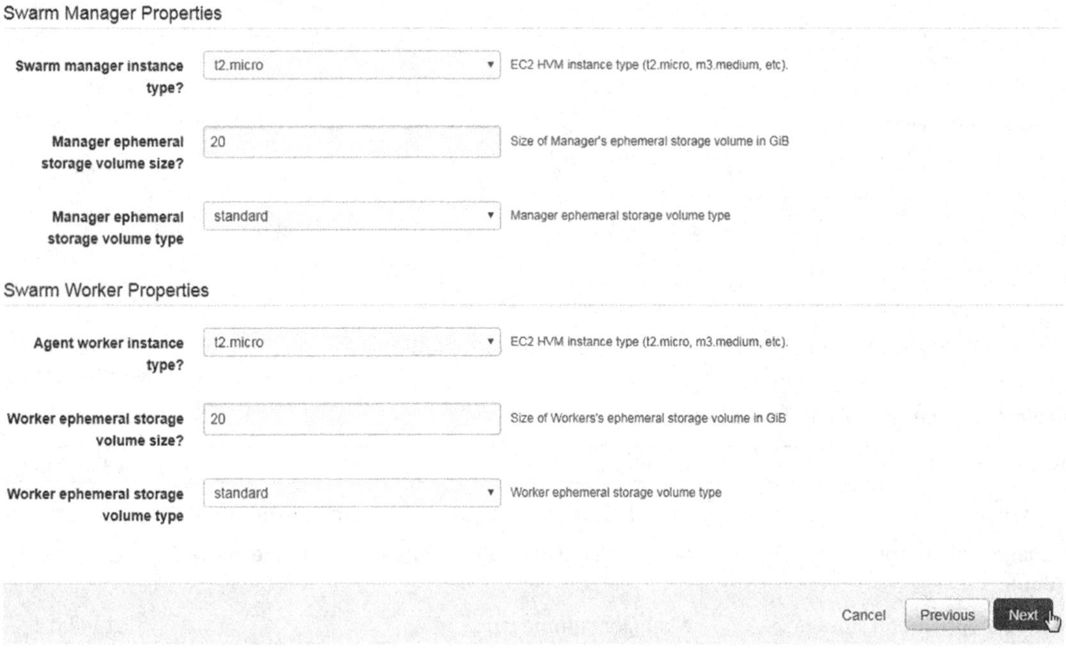

Figure 3-8. *Swarm worker properties*

Next, specify the options for the stack. Tags (key-value pairs) may be specified for resources in a stack. For permissions, an IAM role for CloudFormation may be chosen. None of these options is required to be set, as shown in Figure 3-9.

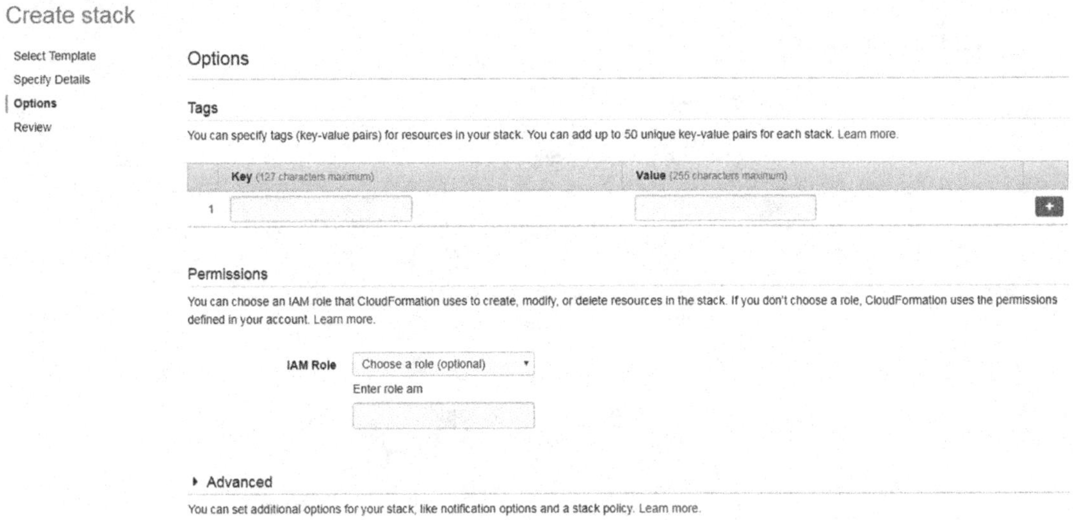

Create stack

Select Template
Specify Details
Options
Review

Options

Tags

You can specify tags (key-value pairs) for resources in your stack. You can add up to 50 unique key-value pairs for each stack. Learn more.

Key (127 characters maximum)	Value (255 characters maximum)	
1		+

Permissions

You can choose an IAM role that CloudFormation uses to create, modify, or delete resources in the stack. If you don't choose a role, CloudFormation uses the permissions defined in your account. Learn more.

IAM Role   Choose a role (optional) ▾

Enter role arn

▸ Advanced

You can set additional options for your stack, like notification options and a stack policy. Learn more.

Figure 3-9. *Optional settings*

For Advanced options, the Notification options are set to No Notification. Set Rollback on Failure to Yes, as shown in Figure 3-10. Click on Next.

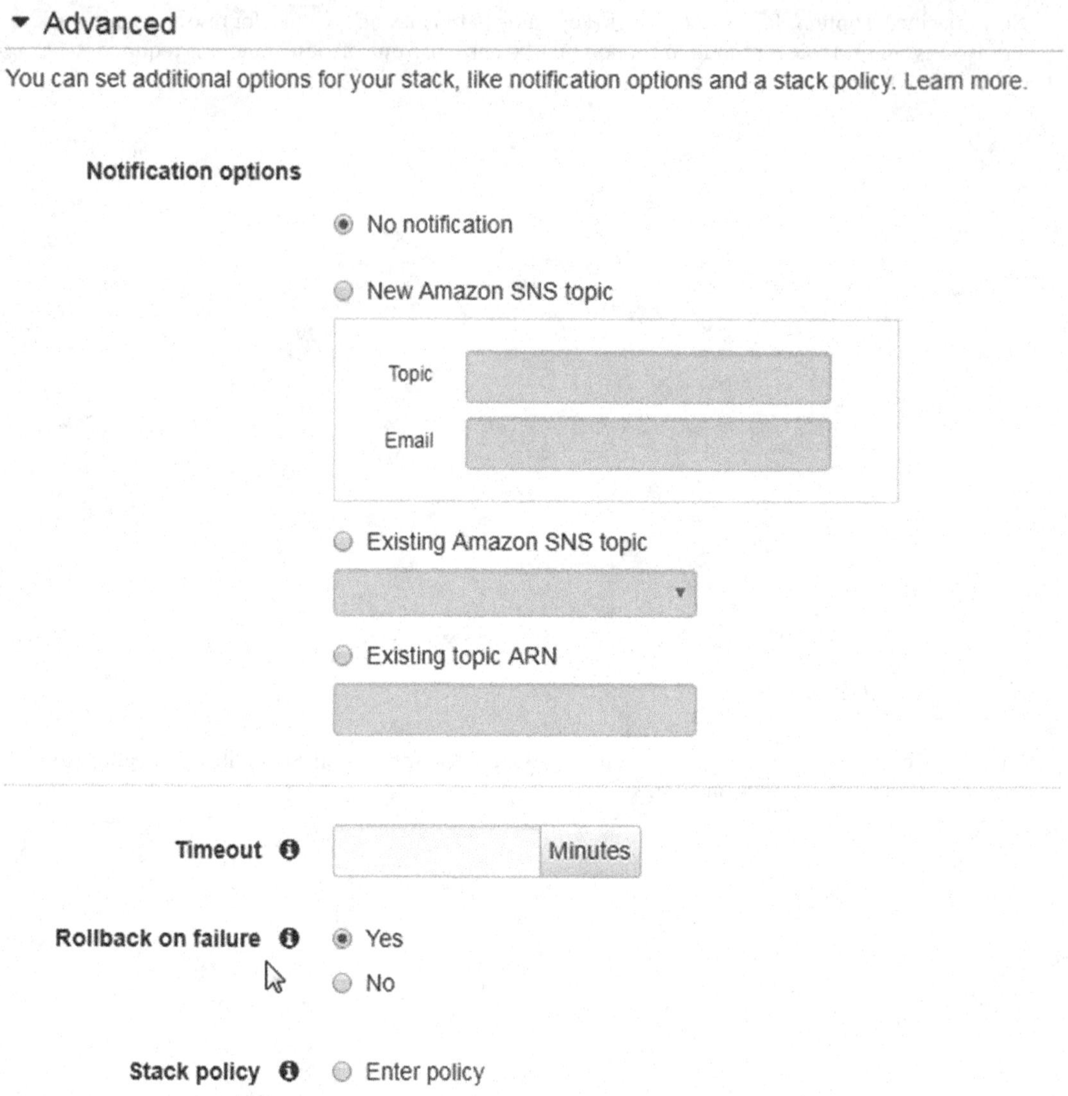

▼ Advanced

You can set additional options for your stack, like notification options and a stack policy. Learn more.

Notification options

○ No notification

○ New Amazon SNS topic

Topic [   ]

Email [   ]

○ Existing Amazon SNS topic

[▼]

○ Existing topic ARN

[   ]

Timeout ❶ [| Minutes]

Rollback on failure ❶   ◉ Yes
                         ○ No

Stack policy ❶   ○ Enter policy

Figure 3-10. *Setting rollback on failure*

Review the stack settings, as shown in Figure 3-11.

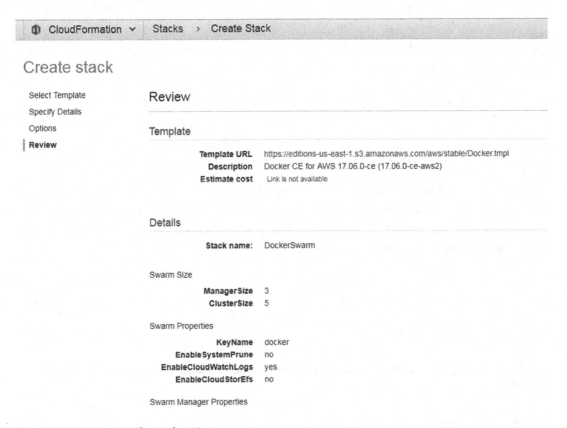

Figure 3-11. *Reviewing the stack settings*

Select the acknowledgement checkbox and then click on Create, as shown in Figure 3-12.

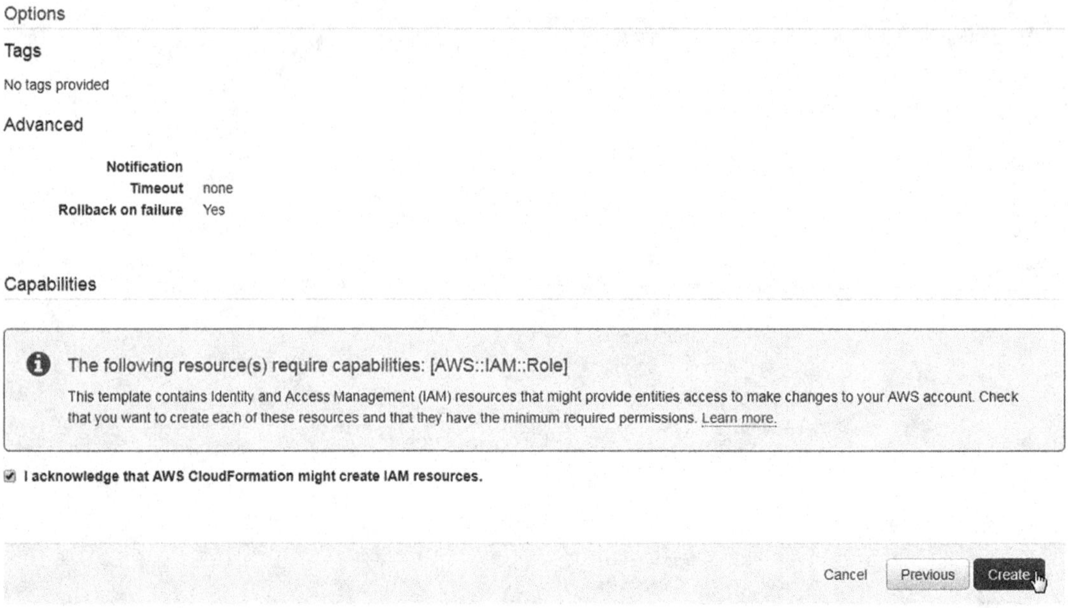

Options

Tags

No tags provided

Advanced

Notification
Timeout   none
Rollback on failure   Yes

Capabilities

> ⓘ   The following resource(s) require capabilities: [AWS::IAM::Role]
>
>   This template contains Identity and Access Management (IAM) resources that might provide entities access to make changes to your AWS account. Check that you want to create each of these resources and that they have the minimum required permissions. Learn more.

☑ I acknowledge that AWS CloudFormation might create IAM resources.

Cancel   Previous   Create

Figure 3-12. *Creating the stack*

A new stack begins to be created. Click on the Refresh button to refresh the stacks listed, as shown in Figure 3-13.

Figure 3-13. *Refresh*

A new stack based on a CloudFormation template for Docker Swarm starts to be created, as indicated by the status CREATE_IN_PROGRESS shown in Figure 3-14.

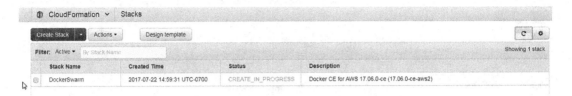

Figure 3-14. *CloudFormation stack status*

The different tabs are provided for the different stack details. The Resources tab shows the AWS resources created by the CloudFormation template, as shown in Figure 3-15.

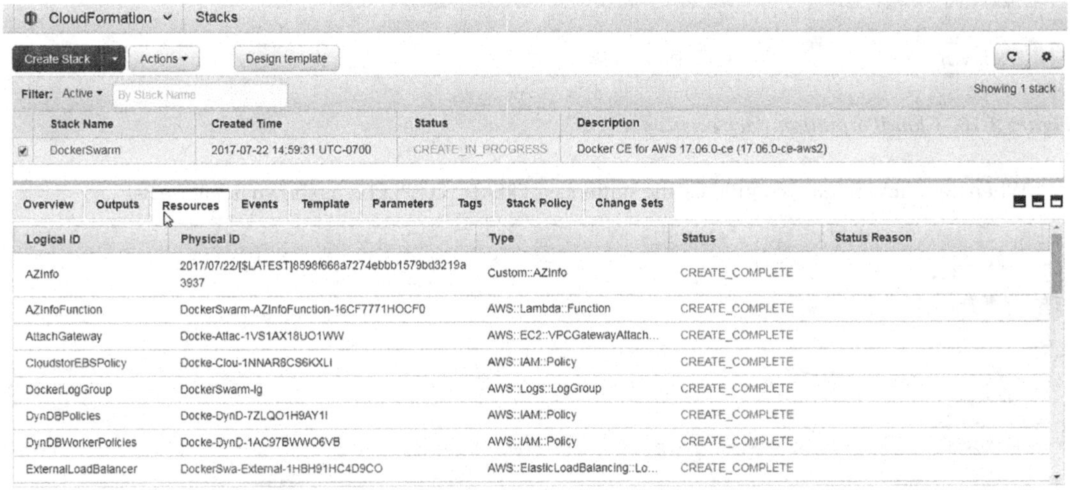

Logical ID	Physical ID	Type	Status	Status Reason
AZInfo	2017/07/22/[$LATEST]8598f668a7274ebbb1579bd3219a3937	Custom::AZInfo	CREATE_COMPLETE	
AZInfoFunction	DockerSwarm-AZInfoFunction-16CF7771HOCF0	AWS::Lambda::Function	CREATE_COMPLETE	
AttachGateway	Docke-Attac-1VS1AX18UO1WW	AWS::EC2::VPCGatewayAttach...	CREATE_COMPLETE	
CloudstorEBSPolicy	Docke-Clou-1NNAR8CS6KXLI	AWS::IAM::Policy	CREATE_COMPLETE	
DockerLogGroup	DockerSwarm-lg	AWS::Logs::LogGroup	CREATE_COMPLETE	
DynDBPolicies	Docke-DynD-7ZLQO1H9AY1I	AWS::IAM::Policy	CREATE_COMPLETE	
DynDBWorkerPolicies	Docke-DynD-1AC97BWWO6VB	AWS::IAM::Policy	CREATE_COMPLETE	
ExternalLoadBalancer	DockerSwa-External-1HBH91HC4D9CO	AWS::ElasticLoadBalancing::Lo...	CREATE_COMPLETE	

Figure 3-15. *CloudFormation stack resources*

The Events tab shows the events that occur in creating a CloudFormation stack, as shown in Figure 3-16.

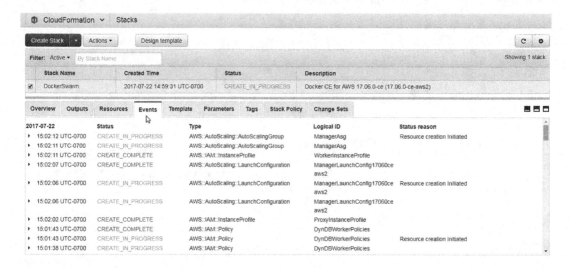

Figure 3-16. *CloudFormation stack events*

When the stack creation completes, the status says CREATE_COMPLETE, as shown in Figure 3-17.

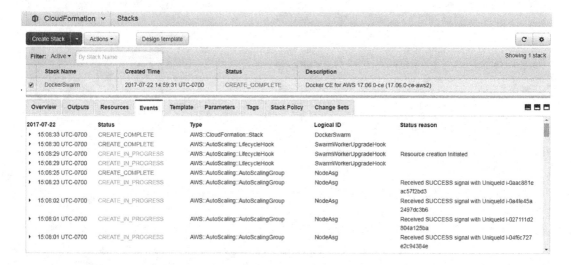

Figure 3-17. *Stack status is CREATE_COMPLETE*

All the required resources—including auto-scaling groups, EC2 Internet Gateway, EC2 security groups, Elastic Load Balancer, IAM policy, Log Group, and VPC Gateway—are created, as shown in Figure 3-18.

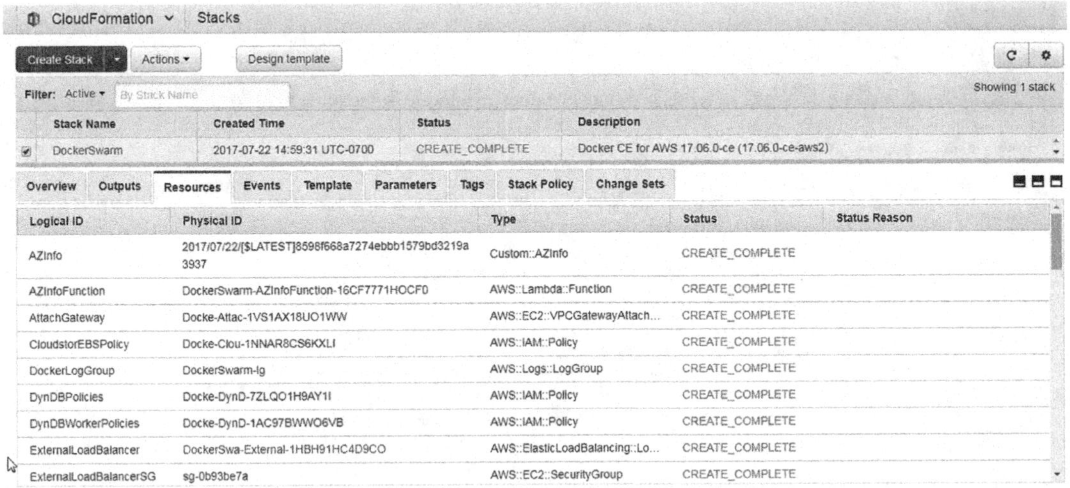

Figure 3-18. *Resources are created*

The Outputs tab lists the Default DNS target, the zone availability comment about the number of availability zones, and the manager nodes, as shown in Figure 3-19.

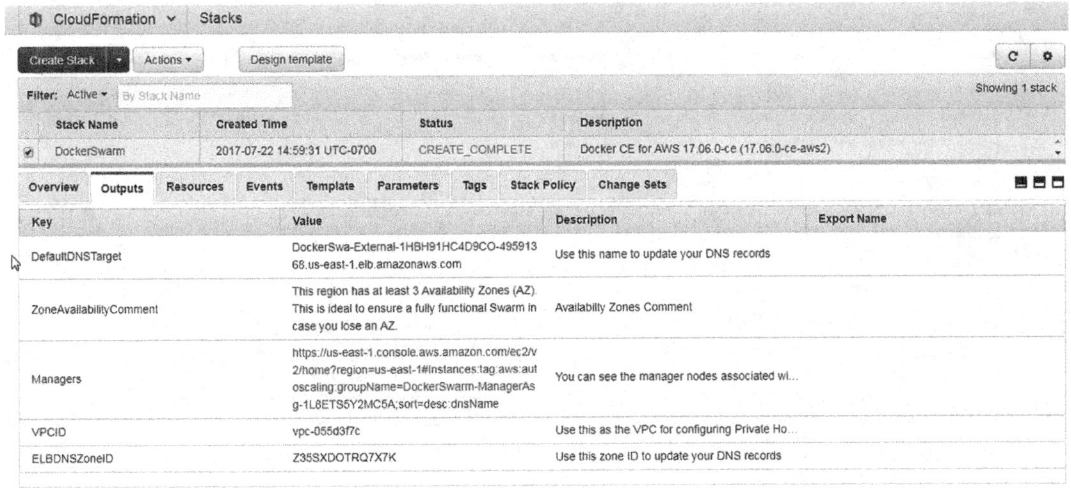

Figure 3-19. *Outputs*

45

To list the EC2 instances for the Swarm managers, click on the link in Managers, as shown in Figure 3-20.

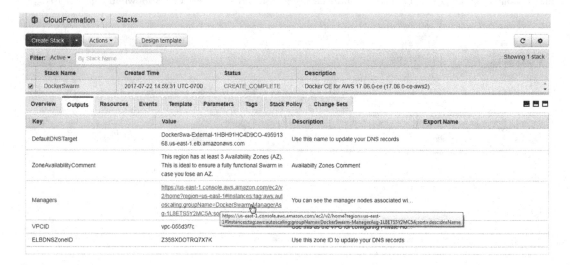

Figure 3-20. *The Managers link*

The three manager instances are all in different availability zones. The public/private IP addresses and the public DNS name for each EC2 instance may be obtained from the EC2 console, as shown in Figure 3-21.

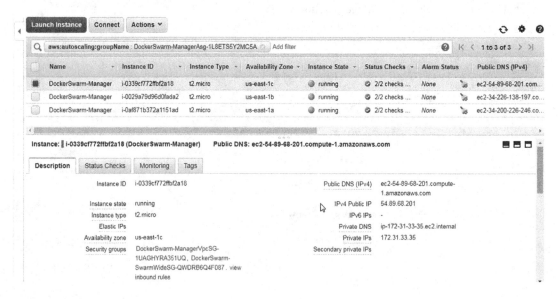

Figure 3-21. *Manager instances on EC2*

The AMI used for the EC2 instances may be found using the AMI ID, as shown in Figure 3-22. A Moby Linux AMI is used for this Swarm, but the AMI could be different for different users and in different AWS regions.

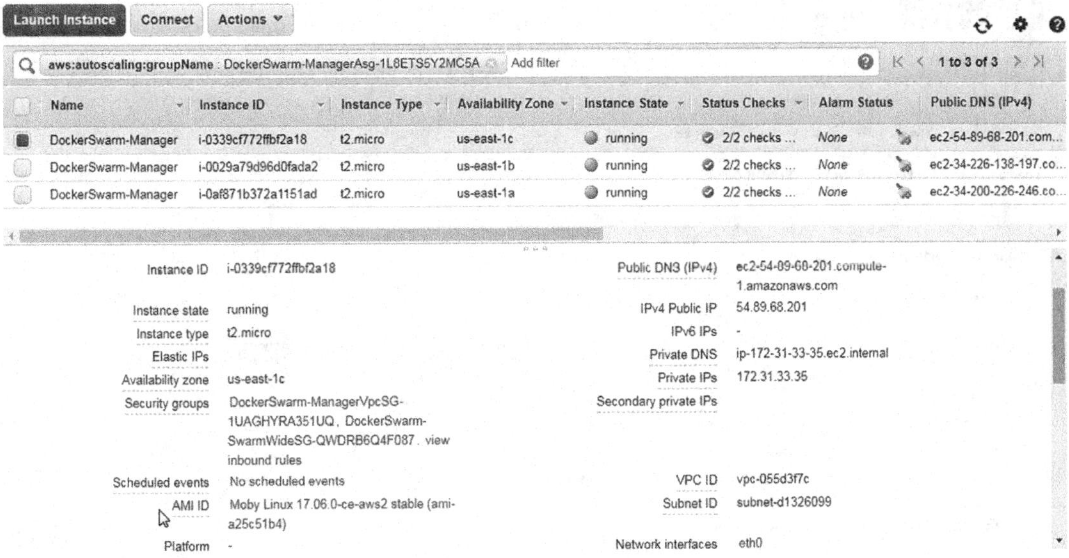

Figure 3-22. *Moby Linux AMI*

You can list all the EC2 instances by setting Instance State to Running. The Docker Swarm manager nodes (three) and worker nodes (five) are listed, as shown in Figure 3-23. The manager and worker nodes are in three different availability zones.

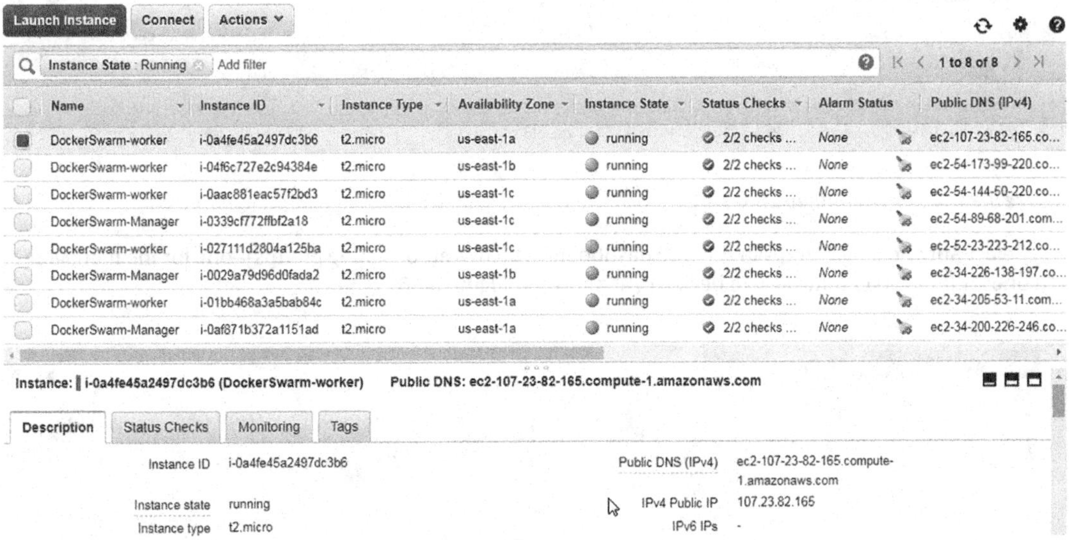

Figure 3-23. *Swarm managers and workers in three different availability zones*

Select Load Balancers in the EC2 dashboard and the provisioned Elastic Load Balancer is listed, as shown in Figure 3-24. Click on the Instances tab to list the instances. All instances should have a status set to InService, as shown in Figure 3-24.

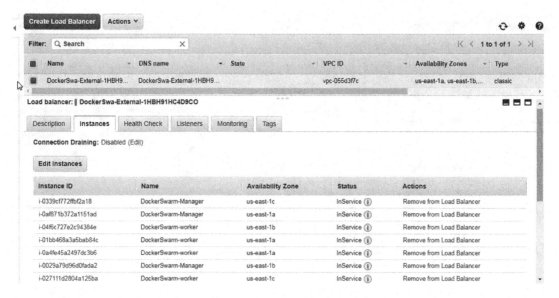

Figure 3-24. *Elastic Load Balancer*

Select Launch Configurations from the EC2 dashboard. The two launch configurations—one for the managers and one for the worker nodes—will be listed, as shown in Figure 3-25.

Name	AMI ID	Instance Type	Spot Price	Creation Time
DockerSwarm-NodeLaunchConfig17060ceaws2-RYA1B9VJKDF3	ami-a25c51b4	t2.micro		July 22, 2017 3:05:29 PM UTC-7
DockerSwarm-ManagerLaunchConfig17060ceaws2-1VOMPPGK1XlVi	ami-a25c51b4	t2.micro		July 22, 2017 3:02:06 PM UTC-7

Figure 3-25. *Launch configurations*

Select Auto Scaling Groups in the EC2 dashboard. The two auto-scaling groups—one for the managers and one for the worker nodes—will be listed, as shown in Figure 3-26.

Name	Launch Configuration	Instances	Desired	Min	Max	Availability Zones	Default Cooldow
DockerSwarm-NodeAsg-1PWVVETKVWXMJ	DockerSwarm-NodeLau...	5	5	0	1,000	us-east-1a, us-east-1b, us-e...	300
DockerSwarm-ManagerAsg-1L8ETS5Y2MC5A	DockerSwarm-Manager...	3	3	0	6	us-east-1a, us-east-1b, us-e...	300

Figure 3-26. *Auto-scaling groups*

Connecting with the Swarm Manager

Next, connect to a Swarm manager node from the local machine on which the key pair docker.pem is copied. Using the public IP address of a manager EC2 instance, SSH login into the instance with user as "docker".

```
ssh -i "docker.pem" docker@54.89.68.201
```

The command prompt for the manager node is displayed.

```
[root@localhost ~]# ssh -i "docker.pem" docker@54.89.68.201

Welcome to Docker!
```

The Docker version of the Swarm node may be listed using docker --version. The version will be 17.06 or greater. Swarm mode is supported on Docker 1.12 or greater.

```
~ $ docker --version
Docker version 17.06.0-ce, build 02c1d87
```

Using the Swarm

List the Swarm nodes with docker node ls and the three manager nodes and five worker nodes will be listed.

```
~ $ docker node ls

ID HOSTNAME STATUS AVAILABILITY MANAGER STATUS

255llm8729rns82bmloaxs6usl ip-172-31-8-37.ec2.internal Ready Active

ikyskl4ysocymoe4pbrj3qnh3 ip-172-31-4-154.ec2.internal Ready Active Reachable

p2ky6meej8tnph5wyuw59xtmr ip-172-31-21-30.ec2.internal Ready Active Leader

r56kkltfgc4zzzfbslinrun2d1 ip-172-31-24-185.ec2.internal Ready Active

soggz5qplcihk8y2y58uj9md4 ip-172-31-1-33.ec2.internal Ready Active

xbdeo8qp9jhi398h478wl2zrv * ip-172-31-33-35.ec2.internal Ready Active Reachable

ykk4odpjps6t6eqc9mriqvo4a ip-172-31-47-162.ec2.internal Ready Active

zrlrmijyj5vklxl3ag7gayb3w ip-172-31-39-210.ec2.internal Ready Active
```

The leader node and two other manager nodes indicated by Manager Status of Leader and Reachable are listed. The worker nodes are all available, as indicated by Active in the Availability column.

Docker services are introduced in the next chapter, but you can run the following docker service create command to create an example Docker service for a MySQL database.

```
docker service create \
  --env MYSQL_ROOT_PASSWORD='mysql'\
  --replicas 1 \
  --name mysql \
  --update-delay 10s \
 --update-parallelism 1  \
 mysql
```

A service gets created:

```
~ $ docker service create \
>    --env MYSQL_ROOT_PASSWORD='mysql'\
>    --replicas 1 \
>    --name mysql \
>    --update-delay 10s \
>   --update-parallelism 1  \
>   mysql
12hg71a3vy793quv14uems5gk
```

List the service with the docker service ls command, which is also discussed in the next chapter, and the service ID, mode, replicas, and image are listed.

```
~S docker service ls

ID NAME MODE REPLICAS IMAGE

n2tomumtl9sbniysql replicated 1/1 mysql:latest
```

Scale the service to three replicas with the docker service scale command. The three replicas are scheduled—one on the leader manager node and two on the worker nodes. The docker service ps command to list service replicas is also discussed in more detail in the next chapter.

```
~ S docker service scale mysql=3

mysql scaled to 3

~ S docker service  ps mysql

ID NAME IMAGE NODE DESIRED STATE CURRENT STATE ERROR PORTS

slqtuf9l4hxo mysql1.1 mysql:latest ip-172-31-35-3.us-east-2.compute.internal

Running Running about a minute ago

exqsthrgszzc mysql.2 mysql:latest ip-172-31-27-83.us-east-2.compute.internal

Running Preparing 8 seconds ago

vtuhsl6mya85 mysql.3 mysql:1atest ip-172-31-29-199.us-east-2.compute.internal Running
Preparing 8 seconds ago
```

Deleting a Swarm

To delete a Swarm, choose Actions ➤ Delete Stack from the CloudFormation console, as shown in Figure 3-27.

Figure 3-27. *Choosing Actions ➤ Delete Stack*

In the Delete Stack confirmation dialog, click on Yes, Delete, as shown in Figure 3-28.

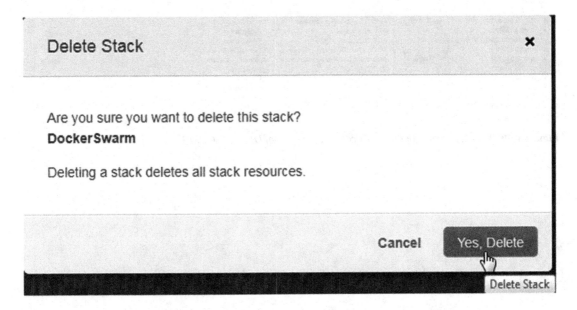

Figure 3-28. *Delete stack confirmation dialog*

The stack's status becomes DELETE_IN_PROGRESS, as shown in Figure 3-29.

Figure 3-29. *Delete in progress*

As each of the stack's resources is deleted, its status becomes DELETE_COMPLETE, as shown for some of the resources on the Events tab in Figure 3-30.

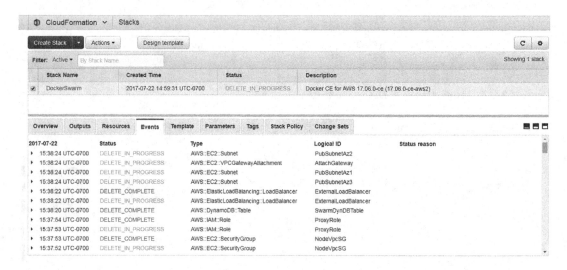

Figure 3-30. *Events list some of the resources with a status of DELETE_COMPLETE*

When the EC2 instances have been deleted, the EC2 console lists their status as terminated, as shown in Figure 3-31.

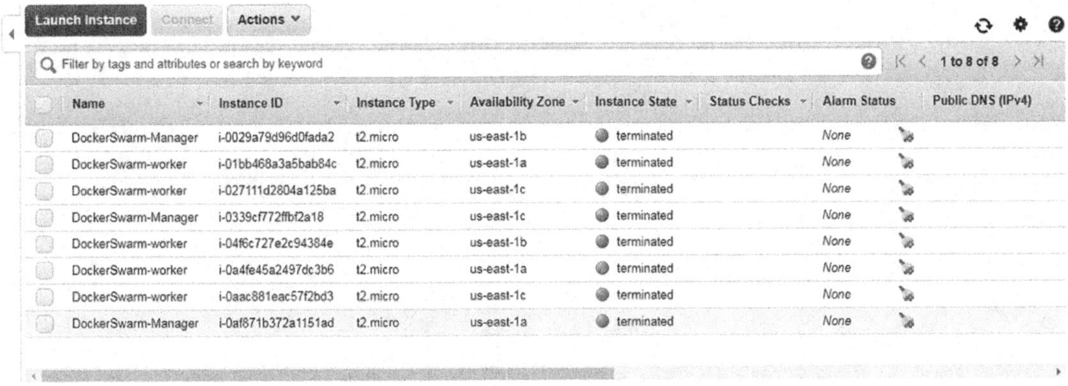

	Name		Instance ID		Instance Type		Availability Zone		Instance State		Status Checks		Alarm Status	Public DNS (IPv4)
	DockerSwarm-Manager		i-0029a79d96d0fada2		t2.micro		us-east-1b		● terminated				None	
	DockerSwarm-worker		i-01bb468a3a5bab84c		t2.micro		us-east-1a		● terminated				None	
	DockerSwarm-worker		i-027111d2804a125ba		t2.micro		us-east-1c		● terminated				None	
	DockerSwarm-Manager		i-0339cf772ffbf2a18		t2.micro		us-east-1c		● terminated				None	
	DockerSwarm-worker		i-04f6c727e2c94384e		t2.micro		us-east-1b		● terminated				None	
	DockerSwarm-worker		i-0a4fe45a2497dc3b6		t2.micro		us-east-1a		● terminated				None	
	DockerSwarm-worker		i-0aac881eac57f2bd3		t2.micro		us-east-1c		● terminated				None	
	DockerSwarm-Manager		i-0af871b372a1151ad		t2.micro		us-east-1a		● terminated				None	

Figure 3-31. EC2 instances with status set to terminated

Summary

This chapter discussed creating a multi-zone Docker Swarm provisioned by a CloudFormation template using the Docker for AWS service. You learned how to connect to the Swarm manager to run docker service commands. The next chapter introduces Docker services.

CHAPTER 4

■ ■ ■

Docker Services

A Docker container contains all the binaries and dependencies required to run an application. A user only needs to run a Docker container to start and access an application. The CoreOS Linux operating system has Docker installed and the Docker commands may be run without even installing Docker.

The Problem

A Docker container, by default, is started only on a single node. However, for production environments, where uptime and redundancy matters, you need to run your applications on multiple hosts.

When a Docker container is started using the docker run command, the container starts only on a single host, as illustrated in Figure 4-1. Software is usually not designed to run on a single host only. A MySQL database in a production environment, for example, may need to run across a cluster of hosts for redundancy and high availability. Applications that are designed for a single host should be able to scale up to multiple hosts as needed. But distributed Docker applications cannot run on a single Docker Engine.

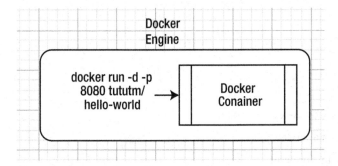

Figure 4-1. *Docker container on a single host*

The Solution

Docker Swarm mode enables a Docker application to run across a distributed cluster of Docker Engines connected by an overlay network, as illustrated in Figure 4-2. A Docker service may be created with a specific number of replicas, with each replica potentially running on a different host in a cluster. A Swarm consists of one or more manager nodes with a single leader for Swarm management and orchestration. Worker nodes run the actual service tasks with the manager nodes being worker nodes by default. A Docker service may be started only from the leader node. Service replicas scheduled on the worker nodes, as a result, run a distributed application. Distributed applications provide several benefits, such as fault tolerance, failover, increased capacity, and load balancing, to list a few.

© Deepak Vohra 2017
D. Vohra, *Docker Management Design Patterns*, https://doi.org/10.1007/978-1-4842-2973-6_4

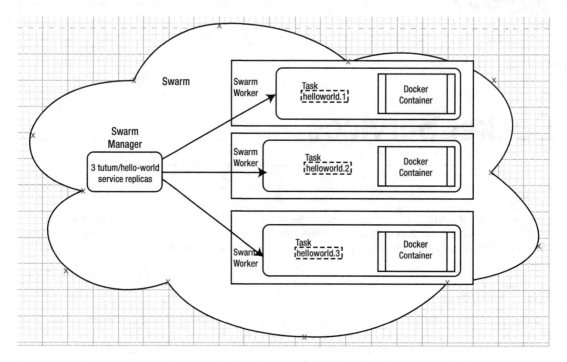

Figure 4-2. *Docker service tasks and containers spread across the nodes*

This chapter covers the following topics:

- Setting the environment
- The Docker service commands
- Types of services
- Creating a service
- Listing the tasks of a service
- Invoking a Hello World service task on the command line
- Getting detailed information about a service
- Invoking the Hello World service in a browser
- Creating a service for a MySQL database
- Scaling a service
- Listing service tasks
- Accessing a MySQL database in a Docker container
- Updating a service
- Updating the replicas
- Updating the Docker image tag
- Updating the placement constraints

- Updating environment variables

- Updating the Docker image

- Updating the container labels

- Updating resources settings

- Removing a service

Setting the Environment

Create a Docker Swarm consisting of one manager and two worker nodes using the procedure discussed in Chapter 3. First, start three CoreOS instances—one for a Swarm manager and two for the Swarm workers. Obtain the public IP address of the Swarm manager, as shown in the EC2 console in Figure 4-3.

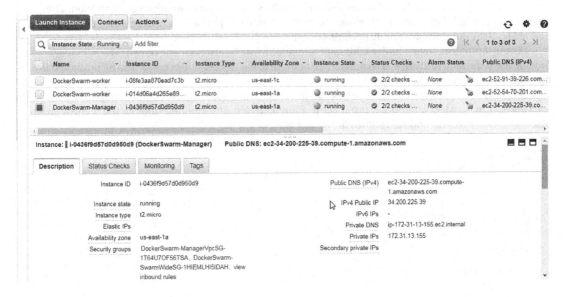

Figure 4-3. *EC2 instances for Swarm*

SSH login to the Swarm manager instance with user as "docker".

```
[root@localhost ~]# ssh -i   "docker.pem"  docker@34.200.225.39
Welcome to Docker!
```

Three nodes should get listed in the Swarm with the docker node ls command—one manager node and two worker nodes.

```
~ $ docker node ls
ID                            HOSTNAME                        STATUS  AVAILABILITY  MANAGER STATUS
ilru4f0i280w2tlsrg9hglwsj     ip-172-31-10-132.ec2.internal   Ready   Active
w5to186ipblpcq390625wyq2e     ip-172-31-37-135.ec2.internal   Ready   Active
zkxle7kafwcmt1sd93kh5cy5e *   ip-172-31-13-155.ec2.internal   Ready   Active        Leader
```

A worker node may be promoted to a manager node using the docker node promote <node ip> command.

```
~ $ docker node promote ilru4f0i280w2tlsrg9hglwsj
Node ilru4f0i280w2tlsrg9hglwsj promoted to a manager in the swarm.
```

If you list the nodes again, two manager nodes should be listed. A manager node is identified by a value in the Manager Status column. One node has a Manager Status of Reachable and the other says Leader.

```
~ $ docker node ls
ID                           HOSTNAME                        STATUS  AVAILABILITY  MANAGER STATUS
ilru4f0i280w2tlsrg9hglwsj    ip-172-31-10-132.ec2.internal   Ready   Active        Reachable
w5to186ipblpcq390625wyq2e    ip-172-31-37-135.ec2.internal   Ready   Active
zkxle7kafwcmt1sd93kh5cy5e *  ip-172-31-13-155.ec2.internal   Ready   Active        Leader
```

The manager node that is the Leader performs all the swarm management and orchestration. The manager node that is Reachable participates in the raft consensus quorum and is eligible for election as the new leader if the current leader node becomes unavailable.

Having multiple manager nodes adds fault tolerance to the Swarm, but one or two Swarm managers provide the same fault tolerance. If required, one or more of the worker nodes could also be promoted to a manager node to increase fault tolerance.

For connectivity to the Swarm instances, modify the inbound rules of the security groups associated with the Swarm manager and worker instances to allow all traffic. The inbound rules for the security group associated with a Swarm node are shown in Figure 4-4.

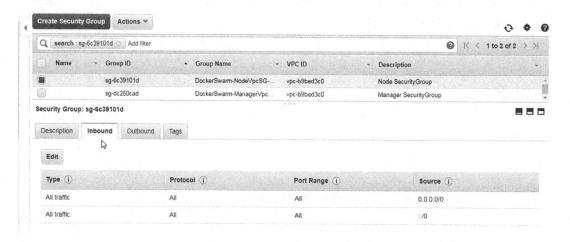

Figure 4-4. *Setting inbound rules on a security group to allow all traffic*

The outbound rules for the security group associated with the Swarm manager are shown in Figure 4-5.

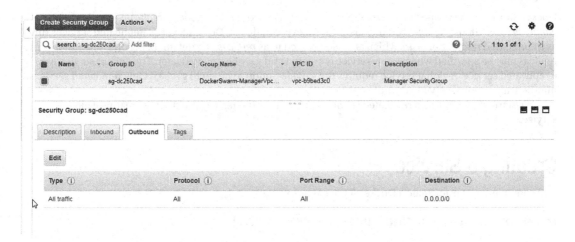

Figure 4-5. *Setting outbound rules on a security group to allow all traffic*

The docker service Commands

The docker service commands are used to manage Docker services. The docker service command provides the sub-commands listed in Table 4-1.

Table 4-1. *The docker service Sub-Commands*

Command	Description
docker service create	Creates a new service.
docker service inspect	Displays detailed information on one or more services.
docker service logs	Fetches the logs of a service. The command was added in Docker 17.0.6.
docker service ls	Lists services.
docker service ps	Lists the tasks of one or more services.
docker service rm	Removes one or more services.
docker service scale	Scales one or multiple replicated services.
docker service update	Updates a service.

To run docker service commands, the following requirements must be met.

- The Docker Swarm mode must be enabled
- The docker service commands must be run from the Swarm manager node that is the Leader

The docker service commands are available only in Swarm mode and cannot be run outside the Swarm mode.

The docker service commands cannot be run from a worker node. Worker nodes cannot be used to view or modify Swarm cluster state.

Types of Services

Docker Swarm mode supports two types of services, also called service modes—*replicated services* and *global services*. Global services run one task only on every node in a Docker Swarm. Replicated services run as a configured number of tasks, which are also referred to as *replicas*, the default being one. The number of replicas may be specified when a new service is created and may be updated later. The default service type is a replicated service. A global service requires the --mode option to be set to global. Only replicated services may be scaled; global services cannot be scaled.

We start off by creating a replicated service. Later in the chapter, we also discuss creating a global service.

Creating a Service

The command syntax to create a Docker service is as follows.

```
docker service create [OPTIONS] IMAGE [COMMAND] [ARG...]
```

Some of the supported options are listed in Table 4-2.

Table 4-2. *Supported Options for Creating a Service*

Option	Description
--constraint	Placement constraints.
--container-label	Container labels.
--env, -e	Sets environment variables.
--env-file	Reads in a file of environment variables. Option not added until Docker 1.13.
--host	Sets one or more custom host-to-IP mappings. Option not added until Docker 1.13. Format is host:ip.
--hostname	Container hostname. Option not added until Docker 1.13.
--label, -l	Service labels.
--limit-cpu	Limits CPUs. Default value is 0.000.
--limit-memory	Limits memory. Default value is 0.
--log-driver	Logging driver for service.
--log-opt	Logging driver options.
--mode	Service mode. Value may be replicated or global. Default is replicated.
--mount	Attaches a filesystem mount to the service.
--name	Service name.
--network	Network attachments. By default, the "ingress" overlay network is used.
--publish, -p	Publishes a port as a node port.
--read-only	Mounts the container's root filesystem as read only. Option not added until Docker 17.03. Default is false.

(continued)

Table 4-2. (*continued*)

Option	Description
--replicas	Number of tasks.
--reserve-cpu	Reserves CPUs. Default is 0.000.
--reserve-memory	Reserves memory. Default is 0.
--restart-condition	Restarts when condition is met. Value may be none, on-failure, or any.
--restart-delay	Delays between restart attempts (ns|us|ms|s|m|h).
--restart-max-attempts	Maximum number of restarts before giving up.
--tty, -t	Whether to allocate a pseudo-TTY. Option not added until Docker 1.13. Default is false.
--update-delay	Delays between updates (ns|us|ms|s|m|h). Default is 0s.
--update-failure-action	Action on update failure. Value may be pause or continue. Default value is pause.
--update-monitor	Duration after each task update to monitor for failure (ns|us|ms|s|m|h). Default is 0s.
--update-parallelism	Maximum number of tasks updated simultaneously. A value of 0 to updates all at once. Default value is 1.
--user, -u	Username or UID in format: <name|uid>[:<group|gid>].
--workdir, -w	Working directory inside the container.

As an example, create a service called hello-world with Docker image tutum/hello-world consisting of two replicas. Expose the service on port 8080 on the host. The docker service create command outputs a service ID if successful.

```
~ $ docker service create \
>   --name hello-world \
>   --publish 8080:80 \
>   --replicas 2 \
>   tutum/hello-world
vyxnpstt351124h12niqm7s64
```

A service gets created.

Listing the Tasks of a Service

You can list the service tasks, also called replicas in the context of a replicated service, with the following command.

```
docker service ps hello-world
```

The two service tasks are listed.

```
~ $ docker service ps hello-world
ID                   NAME           IMAGE                       NODE
DESIRED STATE        CURRENT STATE              ERROR           PORTS
zjm03bjsqyhp         hello-world.1  tutum/hello-world:latest    ip-172-31-10-132.ec2.internal
Running              Running 41 seconds ago
kezidi82ol5c         hello-world.2  tutum/hello-world:latest    ip-172-31-13-155.ec2.internal
Running              Running 41 seconds ago
```

The ID column lists the task ID. The task name is in the format servicename.n; hello-world.1 and hello-world.2 for the two replicas. The Docker image is also listed. The NODE column lists the private DNS of the node on which the task is scheduled. The DESIRED STATE is the state that is desired as defined in the service definition. The CURRENT STATE is the actual state of the task. At times, a task could be in a pending state because of lack of resource capacity in terms of CPU and memory.

A service task is a slot for running a Docker container. On each node on which a task is running, a Docker container should also be running. Docker containers may be listed with the docker ps command.

```
~ $ docker ps
CONTAINER ID         IMAGE                       COMMAND                     CREATED
STATUS               PORTS                       NAMES
0ccdcde64e7d         tutum/hello-world:latest    "/bin/sh -c 'php-f..."     2 minutes ago
Up 2 minutes         80/tcp                      hello-world.2.kezidi82ol5ct81u59jpgfhs1
```

Invoking a Hello World Service Task on the Command Line

Invoke the hello-world service using curl at <hostname>:8080. The curl command output is the HTML markup for the service.

```
~ $ curl ec2-34-200-225-39.compute-1.amazonaws.com:8080
<html>
<head>
        <title>Hello world!</title>
        <link href='http://fonts.googleapis.com/css?family=Open+Sans:400,700' rel='stylesheet'
        type='text/css'>
        <style>
        body {
                background-color: white;
                text-align: center;
                padding: 50px;
                font-family: "Open Sans","Helvetica Neue",Helvetica,Arial,sans-serif;
        }

        #logo {
                margin-bottom: 40px;
        }
        </style>
</head>
<body>
```

```
        <img id="logo" src="logo.png" />
        <h1>Hello world!</h1>
        <h3>My hostname is 20b121986df6</h3>
</body>
</html>
```

Getting Detailed Information About a Service

To get detailed information about the hello-world service, run the docker service inspect command.

```
docker service inspect  hello-world
```

The detailed information includes the container specification, resources, restart policy, placement, mode, update config, ports (target port and published port), virtual IPs, and update status.

```
~ $ docker service inspect  hello-world
[
    {
        "ID": "vyxnpstt351124h12niqm7s64",
        "Version": {
            "Index": 30
        },
        "CreatedAt": "2017-07-23T19:00:09.98992017Z",
        "UpdatedAt": "2017-07-23T19:00:09.9930014872",
        "Spec": {
            "Name": "hello-world",
            "Labels": {},
            "TaskTemplate": {
                "ContainerSpec": {
                    "Image": "tutum/hello-world:latest@sha256:0d57def8055178aafb4c7669cbc25e
                    c17f0acdab97cc587f30150802da8f8d85",
                    "StopGracePeriod": 10000000000,
                    "DNSConfig": {}
                },
                "Resources": {
                    "Limits": {},
                    "Reservations": {}
                },
                "RestartPolicy": {
                    "Condition": "any",
                    "Delay": 5000000000,
                    "MaxAttempts": 0
                },
                "Placement": {
                    "Platforms": [
                        {
                            "Architecture": "amd64",
                            "OS": "linux"
                        }
                    ]
                },
```

```json
                    "ForceUpdate": 0,
                    "Runtime": "container"
                },
                "Mode": {
                    "Replicated": {
                        "Replicas": 2
                    }
                },
                "UpdateConfig": {
                    "Parallelism": 1,
                    "FailureAction": "pause",
                    "Monitor": 5000000000,
                    "MaxFailureRatio": 0,
                    "Order": "stop-first"
                },
                "RollbackConfig": {
                    "Parallelism": 1,
                    "FailureAction": "pause",
                    "Monitor": 5000000000,
                    "MaxFailureRatio": 0,
                    "Order": "stop-first"
                },
                "EndpointSpec": {
                    "Mode": "vip",
                    "Ports": [
                        {
                            "Protocol": "tcp",
                            "TargetPort": 80,
                            "PublishedPort": 8080,
                            "PublishMode": "ingress"
                        }
                    ]
                }
            },
            "Endpoint": {
                "Spec": {
                    "Mode": "vip",
                    "Ports": [
                        {
                            "Protocol": "tcp",
                            "TargetPort": 80,
                            "PublishedPort": 8080,
                            "PublishMode": "ingress"
                        }
                    ]
                },
                "Ports": [
                    {
                        "Protocol": "tcp",
                        "TargetPort": 80,
```

```
                "PublishedPort": 8080,
                "PublishMode": "ingress"
            }
        ],
        "VirtualIPs": [
            {
                "NetworkID": "y3k655bdlp3x102a2bslh4swh",
                "Addr": "10.255.0.5/16"
            }
        ]
    }
  }
]
```

Invoking the Hello World Service in a Browser

The Hello World service may be invoked in a browser using the public DNS of a EC2 instance on which a Swarm node is hosted. A service replica does not have to be running on a node to invoke the service from the node. You obtain the public DNS of a manager node from the EC2 console, as shown in Figure 4-3. Invoke the Hello World service with <Public DNS>:<Published Port> URL. As the Hello World service is exposed or published on port 8080, the URL to invoke in a browser becomes <Public DNS>:8080. The service is invoked and the service output is displayed in the browser, as shown in Figure 4-6.

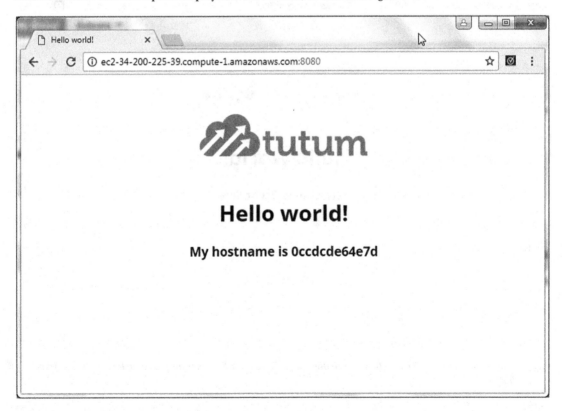

Figure 4-6. *Invoking a service in a browser*

Similarly, you can obtain the public DNS of a EC2 instance on which a Swarm worker node is hosted, as shown in Figure 4-7.

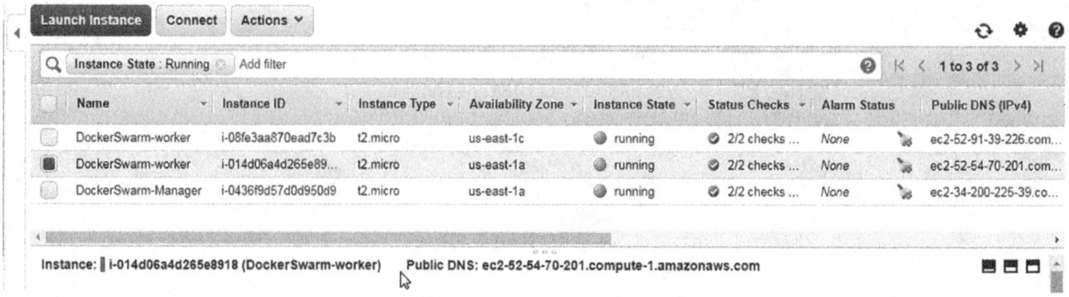

Figure 4-7. *Obtaining the public DNS for a EC2 instance on which a Swarm worker node is hosted*

Invoke the service using the `PublicDNS:8080` URL in a browser, as shown in Figure 4-8.

Figure 4-8. *Invoking a service in a browser using public DNS for a EC2 instance on which a Swarm worker node is hosted*

A manager node is also a worker node by default and service tasks also run on the manager node.

Creating a Service for a MySQL Database

Next, we create a service for a MySQL database. Using the `mysql` Docker image is different than using the `tutum/hello-world` Docker image in two respects.

- The `mysql` Docker image has a mandatory environment variable called `MYSQL_ROOT_PASSWORD`.

- The `mysql` Docker image is based on a Debian Linux and starts the MySQL database server in Docker container, while the `tutum/hello-world` image is based on Alpine Linux and starts Apache Server to run PHP applications.

Run the following `docker service create` command to create one replica of the MySQL database service. Supply a root password with the `MYSQL_ROOT_PASSWORD` environment variable. Include some other options for the restart condition, the restart max attempts, the update delay, and the update failure action. Remove any previously running Docker service called `mysql` with the `docker service rm mysql` command.

```
~ $ docker service create \
   --env MYSQL_ROOT_PASSWORD='mysql'\
   --replicas 1 \
   --restart-condition none \
   --restart-max-attempts 5 \
   --update-failure-action continue \
   --name mysql \
   --update-delay 10s \
  mysql
```

A service gets created for MySQL database and the service ID gets output.

```
~ $ docker service create \
>    --env MYSQL_ROOT_PASSWORD='mysql'\
>    --replicas 1 \
>    --restart-condition none \
>    --restart-max-attempts 5 \
>    --update-failure-action continue \
>    --name mysql \
>    --update-delay 10s \
>  mysql
gzl8k1wy8kf3ms1nu5zwlfxm6
```

List the services with the `docker service ls` command; the `mysql` service should be listed.

```
~ $ docker service ls
ID             NAME          MODE        REPLICAS  IMAGE                       PORTS
gzl8k1wy8kf3   mysql         replicated  1/1       mysql:latest
vyxnpstt3511   hello-world   replicated  2/2       tutum/hello-world:latest    *:8080->80/tcp
```

List the service tasks/replicas with the `docker service ps mysql` command. One task is running on the manager worker node.

```
~ $ docker service ps mysql
ID                NAME          IMAGE            NODE
DESIRED STATE     CURRENT STATE                                      ERROR          PORTS
mfw76m4rxbhp      mysql.1      mysql:latest      ip-172-31-37-135.ec2.internal
Running           Running 16 seconds ago
```

How service tasks are scheduled, including node selection based on node ranking, is discussed in Chapter 8, which covers scheduling.

Scaling a Service

Next, we scale the mysql service. Only replicated services can be scaled and the command syntax to scale one or more services is as follows.

```
docker service scale SERVICE=REPLICAS [SERVICE=REPLICAS...]
```

To scale the mysql service to three tasks, run the following command.

```
docker service scale mysql=3
```

The mysql service gets scaled to three, as indicated by the command output.

```
~ $ docker service scale mysql=3
mysql scaled to 3
```

Listing Service Tasks

The docker service ps command syntax to list service tasks is as follows.

```
docker service ps [OPTIONS] SERVICE [SERVICE...]
```

The command supports the options listed in Table 4-3.

Table 4-3. *Options for the docker service ps Command*

Option	Description
--filter, -f	Filters output based on conditions provided. The following filters are supported:
	id=<task id>
	name=<task name>
	node=<node id or name>
	desired-state=(running | shutdown | accepted)
--no-resolve	Whether to map IDs to names. Default value is false.
--no-trunc	Whether to truncate output. Option not added until Docker 1.13. Default value is false.
--quiet, -q	Whether to only display task IDs. Option not added until Docker 1.13. Default value is false.

As an example, you can list only the service tasks that are running.

```
docker service ps -f desired-state=running mysql
```

Only the running tasks are listed.

```
~ $ docker service ps -f desired-state=running mysql
ID                     NAME                     IMAGE          NODE
DESIRED STATE          CURRENT STATE            ERROR          PORTS
mfw76m4rxbhp           mysql.1                  mysql:latest   ip-172-31-37-135.ec2.internal
Running                Running 46 seconds ago
s4flvtode8od           mysql.2                  mysql:latest   ip-172-31-13-155.ec2.internal
Running                Running 8 seconds ago
j0jd92p5dmd8           mysql.3                  mysql:latest   ip-172-31-10-132.ec2.internal
Running                Running 9 seconds ago
```

All tasks are running; therefore, the effect of using the filter is not very apparent. But, in a subsequent example, you'll list running service tasks when some tasks are not running.

Not all worker nodes are utilized for running service tasks if the number of nodes is more than the number of tasks, as when the hello-world and mysql services had fewer than three tasks running. A node could have more than one service task running if the number of replicas is more than the number of nodes in a Swarm. Scaling up to five replicas starts more than one replica on two of the nodes.

```
~ $ docker service scale mysql=5
mysql scaled to 5
~ $ docker service ps mysql
ID                     NAME                     IMAGE          NODE
DESIRED STATE          CURRENT STATE            ERROR          PORTS
mfw76m4rxbhp           mysql.1                  mysql:latest   ip-172-31-37-135.ec2.internal
Running                Running about a minute ago
s4flvtode8od           mysql.2                  mysql:latest   ip-172-31-13-155.ec2.internal
Running                Running 44 seconds ago
j0jd92p5dmd8           mysql.3                  mysql:latest   ip-172-31-10-132.ec2.internal
Running                Running 45 seconds ago
vh9qxhm452pt           mysql.4                  mysql:latest   ip-172-31-37-135.ec2.internal
Running                Running 26 seconds ago
6jtkvstssnkf           mysql.5                  mysql:latest   ip-172-31-10-132.ec2.internal
Running                Running 26 seconds ago
```

Only one mysql service replica is running on the manager node; therefore, only one Docker container for the mysql service is running on the manager node.

```
~ $ docker ps
CONTAINER ID           IMAGE           COMMAND
CREATED                STATUS          PORTS                 NAMES
6bbe40000874           mysql:latest    "docker-entrypoint..."
About a minute ago     Up About a minute    3306/tcp         mysql.2.s4flvtode8odjjere2z
                                                             si9gdx
```

Scaling to 10 tasks starts multiple tasks on each of the Swarm nodes.

```
~ $ docker service scale mysql=10
mysql scaled to 10
~ $ docker service ps -f desired-state=running mysql
ID                  NAME               IMAGE              NODE
DESIRED STATE       CURRENT STATE                         ERROR           PORTS
s4flvtode8od        mysql.2            mysql:latest       ip-172-31-13-155.ec2.internal
Running             Running about a minute ago
j0jd92p5dmd8        mysql.3            mysql:latest       ip-172-31-10-132.ec2.internal
Running             Running 2 minutes ago
6jtkvstssnkf        mysql.5            mysql:latest       ip-172-31-10-132.ec2.internal
Running             Running about a minute ago
jxunbdec3fnj        mysql.6            mysql:latest       ip-172-31-37-135.ec2.internal
Running             Running 14 seconds ago
t1nz59dyoi2s        mysql.7            mysql:latest       ip-172-31-10-132.ec2.internal
Running             Running 14 seconds ago
lousvchdirn9        mysql.8            mysql:latest       ip-172-31-13-155.ec2.internal
Running             Running 14 seconds ago
94ml0f52344d        mysql.9            mysql:latest       ip-172-31-37-135.ec2.internal
Running             Running 14 seconds ago
pd40sd7qlk3j        mysql.10           mysql:latest       ip-172-31-13-155.ec2.internal
Running             Running 14 seconds ago
```

The number of Docker containers for the mysql service on the manager node increases to three for the three tasks running on the manager node.

```
~ $ docker ps
CONTAINER ID        IMAGE              COMMAND                   CREATED
STATUS              PORTS                            NAMES
15e3253f69f1        mysql:latest       "docker-entrypoint..."    50 seconds ago
Up 49 seconds       3306/tcp                         mysql.8.lousvchdirn9fv8wot5vivk6d
cca7ab20c914        mysql:latest       "docker-entrypoint..."    50 seconds ago
Up 49 seconds       3306/tcp                         mysql.10.pd40sd7qlk3jc0i73huop8e4r
6bbe40000874        mysql:latest       "docker-entrypoint..."    2 minutes ago
Up 2 minutes        3306/tcp                         mysql.2.s4flvtode8odjjere2zsi9gdx
```

Because you'll learn more about Docker services with the MySQL database service example in later sections, and also for completeness, next we discuss using a Docker container for MySQL database to create a database table.

Accessing a MySQL Database in a Docker Container

Next, we access MySQL database in a Docker container. The docker ps command, when run on each instance, lists Docker containers for the mysql service on the instance. Start a bash shell for a Docker container with the docker exec -it <containerid> bash command. The root prompt gets displayed for the Docker container.

```
~ $ docker exec -it 15e3253f69f1 bash
root@15e3253f69f1:/#
```

Start the MySQL CLI with the `mysql` command as user root. Specify the password when prompted; the password used to create the service was specified in the `--env` option to the `docker service create` command using environment variable `MYSQL_ROOT_PASSWORD`. The `mysql>` CLI command prompt is displayed.

```
root@15e3253f69f1:/# mysql -u root -p
Enter password:
Welcome to the MySQL monitor. Commands end with ; or \g.
Your MySQL connection id is 4
Server version: 5.7.19 MySQL Community Server (GPL)
Copyright (c) 2000, 2017, Oracle and/or its affiliates. All rights reserved.
Oracle is a registered trademark of Oracle Corporation and/or its
affiliates. Other names may be trademarks of their respective
owners.
Type 'help;' or '\h' for help. Type '\c' to clear the current input statement.
mysql>
```

Set the database to use as `mysql` with the `use mysql` command.

```
mysql> use mysql;
Reading table information for completion of table and column names
You can turn off this feature to get a quicker startup with -A

Database changed
```

Create a database table with the following SQL script.

```
CREATE  TABLE  wlslog(time_stamp VARCHAR(45) PRIMARY KEY,category VARCHAR(25),type
VARCHAR(25),servername VARCHAR(25),code VARCHAR(25),msg VARCHAR(45));
```

The `wlslog` table is created.

```
mysql> CREATE  TABLE  wlslog(time_stamp VARCHAR(45) PRIMARY KEY,category VARCHAR(25),type
VARCHAR(25),servername VARCHAR(25),code VARCHAR(25),msg VARCHAR(45));
Query OK, 0 rows affected (0.06 sec)
```

Add some data to the `wlslog` table with the following SQL commands run from the MySQL CLI.

```
mysql> INSERT INTO wlslog VALUES('Apr-8-2014-7:06:16-PM-PDT','Notice','WebLogicServer',
'AdminServer','BEA-000365','Server state changed to STANDBY');
Query OK, 1 row affected (0.02 sec)

mysql> INSERT INTO wlslog VALUES('Apr-8-2014-7:06:17-PM-PDT','Notice','WebLogicServer',
'AdminServer','BEA-000365','Server state changed to STARTING');
Query OK, 1 row affected (0.01 sec)
```

```
mysql> INSERT INTO wlslog VALUES('Apr-8-2014-7:06:18-PM-PDT','Notice','WebLogicServer',
'AdminServer','BEA-000365','Server state changed to ADMIN');
Query OK, 1 row affected (0.00 sec)

mysql> INSERT INTO wlslog VALUES('Apr-8-2014-7:06:19-PM-PDT','Notice','WebLogicServer',
'AdminServer','BEA-000365','Server state changed to RESUMING');
Query OK, 1 row affected (0.00 sec)

mysql> INSERT INTO wlslog VALUES('Apr-8-2014-7:06:20-PM-PDT','Notice','WebLogicServer',
'AdminServer','BEA-000331','Started WebLogic AdminServer');
Query OK, 1 row affected (0.01 sec)

mysql> INSERT INTO wlslog VALUES('Apr-8-2014-7:06:21-PM-PDT','Notice','WebLogicServer',
'AdminServer','BEA-000365','Server state changed to RUNNING');
Query OK, 1 row affected (0.00 sec)

mysql> INSERT INTO wlslog VALUES('Apr-8-2014-7:06:22-PM-PDT','Notice','WebLogicServer',
'AdminServer','BEA-000360','Server started in RUNNING mode');
Query OK, 1 row affected (0.00 sec)
```

Run a SQL query to list the database table data.

```
mysql> SELECT * FROM wlslog;
+--------------------------+----------+----------------+------------+------------+--------------------------------+
| time_stamp               | category | type           | servername | code       | msg                            |
+--------------------------+----------+----------------+------------+------------+--------------------------------+
| Apr-8-2014-7:06:16-PM-PDT | Notice   | WebLogicServer | AdminServer | BEA-000365 | Server state changed to STANDBY |
| Apr-8-2014-7:06:17-PM-PDT | Notice   | WebLogicServer | AdminServer | BEA-000365 | Server state changed to STARTING|
| Apr-8-2014-7:06:18-PM-PDT | Notice   | WebLogicServer | AdminServer | BEA-000365 | Server state changed to ADMIN   |
| Apr-8-2014-7:06:19-PM-PDT | Notice   | WebLogicServer | AdminServer | BEA-000365 | Server state changed to RESUMING|
| Apr-8-2014-7:06:20-PM-PDT | Notice   | WebLogicServer | AdminServer | BEA-000331 | Started WebLogic AdminServer    |
| Apr-8-2014-7:06:21-PM-PDT | Notice   | WebLogicServer | AdminServer | BEA-000365 | Server state changed to RUNNING |
| Apr-8-2014-7:06:22-PM-PDT | Notice   | WebLogicServer | AdminServer | BEA-000360 | Server started in RUNNING mode  |
+--------------------------+----------+----------------+------------+------------+--------------------------------+
7 rows in set (0.00 sec)
```

Exit the MySQL CLI and the bash shell using the exit command.

```
mysql> exit
Bye
root@15e3253f69f1:/# exit
exit
```

Updating a Service

A service may be updated subsequent to being created with the docker service update command, which has the following syntax:

```
docker service update [OPTIONS] SERVICE
```

Some of the supported options are listed in Table 4-4.

Table 4-4. *Options for the docker service update Command*

Option	Description
--args	Args for the command.
--constraint-add	Adds or updates a placement constraint.
--constraint-rm	Removes a placement constraint.
--container-label-add	Adds or updates a Docker container label.
--container-label-rm	Removes a container label by its key.
--env-add	Adds or updates an environment variable.
--env-rm	Removes an environment variable.
--force	Whether to force an update even if no changes require it. Option added in Docker 1.13. Default is false.
--group-add	Adds an additional supplementary user group to the container. Option added in Docker 1.13.
--group-rm	Removes a previously added supplementary user group from the container. Option added in Docker 1.13.
--host-add	Adds or updates a custom host-to-IP mapping (host:ip). Option added in Docker 1.13.
--host-rm	Removes a custom host-to-IP mapping (host:ip). Option added in Docker 1.13.
--hostname	Updates the container hostname. Option added in Docker 1.13.
--image	Updates the service image tag.
--label-add	Adds or updates a service label.
--label-rm	Removes a label by its key.
--limit-cpu	Updates the limit CPUs. Default value is 0.000.
--limit-memory	Updates the limit memory. Default value is 0.
--log-driver	Updates logging driver for service.
--log-opt	Updates logging driver options.
--mount-add	Adds or updates a mount on a service.
--mount-rm	Removes a mount by its target path.
--publish-add	Adds or updates a published port.
--publish-rm	Removes a published port by its target port.

(continued)

73

Table 4-4. (*continued*)

Option	Description
--read-only	Mounts the container's root filesystem as read only. Option added in Docker 17.06. Default is false.
--replicas	Updates the number of tasks.
--reserve-cpu	Updates the reserve CPUs. Default is 0.000.
--reserve-memory	Updates the reserve memory. Default is 0.
--restart-condition	Updates the restart when condition is met (none, on-failure, or any).
--restart-delay	Updates the delay between restart attempts (ns|us|ms|s|m|h).
--restart-max-attempts	Updates the maximum number of restarts before giving up.
--rollback	Whether to roll back to a previous specification. Option added in Docker 1.13. Default is false.
--tty, -t	Whether to allocate a pseudo-TTY. Option added in Docker 1.13. Default is false.
--update-delay	Updates delay between updates (ns|us|ms|s|m|h). Default is 0s.
--update-failure-action	Updates action on update failure (pause|continue). Default is pause.
--update-monitor	Duration after each task update to monitor for failure (ns|us|ms|s|m|h). Option added in Docker 1.13. Default 0s.
--update-parallelism	Updates the maximum number of tasks updated simultaneously (0 to update all at once). Default is 1.
--user, -u	Adds the username or UID (format: <name|uid>[:<group|gid>]).
--workdir, -w	Updates the working directory inside the container.

Next, we update some of the parameters of a deployed service.

Updating the Replicas

First, create a mysql service to update.

```
docker service create \
  --env MYSQL_ROOT_PASSWORD='mysql'\
  --replicas 1 \
  --restart-condition on-failure \
  --restart-max-attempts 5 \
  --update-failure-action continue \
  --name mysql \
  --update-delay 10s \
 mysql:5.6
```

A service from Docker image `mysql:5.6` is created and the service ID is output.

```
~ $ docker service rm mysql
mysql
~ $ docker service create \
>    --env MYSQL_ROOT_PASSWORD='mysql'\
>    --replicas 1 \
>    --restart-condition on-failure \
>    --restart-max-attempts 5 \
>    --update-failure-action continue \
>    --name mysql \
>    --update-delay 10s \
>    mysql:5.6
mecdt3zluvlvxqc3hdpw8edg1
```

Update the number of replicas to five using the `docker service update` command. If the command is successful, the service name is output from the command.

```
~ $ docker service update --replicas 5 mysql
mysql
```

Setting replicas to five does not just start four new tasks to make a total of five tasks. When a service is updated to change the number of replicas, all the service tasks are shut down and new tasks are started. Subsequently listing the service tasks lists the first task as being shut down and five new tasks as being started.

```
~ $ docker service ps mysql
ID                  NAME              IMAGE         NODE
DESIRED STATE       CURRENT STATE                   ERROR                      PORTS
jen0fmkjj13k        mysql.1           mysql:5.6     ip-172-31-37-135.ec2.internal
Running             Starting less than a second ago
r616gx588opd        \_ mysql.1        mysql:5.6     ip-172-31-37-135.ec2.internal
Shutdown            Failed 5 seconds ago            "task: non-zero exit (137)"
y350n4e8furo        mysql.2           mysql:5.6     ip-172-31-13-155.ec2.internal
Running             Running 7 seconds ago
ktrwxnn13fug        mysql.3           mysql:5.6     ip-172-31-37-135.ec2.internal
Running             Running 14 seconds ago
2t8j1zd8uts1        mysql.4           mysql:5.6     ip-172-31-10-132.ec2.internal
Running             Running 10 seconds ago
8tf0uuwb8i31        mysql.5           mysql:5.6     ip-172-31-10-132.ec2.internal
Running             Running 10 seconds ago
```

Updating the Docker Image Tag

Starting with a MySQL database service called `mysql` for Docker image `mysql:5.6`, next we update the service to a different Docker image tag—the `mysql:latest` Docker image. Run the following command to update the Docker image; the service name is output to indicate that the update is successful.

```
~ $ docker service update --image mysql:latest mysql
mysql
```

You can list detailed information about the service with the docker service inspect command. The image listed in the ContainerSpec is mysql:latest. The PreviousSpec is also listed.

```
~ $ docker service inspect  mysql
[
    {
        "Spec": {
          "Name": "mysql",
          "Labels": {},
          "TaskTemplate": {
              "ContainerSpec": {
                  "Image": "mysql:latest@sha256:75c563c474f1adc149978011fedfe2e6670483d133
                  b22b07ee32789b626f8de3",
                  "Env": [
                      "MYSQL_ROOT_PASSWORD=mysql"
                  ],
        "PreviousSpec": {
            "Name": "mysql",
            "Labels": {},
            "TaskTemplate": {
                "ContainerSpec": {
                    "Image": "mysql:5.6@sha256:6ad5bd392c9190fa92e65fd21f6debc8b2a76fc54f139
                    49f9b5bc6a0096a5285",
]
```

The update does not get completed immediately even though the docker service update command does. While the service is being updated, the UpdateStatus for the service is listed with State set to "updating" and the Message of "update in progress".

```
"UpdateStatus": {
            "State": "updating",
            "StartedAt": "2017-07-23T19:24:15.539042747Z",
            "Message": "update in progress"
                }
```

When the update completes, the UpdateStatus State becomes "completed" and the Message becomes "update completed".

```
        "UpdateStatus": {
            "State": "completed",
            "StartedAt": "2017-07-23T19:24:15.539042747Z",
            "CompletedAt": "2017-07-23T19:25:25.660907984Z",
            "Message": "update completed"
        }
```

While the service is updating, the service tasks are shutting down and the new service tasks are starting. When the update is starting, some of the running tasks might be based on the previous image mysql:5.6 whereas others could be based on the new image mysql:latest.

```
~ $ docker service ps mysql
ID                  NAME                IMAGE               NODE
DESIRED STATE       CURRENT STATE           ERROR                       PORTS
jen0fmkjj13k        mysql.1             mysql:5.6           ip-172-31-37-135.ec2.internal
Running             Running 38 seconds ago
r616gx588opd          \_ mysql.1         mysql:5.6          ip-172-31-37-135.ec2.internal
Shutdown            Failed 43 seconds ago   "task: non-zero exit (137)"
y350n4e8furo        mysql.2             mysql:5.6           ip-172-31-13-155.ec2.internal
Running             Running 45 seconds ago
bswz4sm8e3vj        mysql.3             mysql:5.6           ip-172-31-37-135.ec2.internal
Running             Running 6 seconds ago
ktrwxnn13fug          \_ mysql.3         mysql:5.6          ip-172-31-37-135.ec2.internal
Shutdown            Failed 12 seconds ago   "task: non-zero exit (1)"
wj1x26wvp0pt        mysql.4             mysql:latest        ip-172-31-13-155.ec2.internal
Running             Running 7 seconds ago
2t8j1zd8uts1          \_ mysql.4         mysql:5.6          ip-172-31-10-132.ec2.internal
Shutdown            Shutdown 7 seconds ago
hppq840ekrh7        mysql.5             mysql:latest        ip-172-31-10-132.ec2.internal
Running             Running 2 seconds ago
8tf0uuwb8i31          \_ mysql.5         mysql:5.6          ip-172-31-10-132.ec2.internal
Shutdown            Failed 8 seconds ago    "task: non-zero exit (1)"
```

The desired state of the tasks with image mysql:5.6 is set to Shutdown. Gradually, all the new service tasks based on the new image mysql:latest are started.

```
~ $ docker service ps mysql
ID                  NAME                IMAGE               NODE
DESIRED STATE       CURRENT STATE           ERROR                       PORTS
2uafxtcbj9qj        mysql.1             mysql:latest        ip-172-31-37-135.ec2.internal
Running             Running 30 seconds ago
jen0fmkjj13k          \_ mysql.1         mysql:5.6          ip-172-31-37-135.ec2.internal
Shutdown            Failed 36 seconds ago   "task: non-zero exit (137)"
r616gx588opd          \_ mysql.1         mysql:5.6          ip-172-31-37-135.ec2.internal
Shutdown            Failed about a minute ago "task: non-zero exit (137)"
mkv95bvx3sl1        mysql.2             mysql:latest        ip-172-31-13-155.ec2.internal
Ready               Ready 3 seconds ago
y350n4e8furo          \_ mysql.2         mysql:5.6          ip-172-31-13-155.ec2.internal
Shutdown            Failed 4 seconds ago    "task: non-zero exit (137)"
yevunzer12vm        mysql.3             mysql:latest        ip-172-31-37-135.ec2.internal
Running             Running 12 seconds ago
bswz4sm8e3vj          \_ mysql.3         mysql:5.6          ip-172-31-37-135.ec2.internal
Shutdown            Shutdown 12 seconds ago
ktrwxnn13fug          \_ mysql.3         mysql:5.6          ip-172-31-37-135.ec2.internal
Shutdown            Failed 48 seconds ago   "task: non-zero exit (1)"
wj1x26wvp0pt        mysql.4             mysql:latest        ip-172-31-13-155.ec2.internal
Running             Running 44 seconds ago
```

```
2t8j1zd8uts1          \_ mysql.4          mysql:5.6           ip-172-31-10-132.ec2.internal
Shutdown              Shutdown 44 seconds ago
hppq840ekrh7          mysql.5             mysql:latest        ip-172-31-10-132.ec2.internal
Running               Running 39 seconds ago
8tf0uuwb8i31          \_ mysql.5          mysql:5.6           ip-172-31-10-132.ec2.internal
Shutdown              Failed 44 seconds ago        "task: non-zero exit (1)"
```

Filtering the service tasks with the –f option was introduced earlier. To find which, if any, tasks are scheduled on a particular node, you run the docker service ps command with the filter set to the node. Filtered tasks, both Running and Shutdown, are then listed.

```
~ $ docker service ps  -f node=ip-172-31-13-155.ec2.internal mysql
ID                   NAME            IMAGE            NODE
DESIRED STATE        CURRENT STATE            ERROR                      PORTS
mkv95bvx3sl1         mysql.2         mysql:latest     ip-172-31-13-155.ec2.internal
Running              Running about a minute ago
y350n4e8furo          \_ mysql.2      mysql:5.6        ip-172-31-13-155.ec2.internal
Shutdown             Failed about a minute ago   "task: non-zero exit (137)"
oksssg7gsh79         mysql.4         mysql:latest     ip-172-31-13-155.ec2.internal
Running              Running 50 seconds ago
wj1x26wvp0pt          \_ mysql.4      mysql:latest     ip-172-31-13-155.ec2.internal
Shutdown             Failed 55 seconds ago       "task: non-zero exit (1)"
```

Service tasks may also be filtered by desired state. To list only running tasks, set the desired-state filter to running.

```
~ $ docker service ps -f desired-state=running mysql
ID                   NAME            IMAGE            NODE
DESIRED STATE        CURRENT STATE            ERROR           PORTS
2uafxtcbj9qj         mysql.1         mysql:latest     ip-172-31-37-135.ec2.internal
Running              Running 3 minutes ago
mkv95bvx3sl1         mysql.2         mysql:latest     ip-172-31-13-155.ec2.internal
Running              Running 2 minutes ago
yevunzer12vm         mysql.3         mysql:latest     ip-172-31-37-135.ec2.internal
Running              Running 2 minutes ago
oksssg7gsh79         mysql.4         mysql:latest     ip-172-31-13-155.ec2.internal
Running              Running 2 minutes ago
hppq840ekrh7         mysql.5         mysql:latest     ip-172-31-10-132.ec2.internal
Running              Running 3 minutes ago
```

Likewise, only the shutdown tasks are listed by setting the desired-state filter to shutdown.

```
~ $ docker service ps -f desired-state=shutdown mysql
ID                   NAME            IMAGE            NODE
DESIRED STATE        CURRENT STATE            ERROR                      PORTS
jen0fmkjj13k         mysql.1         mysql:5.6        ip-172-31-37-135.ec2.internal
Shutdown             Failed 3 minutes ago     "task: non-zero exit (137)"
r616gx588opd          \_ mysql.1      mysql:5.6        ip-172-31-37-135.ec2.internal
Shutdown             Failed 3 minutes ago     "task: non-zero exit (137)"
y350n4e8furo         mysql.2         mysql:5.6        ip-172-31-13-155.ec2.internal
Shutdown             Failed 2 minutes ago     "task: non-zero exit (137)"
```

```
bswz4sm8e3vj          mysql.3             mysql:5.6           ip-172-31-37-135.ec2.internal
Shutdown              Shutdown 2 minutes ago
ktrwxnn13fug          \_ mysql.3          mysql:5.6           ip-172-31-37-135.ec2.internal
Shutdown              Failed 3 minutes ago       "task: non-zero exit (1)"
wj1x26wvp0pt          mysql.4             mysql:latest        ip-172-31-13-155.ec2.internal
Shutdown              Failed 2 minutes ago       "task: non-zero exit (1)"
2t8j1zd8uts1          \_ mysql.4          mysql:5.6           ip-172-31-10-132.ec2.internal
Shutdown              Shutdown 3 minutes ago
8tf0uuwb8i31          mysql.5             mysql:5.6           ip-172-31-10-132.ec2.internal
Shutdown              Failed 3 minutes ago       "task: non-zero exit (1)"
```

Updating the Placement Constraints

The placement constraints may be added/removed with the `--constraint-add` and `--constraint-rm` options. We started with a Swarm consisting of three nodes—one manager and two worker nodes. We then promoted a worker node to a manager, resulting in a Swarm with two manager nodes and one worker node. .

Starting with service replicas running across the Swarm nodes, the replicas may be constrained to run on only worker nodes with the following command. The `docker service update` command outputs the service name if successful.

```
~ $ docker service update --constraint-add  "node.role==worker" mysql
mysql
```

It may take a while (a few seconds or minutes) for the desired state of a service to be reconciled, during which time tasks could be running on manager nodes even though the `node.role` is set to `worker` or less than the required number of tasks could be running. When the update has completed (the update status may be found from the `docker service inspect` command), listing the running tasks for the `mysql` service indicates that the tasks are running only on the worker nodes.

```
~ $ docker service ps -f desired-state=running mysql
ID                    NAME                IMAGE               NODE
DESIRED STATE         CURRENT STATE                 ERROR               PORTS
smk5q4nhu1rw          mysql.1             mysql:latest        ip-172-31-37-135.ec2.internal
Running               Running about a minute ago
wzmou8f6r2tg          mysql.2             mysql:latest        ip-172-31-37-135.ec2.internal
Running               Running 23 seconds ago
byavev89hukv          mysql.3             mysql:latest        ip-172-31-37-135.ec2.internal
Running               Running 23 seconds ago
erx409p0sgcc          mysql.4             mysql:latest        ip-172-31-37-135.ec2.internal
Running               Running 53 seconds ago
q7eqw8jlqig8          mysql.5             mysql:latest        ip-172-31-37-135.ec2.internal
Running               Running 46 seconds ago
```

As another example, service tasks for the `mysql` service may be constrained to run on only manager nodes. Starting with service tasks running on both manager and worker nodes and with no other constraints added, run the following command to place all tasks on the manager nodes.

```
~ $ docker service update --constraint-add 'node.role==manager' mysql
mysql
```

The tasks are not shut down on worker nodes and started on manager nodes immediately and initially may continue to be running on worker nodes.

List the service replicas again after a while. You'll see that all the tasks are listed as running on the manager nodes.

```
~ $ docker service ps -f desired-state=running mysql
ID              NAME            IMAGE           NODE
DESIRED STATE   CURRENT STATE           ERROR           PORTS
7tj8bck4jr5n    mysql.1         mysql:latest    ip-172-31-13-155.ec2.internal
Running         Running 14 seconds ago
uyeu3y67v2rt    mysql.2         mysql:latest    ip-172-31-10-132.ec2.internal
Running         Running about a minute ago
lt9p7479lkta    mysql.3         mysql:latest    ip-172-31-10-132.ec2.internal
Running         Running 1 second ago
t7d9c4viuo5y    mysql.4         mysql:latest    ip-172-31-13-155.ec2.internal
Running         Running 40 seconds ago
8xufz871yx1x    mysql.5         mysql:latest    ip-172-31-13-155.ec2.internal
Running         Running 27 seconds ago
```

Updating Environment Variables

The --env-add and --env-rm options are used to add/remove environment variables to/from a service. The mysql service we created includes only one environment variable—the mandatory MYSQL_ROOT_PASSWORD variable. You can use the docker service update command to add the environment variables MYSQL_DATABASE, MYSQL_PASSWORD, and MYSQL_ALLOW_EMPTY_PASSWORD and to update MYSQL_ROOT_PASSWORD in the same command to an empty password. The command outputs the service name if successful.

```
~ $ docker service update --env-add 'MYSQL _DATABASE=mysql'   --env-add 'MYSQL_
PASSWORD=mysql'  --env-add 'MYSQL_ALLOW_EMPTY_PASSWORD=yes'  --env-add 'MYSQL_ROOT_
PASSWORD=yes'  mysql
mysql
```

When the update has completed, the docker service inspect command lists the environment variables added.

```
~ $ docker service inspect mysql
[...
        "Spec": {
            "Name": "mysql",
...
                    "Env": [
                        "MYSQL_ROOT_PASSWORD=yes",
                        "MYSQL _DATABASE=mysql",
                        "MYSQL_PASSWORD=mysql",
                        "MYSQL_ALLOW_EMPTY_PASSWORD=yes"
                    ],
...
]
```

Updating the environment variables causes the containers to restart. So, simply adding environment variables doesn't cause the new database to be created in the same container. A new container is started with the updated environment variables.

Updating the Docker Image

The Docker image may also be updated, not just the image tag. As an example, update the Docker image for a MySQL database service to use the `postgres` Docker image, which is for the PostgreSQL database. The command outputs the service name if the update is successful.

```
~ $ docker service update --image postgres mysql
mysql
```

After the update has completed, showing the running service tasks lists new tasks for the `postgres` image. The service name stays the same and the Docker image is updated to `postgres`.

```
~ $ docker service ps -f desired-state=running mysql
ID                      NAME            IMAGE               NODE
DESIRED STATE           CURRENT STATE                ERROR          PORTS
hmk7128ls19a            mysql.1         postgres:latest     ip-172-31-13-155.ec2.internal
Running                 Running 18 seconds ago
5ofbkc82gp0i            mysql.2         postgres:latest     ip-172-31-10-132.ec2.internal
Running                 Running about a minute ago
v0gfc65lhw62            mysql.3         postgres:latest     ip-172-31-13-155.ec2.internal
Running                 Running 31 seconds ago
miscjf9n66qq            mysql.4         postgres:latest     ip-172-31-13-155.ec2.internal
Running                 Running 45 seconds ago
g5viy8jyzpi1            mysql.5         postgres:latest     ip-172-31-10-132.ec2.internal
Running                 Running about a minute ago
```

Updating the Docker image does not remove the environment variables associated with the `mysql` Docker image, which are still listed in the service detail.

```
~ $ docker service inspect mysql
[
  ...
      "Spec": {
          "Name": "mysql",
  ...
              "ContainerSpec": {
                  "Env": [
                      "MYSQL_ROOT_PASSWORD=yes",
                      "MYSQL _DATABASE=mysql",
                      "MYSQL_PASSWORD=mysql",
                      "MYSQL_ALLOW_EMPTY_PASSWORD=yes"
                  ],
  ...
]
```

The added environment variables for the MySQL database need to be removed, as the PostgreSQL database Docker image `postgres` does not use the same environment variables. Remove all the environment variables from the `mysql` service with the `--env-rm` option to the `docker service update` command. To remove only the env variable, the name needs to be specified, not the env value.

```
docker service update --env-rm 'MYSQL_DATABASE'   --env-rm 'MYSQL_PASSWORD'   --env-rm
'MYSQL_ALLOW_EMPTY_PASSWORD'   --env-rm 'MYSQL_ROOT_PASSWORD'   mysql
```

81

Updating the Container Labels

The --container-label-add and --container-label-rm options are used to update the Docker container labels for a service. To add a container label to the mysql service, run a docker service update command, which outputs the service name if successful.

```
~ $ docker service update --container-label-add 'com.docker.swarm.service.version=latest'
mysql
mysql
```

On listing detailed information about the service, the added label is listed in the ContainerSpec labels.

```
~ $ docker service inspect mysql
[
...
                "ContainerSpec": {
                    "Labels": {
                        "com.docker.swarm.service.version": "latest"
                    },
...
]
```

The label added may be removed with the --container-label-rm option. To remove only the label, the key needs to be specified, not the label value.

```
~ $ docker service update --container-label-rm  'com.docker.swarm.service.version' mysql
mysql
```

Updating Resources Settings

The --limit-cpu, --limit-memory, --reserve-cpu, and --reserve-memory options of the docker service update command are used to update the resource settings for a service. As an example, update the resource limits and reserves. The command outputs the service name if successful.

```
~ $ docker service update --limit-cpu 0.5  --limit-memory 1GB --reserve-cpu
"0.5"  --reserve-memory "1GB" mysql
mysql
```

The resources settings are updated. Service detail lists the updated resource settings in the Resources JSON object.

```
~ $ docker service inspect mysql
[
   ...
                "ContainerSpec": {
                "Resources": {
                    "Limits": {
                        "NanoCPUs": 500000000,
                        "MemoryBytes": 1073741824
                    },
                    "Reservations": {
```

```
            "NanoCPUs": 500000000,
            "MemoryBytes": 1073741824
          }
        },
  ...
]
```

Removing a Service

The docker service rm command removes a service. If the output of the command is the service name, the service has been removed. All the associated service tasks and Docker containers also are removed.

```
~ $ docker service rm mysql
mysql
```

Creating a Global Service

As discussed earlier, a service has two modes—*replicated* or *global*. The default mode is replicated. The mode may also be explicitly set to replicated with the --mode option of the docker service create command. The service mode cannot be updated after a service has been created, with the docker service update command for example. Create a replicated service for nginx using the --mode option.

```
~ $ docker service create --mode replicated  --name nginx nginx
no177eh3gxsyemb1gfzc99mmd
```

A replicated mode service is created with the default number of replicas, which is 1. List the services with the docker service ls command. The nginx service is listed with one replica.

```
~ $ docker service ls
ID                NAME          MODE          REPLICAS        IMAGE           PORTS
no177eh3gxsy      nginx         replicated    1/1             nginx:latest
```

A global service runs one task on each node in a Swarm by default. A global service may be required at times such as for an agent (logging/monitoring) that needs to run on each node. A global service is used for logging in Chapter 11. Next, we create a nginx Docker image-based service that's global. Remove the replicated service nginx with the docker service rm nginx command. A service name must be unique even if different services are of different modes. Next, create a global mode nginx service with the same command as for the replicated service, except that the --mode option is set to global instead of replicated.

```
~ $ docker service create --mode global  --name nginx  nginx
5prj6c4v4be6ga0odnb22qa4n
```

A global mode service is created. The docker service ls command lists the service. The REPLICAS column for a global service does not list the number of replicas, as no replicas are created. Instead global is listed in the REPLICAS column.

```
~ $ docker service ls
ID                NAME          MODE          REPLICAS        IMAGE           PORTS
5prj6c4v4be6      nginx         global        3/3             nginx:latest
```

A service task is created for a global service on each node in the Swarm on which a task can run. Scheduling constraints may be used with a global service to prevent running a task on each node. Scheduling is discussed in Chapter 8. Global services cannot be scaled.

Summary

This chapter introduced Docker services running on a Docker Swarm. A service consists of service tasks or replicas. A Docker Swarm supports two types of services—*replicated services* and *global services*. A replicated service has the assigned number of replicas and is scalable. A global service has a task on each node in a Swarm. The term "replica" is used in the context of a replicated service to refer to the service tasks that are run across the nodes in a Swarm. A replicated service could run a specified number of tasks for a service, which could imply running no tasks or running multiple tasks on a particular node. The term "replica" is generally not used in the context of a global service, which runs only one task on each node in the Swarm. Each task (replica) is associated with a Docker container. We started with a Hello World service and invoked the service with `curl` on the command line and in a browser. Subsequently, we discussed a service for a MySQL database. We started a bash shell for a MySQL service container and created a database table. Scaling, updating, and removing a service are some of the other service features this chapter covered. The chapter concluded by creating a global service. The next chapter covers the Docker Swarm scaling service in more detail.

■ ■ ■

CHAPTER 5

Scaling Services

Docker Engine is suitable for developing lightweight applications that run in Docker containers that are isolated from each other. Docker containers are able to provide their own networking and filesystem.

The Problem

Docker Engine (prior to native Swarm mode) was designed to run Docker containers that must be started separately. Consider the use case that multiple replicas or instances of a service need to be created. As client load on an application running in a Docker container increases, the application may need to be run on multiple nodes. A limitation of Docker Engine is that the docker run command must be run each time a Docker container is to be started for a Docker image. If a Docker application must run on three nodes, the docker run <img> command must run on each of the nodes as well, as illustrated in Figure 5-1. No provision to scale an application or run multiple replicas is provided in the Docker Engine (prior to Docker 1.12 native Swarm mode support).

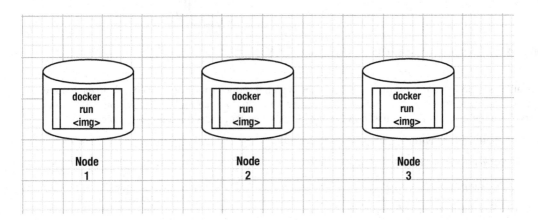

Figure 5-1. *Docker engine without provision for scaling*

© Deepak Vohra 2017

D. Vohra, *Docker Management Design Patterns*, https://doi.org/10.1007/978-1-4842-2973-6_5

The Solution

The Docker Swarm mode has the provision to scale a Docker service. A service abstraction is associated with zero or more replicas (tasks) and each task starts a Docker container for the service. The service may be scaled up or down to run more/fewer replicas, as required. With a single docker service scale <svc>=<replicas> command, a service can run the required number of replicas, as illustrated in Figure 5-2. If 10 service replicas are to be started across a distributed cluster, a single command is able to provision scaling.

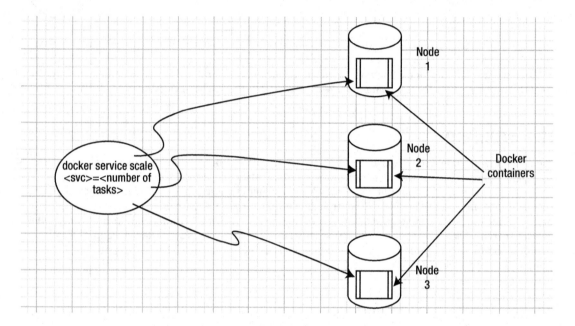

Figure 5-2. *Docker Swarm mode with provision for scaling*

Scaling is supported only for replicated services. A global service runs one service task on each node in a Swarm. Scaling services was introduced in Chapter 3 and, in this chapter, we discuss some of the other aspects of scaling services not discussed in Chapter 3. This chapter covers the following topics:

- Setting the environment
- Creating a replicated service
- Scaling up a service
- Scaling down a service
- Removing a service
- Global services cannot be scaled
- Scaling multiple services in the same command
- Service replicas replacement on a node leaving the Swarm

Setting the Environment

Create a three-node Swarm on Docker for Swarm, which is discussed in Chapter 3. A Docker for AWS Swarm you created in another chapter may be used in this chapter. Obtain the public IP address of the EC2 instance for the Swarm manager.

SSH login to the Swarm manager EC2 instance with user "docker".

```
[root@localhost ~]# ssh -i  "docker.pem"  docker@34.200.225.39
Welcome to Docker!
```

The docker node ls command lists the nodes in the Swarm.

```
~ $ docker node ls
ID                          HOSTNAME                      STATUS   AVAILABILITY  MANAGER STATUS
ilru4f0i280w2tlsrg9hglwsj   ip-172-31-10-132.ec2.internal Ready    Active
w5to186ipblpcq390625wyq2e   ip-172-31-37-135.ec2.internal Ready    Active
zkxle7kafwcmt1sd93kh5cy5e * ip-172-31-13-155.ec2.internal Ready    Active        Leader
```

Creating a Replicated Service

As discussed in Chapter 4, Docker Swarm mode supports two types of services—*global* and *replicated*. The default is the replicated mode. Only the replicated service can be scaled. Next, create a replicated service for MySQL database using the docker service create command, initially consisting of one replica, as specified in the --replicas option. The default number of replicas if the --replicas option is not specified is also one.

```
~ $ docker service create \
>   --env MYSQL_ROOT_PASSWORD='mysql'\
>   --replicas 1 \
>   --name mysql \
>   mysql
ndu4kwqk9ol7e7wxvv5bremr4
```

List the services using docker service ls.

```
~ $ docker service ls
ID              NAME     MODE          REPLICAS      IMAGE           PORTS
ndu4kwqk9ol7    mysql    replicated    1/1           mysql:latest
```

As service replicas take a while (albeit a few seconds) to start, initially 0/1 replicas could be listed in the REPLICAS column, which implies that the desired state of running one service replica has not been achieved yet. Run the same command after a few seconds and 1/1 REPLICAS should be listed as running.

Optionally, the docker service create command may also be run by setting the --mode option. Remove the mysql service if it was created previously and use the --mode option as follows.

```
~ $ docker service rm mysql
mysql
~ $ docker service create \
>   --mode replicated \
>   --env MYSQL_ROOT_PASSWORD='mysql'\
>   --replicas 1 \
>   --name mysql \
>   mysql
rl2s2ptgbs9z2t7fy5e63wf2j
```

The mysql service is created as without the --mode replicated option. List the service replicas or tasks with docker service ps mysql. A single replica is listed.

```
~ $ docker service ps mysql
ID              NAME        IMAGE    NODE            DESIRED STATE   CURRENT STATE   ERROR   PORTS
yrikmh7mciv7    mysql.1     mysql:   ip-172-31-13-   Running         Running 21
                            latest   155.ec2.internal                seconds ago
```

One service replica is created by default if the --replicas option is omitted. It should be mentioned that running multiple replicas of the MySQL database does not automatically imply that they are sharing data, so accessing one replica will not give you the same data as another replica. Sharing data using mounts is discussed in Chapter 6.

Scaling Up a Service

The docker service scale command, which has the following syntax, may be used to scale up/down a service, which changes the desired state of the service.

```
docker service scale SERVICE=REPLICAS [SERVICE=REPLICAS...]
```

First, scale up the service to three replicas.

```
~ $ docker service scale mysql=3
mysql scaled to 3
```

Subsequently, three tasks are listed as scheduled on the three nodes in the Swarm.

```
~ $ docker service ps mysql
ID              NAME        IMAGE    NODE            DESIRED STATE  CURRENT STATE   ERROR   PORTS
yrikmh7mciv7    mysql.1     mysql:   ip-172-31-13-   Running        Running 37
                            latest   155.ec2.internal               seconds ago
3zxmotmy6n2t    mysql.2     mysql:   ip-172-31-37-   Running        Running 7
                            latest   135.ec2.internal               seconds ago
rdfsowttd3b9    mysql.3     mysql:   ip-172-31-10-   Running        Running 7
                            latest   132.ec2.internal               seconds ago
```

In addition to one replica on the manager node, one replica each is started on each of the two worker nodes. If the docker ps command is run on the manager node, only one Docker container for the mysql Docker image is listed.

```
~ $ docker ps
CONTAINER ID    IMAGE      COMMAND         CREATED         STATUS   PORTS      NAMES
6d2161a3b282    mysql:     "docker-        50 seconds ago  Up 49    3306/tcp   mysql.1.yrikmh7mci
                latest     entrypoint..."                  seconds             v7dsmql1nhdi62l
```

A service may also be scaled using the docker service update command with the --replicas option. As an example, scale it to 50 replicas.

```
~ $ docker service update --replicas=50  mysql
mysql
```

The service is scaled to 50 replicas and, subsequently, 50 service tasks are listed.

```
~ $ docker service ps -f desired-state=running mysql
ID                  NAME                IMAGE               NODE
DESIRED STATE       CURRENT STATE           ERROR              PORTS
to26kjbsgzmq        mysql.1             mysql:latest        ip-172-31-37-135.ec2.internal
Running             Running 11 seconds ago
f3tx2kbe55dh        mysql.2             mysql:latest        ip-172-31-10-132.ec2.internal
Running             Running 20 seconds ago
5mzej75us115        mysql.3             mysql:latest        ip-172-31-10-132.ec2.internal
Running             Running 13 seconds ago
wluix1b3z863        mysql.4             mysql:latest        ip-172-31-13-155.ec2.internal
Running             Preparing 13 seconds ago
9ld8smvahk9g        mysql.5             mysql:latest        ip-172-31-13-155.ec2.internal
Running             Running 47 seconds ago
3tgw8ni5mfi1        mysql.6             mysql:latest        ip-172-31-10-132.ec2.internal
Running             Running 46 seconds ago
1gm8e7pxkg0o        mysql.7             mysql:latest        ip-172-31-13-155.ec2.internal
Running             Running 46 seconds ago
iq5p2g48oagq        mysql.8             mysql:latest        ip-172-31-37-135.ec2.internal
Running             Running 45 seconds ago
i4yh072h1gs6        mysql.9             mysql:latest        ip-172-31-13-155.ec2.internal
Running             Running 46 seconds ago
r1z5tgu0dg13        mysql.10            mysql:latest        ip-172-31-13-155.ec2.internal
Running             Running 45 seconds ago
mekfjvxi9pds        mysql.11            mysql:latest        ip-172-31-10-132.ec2.internal
Running             Running 46 seconds ago
nd8f2pr4oivc        mysql.12            mysql:latest        ip-172-31-13-155.ec2.internal
Running             Running 45 seconds ago
xou9hztlj637        mysql.13            mysql:latest        ip-172-31-13-155.ec2.internal
Running             Running 45 seconds ago
t95flokvca2y        mysql.14            mysql:latest        ip-172-31-37-135.ec2.internal
Running             Running 45 seconds ago
rda5shwwfmsc        mysql.15            mysql:latest        ip-172-31-37-135.ec2.internal
Running             Running 45 seconds ago
ibb2fk2llm3w        mysql.16            mysql:latest        ip-172-31-13-155.ec2.internal
Running             Running 47 seconds ago
st4ofpvrfaip        mysql.17            mysql:latest        ip-172-31-13-155.ec2.internal
Running             Running 45 seconds ago
iw4daunt6s63        mysql.18            mysql:latest        ip-172-31-37-135.ec2.internal
Running             Running 47 seconds ago
vk4nzq7utyl2        mysql.19            mysql:latest        ip-172-31-10-132.ec2.internal
Running             Running 46 seconds ago
oj59qjcy51qw        mysql.20            mysql:latest        ip-172-31-37-135.ec2.internal
Running             Running 45 seconds ago
```

```
wiou769z8xeh          mysql.21           mysql:latest          ip-172-31-10-132.ec2.internal
Running               Running 47 seconds ago
5exwimn64w94          mysql.22           mysql:latest          ip-172-31-10-132.ec2.internal
Running               Running 48 seconds ago
agqongnh9uu3          mysql.23           mysql:latest          ip-172-31-37-135.ec2.internal
Running               Running 45 seconds ago
ynkvjwgqqqlx          mysql.24           mysql:latest          ip-172-31-37-135.ec2.internal
Running               Running 47 seconds ago
yf87kbsn1cga          mysql.25           mysql:latest          ip-172-31-13-155.ec2.internal
Running               Running 10 seconds ago
xxqj62o07cxd          mysql.26           mysql:latest          ip-172-31-37-135.ec2.internal
Running               Running 45 seconds ago
5oym9i8tjwd5          mysql.27           mysql:latest          ip-172-31-37-135.ec2.internal
Running               Running 45 seconds ago
7btl2pga1l5o          mysql.28           mysql:latest          ip-172-31-10-132.ec2.internal
Running               Running 46 seconds ago
62dqj60q1ol8          mysql.29           mysql:latest          ip-172-31-13-155.ec2.internal
Running               Running 45 seconds ago
psn7zl4th2zb          mysql.30           mysql:latest          ip-172-31-37-135.ec2.internal
Running               Preparing 16 seconds ago
khsj2an2f5gk          mysql.31           mysql:latest          ip-172-31-37-135.ec2.internal
Running               Running 45 seconds ago
rzpndzjpmuj7          mysql.32           mysql:latest          ip-172-31-13-155.ec2.internal
Running               Running 45 seconds ago
9zrcga93u5fi          mysql.33           mysql:latest          ip-172-31-13-155.ec2.internal
Running               Running 45 seconds ago
x565ry5ugj8m          mysql.34           mysql:latest          ip-172-31-10-132.ec2.internal
Running               Running 48 seconds ago
o1os5dievj37          mysql.35           mysql:latest          ip-172-31-10-132.ec2.internal
Running               Running 46 seconds ago
dritgxq0zrua          mysql.36           mysql:latest          ip-172-31-37-135.ec2.internal
Running               Running 45 seconds ago
n8hs01m8picr          mysql.37           mysql:latest          ip-172-31-37-135.ec2.internal
Running               Running 47 seconds ago
dk5w0qnkfb63          mysql.38           mysql:latest          ip-172-31-13-155.ec2.internal
Running               Running 45 seconds ago
joii103na4ao          mysql.39           mysql:latest          ip-172-31-37-135.ec2.internal
Running               Running 45 seconds ago
db5hz7m2vac1          mysql.40           mysql:latest          ip-172-31-13-155.ec2.internal
Running               Running 46 seconds ago
ghk6s12eeo48          mysql.41           mysql:latest          ip-172-31-37-135.ec2.internal
Running               Running 45 seconds ago
jbi8aksksozs          mysql.42           mysql:latest          ip-172-31-13-155.ec2.internal
Running               Running 47 seconds ago
rx3rded30oa4          mysql.43           mysql:latest          ip-172-31-37-135.ec2.internal
Running               Running 47 seconds ago
c3zaacke440s          mysql.44           mysql:latest          ip-172-31-13-155.ec2.internal
Running               Running 45 seconds ago
l6ppiurx4306          mysql.46           mysql:latest          ip-172-31-10-132.ec2.internal
Running               Running 46 seconds ago
```

```
of06zibtlsum        mysql.47             mysql:latest        ip-172-31-10-132.ec2.internal
Running             Running 46 seconds ago
kgjjwlc9zmp8        mysql.48             mysql:latest        ip-172-31-10-132.ec2.internal
Running             Running 46 seconds ago
rw1icgkyw61u        mysql.49             mysql:latest        ip-172-31-10-132.ec2.internal
Running             Running 46 seconds ago
j5jpl9a5jgbj        mysql.50             mysql:latest        ip-172-31-10-132.ec2.internal
Running             Running 47 seconds ago
```

A small-scale MySQL database service probably wouldn't benefit from scaling to 50 replicas, but an enterprise-scale application could use 50 or even more replicas.

Scaling Down a Service

A service may be scaled down just as it is scaled up. A service may even be scaled down to no replicas. The mysql service may be scaled down to no replicas by setting the number of replicas to 0 using the docker service update or docker service scale command.

```
~ $ docker service scale mysql=0
mysql scaled to 0
```

The service gets scaled down to no replicas. No service replicas that are running are listed.

```
~ $ docker service ps -f desired-state=running mysql
ID              NAME            IMAGE           NODE            DESIRED STATE
CURRENT STATE        ERROR           PORTS
```

The actual service tasks could take a while to shut down, but the desired state of all tasks is set to Shutdown.

Scaling a service to no tasks does not run any tasks, but the service is not removed. The mysql service may be scaled back up again from none to three tasks as an example.

```
~ $ docker service scale mysql=3
mysql scaled to 3
```

Three service tasks start running.

```
~ $ docker service ps -f desired-state=running mysql
ID              NAME            IMAGE           NODE
DESIRED STATE        CURRENT STATE        ERROR           PORTS
py7aqwy2reku    mysql.1         mysql:latest    ip-172-31-37-135.ec2.internal
Running         Running 9 seconds ago
re1l3q3iwmvo    mysql.2         mysql:latest    ip-172-31-37-135.ec2.internal
Running         Running 9 seconds ago
h7my2ucpfz3u    mysql.3         mysql:latest    ip-172-31-37-135.ec2.internal
Running         Running 9 seconds ago
```

Removing a Service

A service may be removed using the docker service rm command.

```
~ $ docker service rm mysql
mysql
```

The mysql service is not listed after having been removed.

```
~ $ docker service ls
ID              NAME            MODE              REPLICAS          IMAGE              PORTS
```

Multiple services may be removed using the docker service rm command. To demonstrate, you can create two services, hello-world and nginx.

```
~ $ docker service create \
>   --name hello-world \
>   --publish 8080:80 \
>   --replicas 2 \
>   tutum/hello-world
t3msb25rc8b6xcm30k0zoh4ws
~ $ docker service create --name nginx nginx
ncn4aqkgzrcjc8w1uorjo5jrd
~ $ docker service ls
ID              NAME        MODE         REPLICAS   IMAGE                      PORTS
ncn4aqkgzrcj    nginx       replicated   1/1        nginx:latest
t3msb25rc8b6    hello-world replicated   2/2        tutum/hello-world:latest   *:8080->80/tcp
```

Subsequently, remove both the services with one docker service rm command. The services removed are output if the command is successful.

```
~ $ docker service rm nginx hello-world
nginx
hello-world
```

Global Services Cannot Be Scaled

A global service creates a service task on each node in the Swarm and cannot be scaled. Create a global service for a MySQL database using the docker service create command. Notable differences in the command are that the --mode is set to global and the --replicas option is not included.

```
~ $ docker service create \
>   --mode global \
>   --env MYSQL_ROOT_PASSWORD='mysql'\
>   --name mysql-global \
>   mysql
nxhnrsiulymd9n4171cie9a8j
```

The global service is created and listing the service should indicate a Mode set to global.

```
~ $ docker service ls
ID                  NAME              MODE       REPLICAS           IMAGE              PORTS
nxhnrsiulymd        mysql-global      global     3/3                mysql:latest
```

One service task is created on each node in the Swarm.

```
~ $ docker service ps mysql-global
ID                        NAME                                     IMAGE
NODE                            DESIRED STATE     CURRENT STATE          ERROR        PORTS
nfbmkqdh46k0              mysql-global.zkxle7kafwcmt1sd93kh5cy5e    mysql:latest
ip-172-31-13-155.ec2.internal   Running           Running 22 seconds ago
t55ba3bobwzf              mysql-global.w5to186ipblpcq390625wyq2e    mysql:latest
ip-172-31-37-135.ec2.internal   Running           Running 22 seconds ago
kqg656m3olj3              mysql-global.ilru4f0i280w2tlsrg9hglwsj    mysql:latest
ip-172-31-10-132.ec2.internal   Running           Running 22 seconds ago
```

If another node is added to the Swarm, a service task automatically starts on the new node.

If the docker service scale command is run for the global service, the service does not get scaled. Instead, the following message is output.

```
~ $ docker service scale mysql-global=5
mysql-global: scale can only be used with replicated mode
```

A global service may be removed just as a replicated service, using the docker service rm command.

```
~ $ docker service rm mysql-global
mysql-global
```

Scaling Multiple Services Using the Same Command

Multiple services may be scaled using a single docker service scale command. To demonstrate, create two services: nginx and mysql.

```
~ $ docker service create \
>    --replicas 1 \
>    --name nginx \
>    nginx
u6i4e8eg720dwzz425inhxqrp
```

```
~ $ docker service create \
>    --env MYSQL_ROOT_PASSWORD='mysql'\
>    --name mysql \
>    mysql
1umb7e2gr68s54utujr6khjgd
```

List the two services. One replica for each service should be running.

```
~ $ docker service ls
ID                  NAME       MODE         REPLICAS          IMAGE              PORTS
1umb7e2gr68s        mysql      replicated   1/1               mysql:latest
u6i4e8eg720d        nginx      replicated   1/1               nginx:latest
```

Scale the `nginx` service and the `mysql` service with a single command. Different services may be scaled to a different number of replicas.

```
~ $ docker service scale mysql=5 nginx=10
mysql scaled to 5
nginx scaled to 10
```

The `mysql` service gets scaled to five tasks and the `nginx` service gets scaled to 10 replicas. Initially, some of the new tasks for a service may not have started, as for the `nginx` service, which lists only 8 of the 10 tasks as running.

```
~ $ docker service ls
ID                NAME      MODE         REPLICAS      IMAGE              PORTS
1umb7e2gr68s      mysql     replicated   5/5           mysql:latest
u6i4e8eg720d      nginx     replicated   8/10          nginx:latest
```

After a while, all service tasks should be listed as running, as indicated by 10/10 for the `nginx` service.

```
~ $ docker service ls
ID                NAME      MODE         REPLICAS      IMAGE              PORTS
1umb7e2gr68s      mysql     replicated   5/5           mysql:latest
u6i4e8eg720d      nginx     replicated   10/10         nginx:latest
```

The service tasks for the two services may be listed using a single `docker service ps` command.

```
~ $ docker service ps nginx mysql
ID                NAME            IMAGE          NODE
DESIRED STATE     CURRENT STATE             ERROR         PORTS
f9g1tw88nppk      mysql.1         mysql:latest   ip-172-31-26-234.ec2.internal
Running           Running about a minute ago
zcl1qfdiqrvu      nginx.1         nginx:latest   ip-172-31-10-132.ec2.internal
Running           Running about a minute ago
vu4xo99xr0y4      nginx.2         nginx:latest   ip-172-31-13-155.ec2.internal
Running           Running 40 seconds ago
xvxgfoacxjos      mysql.2         mysql:latest   ip-172-31-37-135.ec2.internal
Running           Running 41 seconds ago
ywOopq5y0x20      nginx.3         nginx:latest   ip-172-31-13-155.ec2.internal
Running           Running 41 seconds ago
vb92hkua6eyo      mysql.3         mysql:latest   ip-172-31-13-155.ec2.internal
Running           Running 40 seconds ago
1cnqwtb24zvy      nginx.4         nginx:latest   ip-172-31-13-155.ec2.internal
Running           Running 41 seconds ago
hclu53xkosva      mysql.4         mysql:latest   ip-172-31-26-234.ec2.internal
Running           Running 40 seconds ago
2xjcw4i9xw89      nginx.5         nginx:latest   ip-172-31-10-132.ec2.internal
Running           Running 41 seconds ago
ocvb2qctuids      mysql.5         mysql:latest   ip-172-31-10-132.ec2.internal
Running           Running 41 seconds ago
18mlu3jpp9cx      nginx.6         nginx:latest   ip-172-31-10-132.ec2.internal
Running           Running 41 seconds ago
```

```
p84m8yh5if5t          nginx.7              nginx:latest         ip-172-31-37-135.ec2.internal
Running               Running 41 seconds ago
7yp8m7ytt7z4          nginx.8              nginx:latest         ip-172-31-26-234.ec2.internal
Running               Running 24 seconds ago
zegs90r015nn          nginx.9              nginx:latest         ip-172-31-37-135.ec2.internal
Running               Running 41 seconds ago
qfkpvy28g1g6          nginx.10             nginx:latest         ip-172-31-26-234.ec2.internal
Running               Running 24 seconds ago
```

Service Tasks Replacement on a Node Leaving the Swarm

The desired state reconciliation in Docker Swarm mode ensures that the desired number of replicas are running if resources are available. If a node is made to leave a Swarm, the replicas running on the node are scheduled on another node. Starting with a mysql service replica running on each node in a three-node Swarm, you can make one worker node leave the Swarm.

```
~ docker swarm leave
Node left the swarm.
```

A replacement service task for the service task running on the shutdown node gets scheduled on another node.

```
~ s docker service ps mysql
```

NAME IMAGE NODE DESIRED STATE CURRENT STATE ERROR

```
6zu7a59ejdxip3y9oeu548hv5 mysql.l mysql ip-10-0-0-46.ec2.internal Running Running 3 minutes ago
441cuufa7sa9möeatqbiq7vi3 mysql.2 mysql ip-10-0-0-28.ec2.internal Running Running about a minute ago
blcdm8Bh6v86gl..pwp6zx3janv mysql.3 mysql ip-10-0-0-28.ec2.internal Running Running 4 seconds ago
Or3oki4acf3d6ils5iazmg425 \_ mysql.3 mysql ip-10-0-0-106.ec2.internal Shutdown Running about a minute ago
```

Make the other worker node also leave the Swarm. The service replicas on the other worker node also get shut down and scheduled on the only remaining node in the Swarm.

```
~ s docker service ps mysql
```

NAME IMAGE NODE DESIRED STATE CURRENT STATE ERROR

```
6zu7a59ejdxip3y9oeu548hv5 mysql.1 mysql ip-10-0-0-46.ec2. internal Running Running 5 minutes ago

dbdaxvl6lohlxrsxh5aobjxi8 mysq.2 mysql ip-10-0-0-46.ec2.internal Running Running 7 seconds ago

44tcuufa7sa9m6eatqbiq7vi3 \_ mysql.2 mysql ip-10-0-0-28.ec2.internal Shutdown Running 2 minutes ago

216iu28xh5hztm3bgtvy7ttk8 mysql.3 mysql ip-10-0-0-46.ec2.internal Running Running 7 seconds ago

blcdm88h6v86gLpwp6zx3janv \_ mysql.3 mysql ip-10-0-0-28.ec2.internal Shutdown Running about a minute ago

Or3oki4acf3d6ils5iazmg425 \_ mysql.3 mysql ip-10-0-0-106.ec2.internal Shutdown Running 2 minutes ago
```

If only the replicas with desired state as running are listed, all replicas are listed as running on the manager node.

```
~s docker service ps -f desired-state=running mysql

ID NAME IMAGE NODE DESIRED STATE CURRENT STATE ERROR

6zu7a59ejdxip3y9oeu548hv5 mysql.1 mysql ip-10-0-0-46.ec2.internal Running Running 7 minutes ago

dbdaxvl6lohlxrsxh5aobjxi8 mysql.2 mysql ip-10-0-0-46.ec2.internal Running Running 2 minutes ago

216iu28xh5hztm3bgtvy7ttk8 mysql.3 mysql ip-10-0-0-46.ec2.internal Running Running 2 minutes ago
```

Summary

This chapter discussed service scaling in Swarm mode. Only a replicated service can be scaled and not a global service. A service may be scaled up to as many replicas as resources can support and can be scaled down to no replicas. Multiple services may be scaled using the same command. Desire state reconciliation ensures that the desired number of service replicas are running. The next chapter covers Docker service mounts.

CHAPTER 6

■ ■ ■

Using Mounts

A service task container in a Swarm has access to the filesystem inherited from its Docker image. The data is made integral to a Docker container via its Docker image. At times, a Docker container may need to store or access data on a persistent filesystem. While a container has a filesystem, it is removed once the container exits. In order to store data across container restarts, that data must be persisted somewhere outside the container.

The Problem

Data stored only within a container could result in the following issues:

- The data is not persistent. The data is removed when a Docker container is stopped.

- The data cannot be shared with other Docker containers or with the host filesystem.

The Solution

Modular design based on the Single Responsibility Principle (SRP) recommends that data be decoupled from the Docker container. Docker Swarm mode provides *mounts* for sharing data and making data persistent across a container startup and shutdown. Docker Swarm mode provides two types of mounts for services:

- Volume mounts

- Bind mounts

The default is the volume mount. A mount for a service is created using the `--mount` option of the `docker service create` command.

Volume Mounts

Volume mounts are named volumes on the host mounted into a service task's container. The named volumes on the host persist even after a container has been stopped and removed. The named volume may be created before creating the service in which the volume is to be used or the volume may be created at service deployment time. Named volumes created at deployment time are created just prior to starting a service task's container. If created at service deployment time, the named volume is given an auto-generated name if a volume name is not specified. An example of a volume mount is shown in Figure 6-1, in which a named volume `mysql-scripts`, which exists prior to creating a service, is mounted into service task containers at the directory path `/etc/mysql/scripts`.

© Deepak Vohra 2017
D. Vohra, *Docker Management Design Patterns*, https://doi.org/10.1007/978-1-4842-2973-6_6

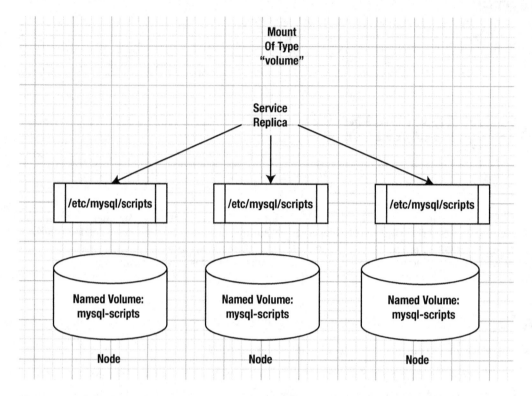

Figure 6-1. *Volume mount*

Each container in the service has access to the same named volume on the host on which the container is running, but the host named volume could store the same or different data.

When using volume mounts, contents are not replicated across the cluster. For example, if you put something into the `mysql-scripts` directory you're using, those new files will only be accessible to other tasks running on that same node. Replicas running on other nodes will not have access to those files.

Bind Mounts

Bind mounts are filesystem paths on the host on which the service task is to be scheduled. The host filesystem path is mounted into a service task's container at the specified directory path. The host filesystem path must exist on each host in the Swarm on which a task may be scheduled prior to a service being created. If certain nodes are to be excluded for service deployment, using node constraints, the bind mount host filesystem does not have to exist on those nodes. When using bind mounts, keep in mind that the service using a bind mount is not portable as such. If the service is to be deployed in production, the host directory path must exist on each host in the Swarm in the production cluster.

The host filesystem path does not have to be the same as the destination directory path in a task container. As an example, the host path `/db/mysql/data` is mounted as a bind mount into a service's containers at directory path `/etc/mysql/data` in Figure 6-2. A bind mount is read-write by default, but could be made read-only at service deployment time. Each container in the service has access to the same directory path on the host on which the container is running, but the host directory path could store different or the same data.

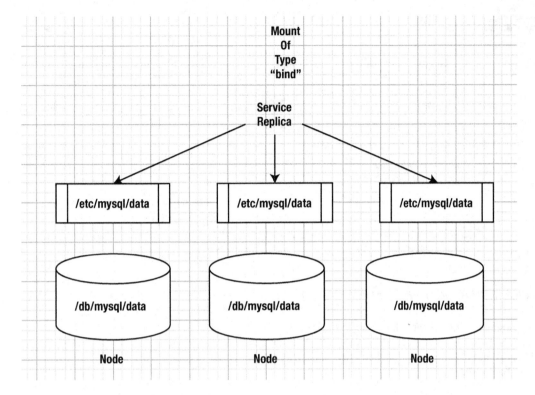

Figure 6-2. *Bind mount*

Swarm mode mounts provide shareable named volumes and filesystem paths on the host that persist across a service task startup and shutdown. A Docker image's filesystem is still at the root of the filesystem hierarchy and a mount can only be mounted on a directory path within the root filesystem.

This chapter covers the following topics:

- Setting the environment
- Types of mounts
- Creating a named volume
- Using a volume mount to get detailed info about a volume
- Removing a volume
- Creating and using a bind mount

Setting the Environment

Create a Docker for AWS-based Swarm consisting of one manager node and two worker nodes, as discussed in Chapter 3. The Docker for AWS Swarm will be used for one type of mount, the *volume* mount. For the *bind* mount, create a three-node Swarm consisting of one manager and two worker nodes on CoreOS instances. Creating a Swarm on CoreOS instances is discussed in Chapter 2. A CoreOS-based Swarm is used because Docker for AWS Swarm does not support bind mounts out-of-the-box. Obtain the public IP address of the manager instance for the Docker for AWS Swarm from the EC2 console, as shown in Figure 6-3.

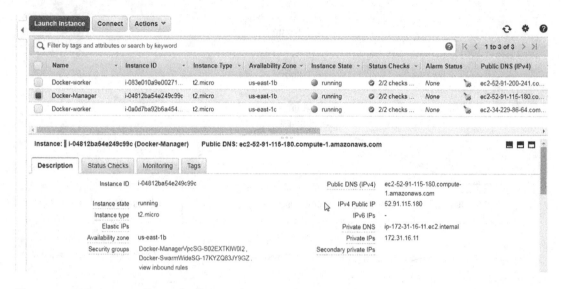

Figure 6-3. *EC2 instances for Docker for AWS Swarm nodes*

SSH login into the manager instance.

```
[root@localhost ~]# ssh -i "docker.pem" docker@52.91.115.180
Welcome to Docker!
```

List the nodes in the Swarm. A manager node and two worker nodes are listed.

```
~ $ docker node ls
ID                         HOSTNAME                      STATUS AVAILABILITY MANAGER STATUS
8ynq7exfo5v74ymoe7hrsghxh  ip-172-31-33-230.ec2.internal Ready  Active
o0h7oo9a61ico7n1t8ooe281g * ip-172-31-16-11.ec2.internal  Ready  Active       Leader
yzlv7c3qwcwozhxz439dbknj4  ip-172-31-25-163.ec2.internal Ready  Active
```

Creating a Named Volume

A named volume to be used in a service as a mount of type volume may either be created prior to creating the service or at deployment time. A new named volume is created with the following command syntax.

```
docker volume create [OPTIONS] [VOLUME]
```

The options discussed in Table 6-1 are supported.

Table 6-1. *Options for the docker volume create Command for a Named Volume*

Option	Description	Type	Default Value
--driver, -d	Specifies volume driver name	string	local
--label	Sets metadata for a volume	value	[]
--name	Specifies volume name	string	
--opt, -o	Sets driver specific options	value	map[]

Create a named volume called hello using the docker volume create command.

```
~ $ docker volume create --name  hello
hello
```

Subsequently, list the volumes with the docker volume ls command. The hello volume is listed in addition to other named volumes that may exist.

```
~ $ docker volume ls
DRIVER              VOLUME NAME
local               hello
```

You can find detailed info about the volume using the following command.

```
docker volume inspect hello
```

In addition to the volume name and driver, the mountpoint of the volume also is listed.

```
~ $ docker volume inspect hello
[
    {
        "Driver": "local",
        "Labels": {},
        "Mountpoint": "/var/lib/docker/volumes/hello/_data",
        "Name": "hello",
        "Options": {},
        "Scope": "local"
    }
]
```

The scope of a local driver volume is local. The other supported scope is global. A local volume is created on a single Docker host and a global volume is created on each Docker host in the cluster.

Using a Volume Mount

Use the hello volume in the docker service create command with the --mount option. The options discussed in Table 6-2 may be used both with bind mounts and volume mounts.

***Table** 6-2. Options for Volume and Bind Mounts*

Option	Required	Description	Default
type	No	Specifies the type of mount. One of three values may be specified:	volume
		volume-Mounts is a named volume in a container. bind-Bind-mounts is a directory or file from the host into a container. tmpfs-Mounts is a tmpfs into a container.	
src or source	Yes for type=bind only. No for type=volume	The source directory or volume. The option has different meanings for different types of mounts.	
		type=volume: src specifies the name of the volume. If the named volume does not exist, it is created. If src is omitted, the named volume is created with an auto-generated name, which is unique on the host but may not be unique cluster-wide. An auto-generated named volume is removed when the container using the volume is removed. The docker service update command shuts down task containers and starts new task containers and so does scaling a service. volume source must not be an absolute path.	
		type=bind: src specifies the absolute path to the directory or file to bind-mount. The directory path must be an absolute and not a relative path. The src option is required for a mount of type bind and an error is generated if it's not specified. type=tmpfs: is not supported.	
dst or destination or target	Yes	Specifies the mount path inside a container. If the path does not exist in a container's filesystem, the Docker engine creates the mount path before mounting the bind or volume mount. The volume target must be a relative path.	
readonly or ro	No	A boolean (true/false) or (1/0) to indicate whether the Docker Engine should mount volumes and bind read-write or read-only. If the option is not specified, the engine mounts the bind or volume read-write. If the option is specified with a value of true or 1 or no value, the engine mounts the volume or bind read-only. If the option is specified with a value of false or 0, the engine mounts the volume or bind read-write.	

Some of the mount options are only supported for volume mounts and are discussed in Table 6-3.

Table 6-3. *Options for Volume Mounts*

Option	Required	Description	Default Value
volume-driver	No	Specifies the name of the volume-driver plugin to use for the volume. If a named volume is not specified in src, the volume-driver is used to create a named volume.	local
volume-label	No	Specifies one or more comma-separated metadata labels to apply to the volume. Example: volume-label=label-1=hello-world,label-2=hello.	
volume-nocopy	No	Applies to an empty volume that is mounted in a container at a mount path at which files and directories already existed. Specifies whether a container's filesystem files and directories at the mount path (dst) are to be copied to the volume. A host is able to access the files and directories copied from the container to the named volume. A value of true or 1 disables copying of files from the container's filesystem to the host volume. A value of false or 0 enables copying.	true or 1
volume-opt	No	Specifies the options to be supplied to the volume-driver in creating a named volume if one does not exist. The volume-opt options are specified as a comma-separated list of key/value pairs. Example: volume-opt-1=option-1=value1,option-2=value2. A named volume has to exist on each host on which a mount of type volume is to be mounted. Creating a named volume on the Swarm manager does not also create the named volume on the worker nodes. The volume-driver and volume-opt options are used to create the named volume on the worker nodes.	

The options discussed in Table 6-4 are supported only with a mount of type tmpfs.

Table 6-4. *Options for the tmpfs Mount*

Option	Required	Description	Default Value
tmpfs-size	No	Size of the tmpfs mount in bytes	Unlimited value on Linux
tmpfs-mode	No	Specifies the file mode of the tmpfs in octal	1777 in Linux

Next, we will use the named volume hello in a service created with Docker image tutum/hello-world. In the following docker service create command, the --mount option specifies the src as hello and includes some volume-label labels for the volume.

```
~ $ docker service create \
  --name hello-world \
  --mount src=hello,dst=/hello,volume-label="msg=hello",volume-label="msg2=world" \
  --publish 8080:80 \
  --replicas 2 \
  tutum/hello-world
```

The service is created and the service ID is output.

```
~ $ docker service create \
>   --name hello-world \
>   --mount src=hello,dst=/hello,volume-label="msg=hello",volume-label="msg2=world" \
>   --publish 8080:80 \
>   --replicas 2 \
>   tutum/hello-world
8ily37o72wyxkyw2jt60kdqoz
```

Two service replicas are created.

```
~ $ docker service ls
ID              NAME           MODE         REPLICAS   IMAGE                        PORTS
8ily37o72wyx    hello-world    replicated   2/2        tutum/hello-world:latest     *:8080->80/tcp
~ $ docker service ps hello-world
ID              NAME                   IMAGE                       NODE
DESIRED STATE           CURRENT STATE              ERROR          PORTS
uw6coztxwqhf    hello-world.1          tutum/hello-world:latest    ip-172-31-25-163.ec2.internal
Running                 Running 20 seconds ago
cfkwefwadkki    hello-world.2          tutum/hello-world:latest    ip-172-31-16-11.ec2.internal
Running                 Running 21 seconds ago
```

The named volume is mounted in each task container in the service.
The service definition lists the mounts, including the mount labels.

```
~ $ docker service inspect hello-world
[
    ...
        "Spec": {
            "ContainerSpec": {
                "Image": "tutum/hello-world:latest@sha256:0d57def8055178aafb4c7669cbc25e
                c17f0acdab97cc587f30150802da8f8d85",
                "Mounts": [
                    {
                        "Type": "volume",
                        "Source": "hello",
                        "Target": "/hello",
                        "VolumeOptions": {
                            "Labels": {
                                "msg": "hello",
                                "msg2": "world"
                            },
    ...
]
```

In the preceding example, a named volume is created before using the volume in a volume mount. As another example, create a named volume at deployment time. In the following `docker service create` command, the `--mount` option is set to `type=volume` with the source set to `nginx-root`. The named volume `nginx-root` does not exist prior to creating the service.

```
~ $ docker service create \
>     --name nginx-service \
>     --replicas 3 \
>     --mount type=volume,source="nginx-root",destination="/var/lib/nginx",volume-
label="type=nginx root dir" \
>     nginx:alpine
rtz1ldok405mr03uhdk1htlnk
```

When the command is run, a service is created. Service description includes the volume mount in mounts.

```
~ $ docker service inspect nginx-service
[
...
        "Spec": {
            "Name": "nginx-service",
...
                    "Mounts": [
                        {
                            "Type": "volume",
                            "Source": "nginx-root",
                            "Target": "/var/lib/nginx",
                            "VolumeOptions": {
                                "Labels": {
                                    "type": "nginx root dir"
                                },
...
]
```

The named volume `nginx-root` was not created prior to creating the service and is therefore created before starting containers for service tasks. The named volume `nginx-root` is created only on nodes on which a task is scheduled. One service task is scheduled on each of the three nodes.

```
~ $ docker service ps nginx-service
ID                   NAME                IMAGE              NODE
DESIRED STATE        CURRENT STATE          ERROR              PORTS
pfqinizqmgur         nginx-service.1     nginx:alpine       ip-172-31-33-230.ec2.internal
Running              Running 19 seconds ago
mn8h3p40chgs         nginx-service.2     nginx:alpine       ip-172-31-25-163.ec2.internal
Running              Running 19 seconds ago
k8n5zzlnn46s         nginx-service.3     nginx:alpine       ip-172-31-16-11.ec2.internal
Running              Running 18 seconds ago
```

As a task is scheduled on the manager node, a named volume called `nginx-root` is created on the manager node, as listed in the output of the `docker volume ls` command.

```
~ $ docker volume ls
DRIVER              VOLUME NAME
local               hello
local               nginx-root
```

Service tasks and task containers are started on each of the two worker nodes. A `nginx-root` named volume is created on each of the worker nodes. Listing the volumes on the worker nodes lists the `nginx-root` volume.

```
[root@localhost ~]# ssh -i "docker.pem" docker@34.229.86.64
Welcome to Docker!
~ $ docker volume ls
DRIVER              VOLUME NAME
local               hello
local               nginx-root

[root@localhost ~]# ssh -i "docker.pem" docker@52.91.200.241
Welcome to Docker!
~ $ docker volume ls
DRIVER              VOLUME NAME
local               hello
local               nginx-root
```

A named volume was specified in `src` in the preceding example. The named volume may be omitted as in the following service definition.

```
~ $ docker service create \
>    --name nginx-service-2 \
>    --replicas 3 \
>    --mount type=volume,destination=/var/lib/nginx    \
>    nginx:alpine
q8ordkmkwqrwiwhmaemvcypc3
```

The service is created with a replica and is scheduled on each of the Swarm nodes.

```
~ $ docker service ps nginx-service-2
ID                  NAME                IMAGE               NODE
DESIRED STATE       CURRENT STATE            ERROR              PORTS
kz8d8k6bxp7u        nginx-service-2.1   nginx:alpine        ip-172-31-25-163.ec2.internal
Running             Running 27 seconds ago
wd65qsmqixpg        nginx-service-2.2   nginx:alpine        ip-172-31-16-11.ec2.internal
Running             Running 27 seconds ago
mbnmzldtaaed        nginx-service-2.3   nginx:alpine        ip-172-31-33-230.ec2.internal
Running             Running 26 seconds ago
```

The service definition does not list a named volume.

```
~ $ docker service inspect nginx-service-2
[
        "Spec": {
            "Name": "nginx-service-2",
                "ContainerSpec": {
                    "Mounts": [
                        {
                            "Type": "volume",
                            "Target": "/var/lib/nginx"
                        }
                    ],
...
]
```

Named volumes with auto-generated names are created when a volume name is not specified explicitly. One auto-generated named volume with an auto-generated name is created on each node on which a service task is run. One of the named volumes listed on the manager node is an auto-generated named volume with an auto-generated name.

```
~ $ docker volume ls
DRIVER              VOLUME NAME
local               305f1fa3673e811b3b320fad0e2dd5786567bcec49b3e66480eab2309101e233
local               hello
local               nginx-root
```

As another example of using named volumes as mounts in a service, create a named volume called mysql-scripts for a MySQL database service.

```
~ $ docker volume create --name mysql-scripts
mysql-scripts
```

The named volume is created and listed.

```
~ $ docker volume ls
DRIVER              VOLUME NAME
local               305f1fa3673e811b3b320fad0e2dd5786567bcec49b3e66480eab2309101e233
local               hello
local               mysql-scripts
local               nginx-root
```

The volume description lists the scope as local and lists the mountpoint.

```
~ $ docker volume inspect mysql-scripts
[
    {
        "Driver": "local",
        "Labels": {},
        "Mountpoint": "/var/lib/docker/volumes/mysql-scripts/_data",
        "Name": "mysql-scripts",
        "Options": {},
        "Scope": "local"
    }
]
```

Next, create a service that uses the named volume in a volume mount.

```
~ $ docker service create \
>    --env MYSQL_ROOT_PASSWORD='mysql'\
>    --mount type=volume,src="mysql-scripts",dst="/etc/mysql/scripts",
      el="msg=mysql",volume-label="msg2=scripts" \
> --publish 3306:3306\
>    --replicas 2 \
>    --name mysql \
>  mysql
cghaz4zoxurpyqil5iknqf4c1
```

The service is created and listed.

```
~ $ docker service ls
ID            NAME          MODE         REPLICAS  IMAGE                       PORTS
8ily37o72wyx  hello-world   replicated   2/2       tutum/hello-world:latest    *:8080->80/tcp
cghaz4zoxurp  ysql          replicated   1/2       mysql:latest                *:3306->3306/tcp
```

Listing the service tasks indicates that the tasks are scheduled on the manager node and one of the worker nodes.

```
~ $ docker service ps mysql
ID             NAME             IMAGE           NODE
DESIRED STATE  CURRENT STATE                      ERROR          PORTS
y59yhzwch2fj   mysql.1          mysql:latest    ip-172-31-33-230.ec2.internal
Running        Preparing 12 seconds ago
zg7wrludkr84   mysql.2          mysql:latest    ip-172-31-16-11.ec2.internal
Running        Running less than a second ago
```

The destination directory for the named volume is created in the Docker container. The Docker container on the manager node may be listed with docker ps and a bash shell on the container may be started with the docker exec -it <containerid> bash command.

```
~ $ docker ps
CONTAINER ID          IMAGE                               COMMAND
CREATED               STATUS           PORTS               NAMES
a855826cdc75          mysql:latest                        "docker-entrypoint..."
22 seconds ago        Up 21 seconds    3306/tcp            mysql.2.zg7wrludkr84zf
                                                           8vhdkf8wnlh
~ $ docker exec -it a855826cdc75 bash
root@a855826cd75:/#
```

Change the directory to /etc/mysql/scripts in the container. Initially, the directory is empty.

```
root@a855826cdc75:/# cd /etc/mysql/scripts
root@a855826cdc75:/etc/mysql/scripts# ls -l
total 0
root@a855826cdc75:/etc/mysql/scripts# exit
exit
```

A task container for the service is created on one of the worker nodes and may be listed on the worker node.

```
~ $ docker ps
CONTAINER ID          IMAGE                           COMMAND
CREATED               STATUS           PORTS           NAMES
eb8d59cc2dff          mysql:latest                    "docker-entrypoint..."
8 minutes ago         Up 8 minutes     3306/tcp        mysql.1.xjmx7qviihyq2so7n0oxi1muq
```

Start a bash shell for the Docker container on the worker node. The /etc/mysql/scripts directory on which the named volume is mounted is created in the Docker container.

```
~ $ docker exec -it eb8d59cc2dff bash
root@eb8d59cc2dff:/# cd /etc/mysql/scripts
root@eb8d59cc2dff:/etc/mysql/scripts# exit
exit
```

If a service using an auto-generated named volume is scaled to run a task on nodes on which a task was not running previously, named volumes are auto-generated on those nodes also. As an example of finding the effect of scaling a service when using an auto-generated named volume as a mount in the service, create a MySQL database service with a volume mount. The volume mysql-scripts does not exist prior to creating the service; remove the mysql-scripts volume if it exists.

```
~ $ docker service create \
>    --env MYSQL_ROOT_PASSWORD='mysql'\
>    --replicas 1 \
>    --mount type=volume,src="mysql-scripts",dst="/etc/mysql/scripts"\
>    --name mysql \
>    mysql
088ddf5pt4yb3yvr5s7elyhpn
```

The service task is scheduled on a node.

```
~ $ docker service ps mysql
ID                        NAME                      IMAGE                NODE
DESIRED STATE             CURRENT STATE             ERROR                  PORTS
xlix91njbaq0              mysql.1                   mysql:latest         ip-172-31-13-122.ec2.internal
Running                   Preparing 12 seconds ago
```

List the nodes; the node on which the service task is scheduled is the manager node.

```
~ $ docker node ls
ID                          HOSTNAME                      STATUS  AVAILABILITY  MANAGER STATUS
o5hyue3hzuds8vtyughswbosl   ip-172-31-11-41.ec2.internal  Ready   Active
p6uuzp8pmoahlcwexr3wdulxv   ip-172-31-23-247.ec2.internal Ready   Active
qnk35m01411x8jljp87ggnsnq * ip-172-31-13-122.ec2.internal Ready   Active        Leader
```

A named volume mysql-scripts and an ancillary named volume with an auto-generated name are created on the manager node on which a task is scheduled.

```
~ $ docker volume ls
DRIVER          VOLUME NAME
local           a2bc631f1b1da354d30aaea37935c65f9d99c5f084d92341c6506f1e2aab1d55
local           mysql-scripts
```

The worker nodes do not list the mysql-scripts named volume, as a task is not scheduled on the worker nodes.

```
~ $ docker volume ls
DRIVER          VOLUME NAME
```

Scale the service to three replicas. A replica is scheduled on each of the three nodes.

```
~ $ docker service scale mysql=3
mysql scaled to 3
```

```
~ $ docker service ps mysql
ID                NAME          IMAGE                NODE
DESIRED STATE     CURRENT STATE                ERROR          PORTS
xlix91njbaq0      mysql.1           mysql:latest         ip-172-31-13-122.ec2.internal
Running           Running about a minute ago
ifk7xuvfp9p2      mysql.2           mysql:latest         ip-172-31-23-247.ec2.internal
Running           Running less than a second ago
3c53fxgcjqyt      mysql.3           mysql:latest         ip-172-31-11-41.ec2.internal
Running           Running less than a second ago
```

A named volume `mysql-scripts` and an ancillary named volume with an auto-generated name are created on the worker nodes because a replica is scheduled.

```
[root@localhost ~]# ssh -i "docker.pem" docker@54.165.69.9
Welcome to Docker!

~ $ docker volume ls
DRIVER              VOLUME NAME
local               431a792646d0b04b5ace49a32e6c0631ec5e92f3dda57008b1987e4fe2a1b561
local               mysql-scripts
[root@localhost ~]# ssh -i "docker.pem" docker@34.232.95.243
Welcome to Docker!

~ $ docker volume ls
DRIVER              VOLUME NAME
local               afb2401a9a916a365304b8aa0cc96b1be0c161462d375745c9829f2b6f180873
local               mysql-scripts
```

The auto-generated named volumes are persistent and do not get removed when a service replica is shut down. The named volumes with auto-generated names are not persistent volumes. As an example, scale the service back to one replica. Two of the replicas shut down, including the replica on the manager node.

```
~ $ docker service scale mysql=1
mysql scaled to 1
~ $ docker service ps mysql
ID              NAME            IMAGE           NODE
DESIRED STATE   CURRENT STATE       ERROR           PORTS
3c53fxgcjqyt    mysql.3         mysql:latest    ip-172-31-11-41.ec2.internal
Running         Running 2 minutes ago
```

But the named volume `mysql-scripts` on the manager node is not removed even though no Docker container using the volume is running.

```
~ $ docker volume ls
DRIVER              VOLUME NAME
local               mysql-scripts
```

Similarly, the named volume on a worker node on which a service replica is shut down also does not get removed even though no Docker container using the named volume is running. The named volume with the auto-generated name is removed when no container is using it, but the `mysql-scripts` named volume does not.

Remove the volume `mysql-scripts` still does not get removed.

```
~ $ docker service rm mysql
mysql
~ $ docker volume ls
DRIVER              VOLUME NAME
local               mysql-scripts
```

Removing a Volume

A named volume may be removed using the following command.

```
docker volume rm  <VOL>
```

As an example, remove the named volume `mysql-scripts`.

```
~ $ docker volume rm mysql-scripts
mysql-scripts
```

If the volume you try to delete is used in a Docker container, an error is generated instead and the volume will not be removed. Even a named volume with an auto-generated name cannot be removed if it's being used in a container.

Creating and Using a Bind Mount

In this section, we create a mount of type *bind*. Bind mounts are suitable if data in directories that already exist on the host needs to be accessed from within Docker containers. `type=bind` must be specified with the `--mount` option when creating a service with mount of type *bind*. The host source directory and the volume target must both be absolute paths. The host source directory must exist prior to creating a service. The target directory within each Docker container of the service is created automatically. Create a directory on the manager node and then add a file called `createtable.sql` to the directory.

```
core@ip-10-0-0-143 ~ $ sudo mkdir -p /etc/mysql/scripts
core@ip-10-0-0-143 ~ $ cd /etc/mysql/scripts
core@ip-10-0-0-143 /etc/mysql/scripts $ sudo vi createtable.sql
```

Save a SQL script in the sample SQL file, as shown in Figure 6-4.

```
                          root@localhost:~                          _ □ ×
File  Edit  View  Search  Terminal  Help
CREATE TABLE wlslog(time_stamp VARCHAR(255) PRIMARY KEY,category VARCHAR(255),ty
INSERT INTO wlslog(time_stamp,category,type,servername,code,msg) VALUES('Apr-8-2
INSERT INTO wlslog(time_stamp,category,type,servername,code,msg) VALUES('Apr-8-2
INSERT INTO wlslog(time_stamp,category,type,servername,code,msg) VALUES('Apr-8-2
INSERT INTO wlslog(time_stamp,category,type,servername,code,msg) VALUES('Apr-8-2
INSERT INTO wlslog(time_stamp,category,type,servername,code,msg) VALUES('Apr-8-2
INSERT INTO wlslog(time_stamp,category,type,servername,code,msg) VALUES('Apr-8-2
INSERT INTO wlslog(time_stamp,category,type,servername,code,msg) VALUES('Apr-8-2

~
~
~
:wq
```

Figure 6-4. Adding a SQL script to the host directory

Similarly, create a directory and add a SQL script to the worker nodes.

Create a service with a bind mount that's using the host directory. The destination directory is specified as /scripts.

```
core@ip-10-0-0-143 ~ $ docker service create \
>    --env MYSQL_ROOT_PASSWORD='mysql' \
>    --replicas 3 \
>    --mount type=bind,src="/etc/mysql/scripts",dst="/scripts" \
>    --name mysql \
>       mysql
0kvk2hk2qigqyeem8x1r8qkvk
```

Start a bash shell for the service container from the node on which a task is scheduled. The destination directory /scripts is listed.

```
core@ip-10-0-0-143 ~ $ docker ps
CONTAINER ID      IMAGE           COMMAND               CREATED
STATUS            PORTS           NAMES
e71275e6c65c      mysql:latest    "docker-entrypoint.sh"  5 seconds ago
Up 4 seconds      3306/tcp        mysql.1.btqfrx7uffym2xvc441pubaza

core@ip-10-0-0-143 ~ $ docker exec -it e71275e6c65c bash
root@e71275e6c65c:/# ls -l
drwxr-xr-x.  2 root root 4096 Jul 24 20:44 scripts
```

Change the directory (cd) to the destination mount path /scripts. The createtable.sql script is listed in the destination mount path of the bind mount.

```
root@e71275e6c65c:/# cd /scripts
root@e71275e6c65c:/scripts# ls -l
-rw-r--r--. 1 root root 1478 Jul 24 20:44 createtable.sql
```

113

Each service task Docker container has its own copy of the file on the host. Because, by default, the mount is read-write, the files in the mount path may be modified or removed. As an example, remove the createtable.sql script from a container.

```
core@ip-10-0-0-137 ~ $ docker exec -it 995b9455aff2 bash
root@995b9455aff2:/# cd /scripts
root@995b9455aff2:/scripts# ls -l
total 8
-rw-r--r--. 1 root root 1478 Jul 24 20:45 createtable.sql
root@995b9455aff2:/scripts# rm createtable.sql
root@995b9455aff2:/scripts# ls -l
total 0
root@995b9455aff2:/scripts#
```

A mount may be made read-only by including an additional option in the --mount arg, as discussed earlier. To demonstrate a readonly mount, first remove the mysql service that's already running. Create a service and mount a readonly bind with the same command as before, except include an additional readonly option.

```
core@ip-10-0-0-143 ~ $ docker service create \
>    --env MYSQL_ROOT_PASSWORD='mysql' \
>    --replicas 3 \
>    --mount type=bind,src="/etc/mysql/scripts",dst="/scripts",readonly \
>    --name mysql \
>       mysql
c27se8vfygk2z57rtswentrix
```

A bind of type mount which is readonly is mounted.

Access the container on a node on which a task is scheduled and list the sample script from the host directory.

```
core@ip-10-0-0-143 ~ $ docker exec -it 3bf9cf777d25 bash
root@3bf9cf777d25:/# cd /scripts
root@3bf9cf777d25:/scripts# ls -l
-rw-r--r--. 1 root root 1478 Jul 24 20:44 createtable.sql
```

Remove, or try to remove, the sample script. An error is generated.

```
root@3bf9cf777d25:/scripts# rm createtable.sql
rm: cannot remove 'createtable.sql': Read-only file system
```

Summary

This chapter introduced mounts in Swarm mode. Two types of mounts are supported—*bind* mount and *volume* mount. A bind mount mounts a pre-existing directory or file from the host into each container of a service. A volume mount mounts a named volume, which may or may not exist prior to creating a service, into each container in a service. The next chapter discusses configuring resources.

CHAPTER 7

■ ■ ■

Configuring Resources

Docker containers run in isolation on the underlying OS kernel and require resources to run. Docker Swarm mode supports two types of resources—CPU and memory—as illustrated in Figure 7-1.

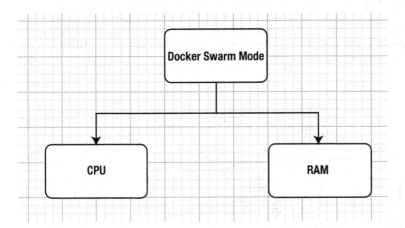

Figure 7-1. *Types of resources supported by Docker Swarm mode*

The Problem

By default, Docker Swarm mode does not impose any limit on how many resources (CPU cycles or memory) a service task may consume. Nor does Swarm mode guarantee minimum resources. Two issues can result if no resource configuration is specified in Docker Swarm mode.

Some of the service tasks could consume a disproportionate amount of resources, while the other service tasks are not able to get scheduled due to lack of resources. As an example, consider a node with resource capacity of 3GB and 3 CPUs. Without any resource guarantees and limits, one service task container could consume most of the resources (2.8GB and 2.8 CPUs), while two other service task containers each have only 0.1GB and 0.1 CPU of resources remaining to be used and do not get scheduled, as illustrated in Figure 7-2. A Docker service task that does not have enough resources to get scheduled is put in Pending state.

© Deepak Vohra 2017
D. Vohra, *Docker Management Design Patterns*, https://doi.org/10.1007/978-1-4842-2973-6_7

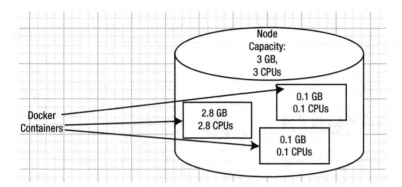

Figure 7-2. *Unequal allocation of resources*

The second issue that can result is that the resource capacity of a node can get fully used up without any provision to schedule any more service tasks. As an example, a node with a resource capacity of 9GB and 9 CPUs has three service task containers running, with each using 3GB and 3 CPUs, as illustrated in Figure 7-3. If a new service task is created for the same or another service, it does not have any available resources on the node.

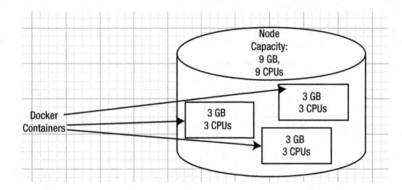

Figure 7-3. *Fully resource-utilized node*

The Solution

Docker Swarm mode has a provision to set resource guarantees (or reserves) and resource limits, as illustrated in Figure 7-4. A *resource reserve* is the minimum amount of a resource that is guaranteed or reserved for a service task. A *resource limit* is the maximum amount of a resource that a service task can use regardless of how much of a resource is available.

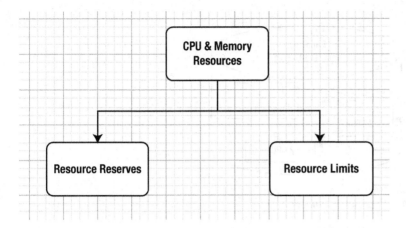

Figure 7-4. *Managing Swarm resources with resource reserves and limits*

With resource reserves, each service task container can be guaranteed 1 CPU and 1GB in the issue discussed previously, as illustrated in Figure 7-5.

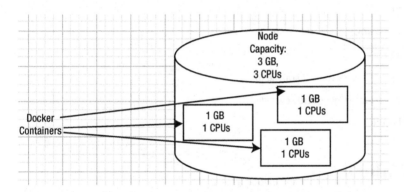

Figure 7-5. *Resource allocation with resource reserves set*

And, if resource limits are implemented for service task containers, excess resources would be available to start new service task containers. In the example discussed previously, a limit of 2GB and 2 CPUs per service task would keep the excess resources of 3GB and 3 CPUs available for new service task containers, as illustrated in Figure 7-6.

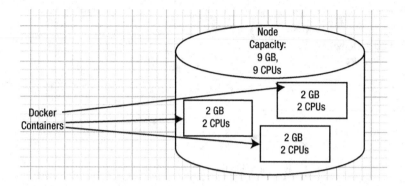

Figure 7-6. *Resource allocation with resource limits set*

This chapter covers the following topics:

- Setting the environment

- Creating a service without resource specification

- Reserving resources

- Setting resource limits

- Creating a service with resource specification

- Scaling and resources

- Reserved resources must be less than resource limits

- Rolling update to set resource limits and reserves

- Resource usage and node capacity

Setting the Environment

Create a three-node Swarm on Docker for AWS with one manager node and two worker nodes. Creating a Swarm on Docker for AWS is discussed in Chapter 3. We use the three-node Swarm created in Chapter 6 for this chapter also. Obtain the public IP address of the Swarm manager instance, as shown in Figure 7-7.

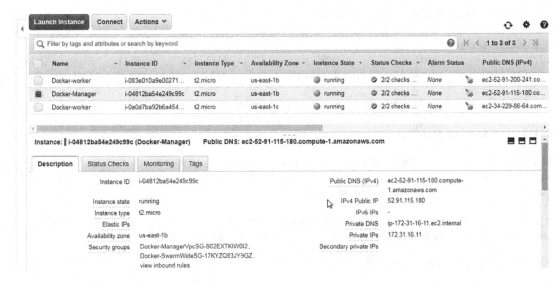

Figure 7-7. *EC2 instances for Swarm nodes*

SSH login into the manager instance with user as "docker".

```
[root@localhost ~]# ssh -i "docker.pem" docker@52.91.115.180
Welcome to Docker!
```

List the Swarm nodes; a manager node and two worker nodes are listed.

```
~ $ docker node ls
ID                          HOSTNAME                        STATUS  AVAILABILITY MANAGER STATUS
8ynq7exfo5v74ymoe7hrsghxh   ip-172-31-33-230.ec2.internal   Ready   Active
oOh7oo9a61ico7n1t8ooe281g * ip-172-31-16-11.ec2.internal    Ready   Active       Leader
yzlv7c3qwcwozhxz439dbknj4   ip-172-31-25-163.ec2.internal   Ready   Active
```

Creating a Service Without Resource Specification

We start by creating a service without any resource specification. Create a MySQL database service without setting any resource reserves or limits.

```
docker service create \
  --env MYSQL_ROOT_PASSWORD='mysql'\
  --replicas 1 \
  --name mysql \
 mysql
```

A single service replica is created. The output of the command is the service ID (shown in italics).

```
~ $ docker service create \
>   --env MYSQL_ROOT_PASSWORD='mysql'\
>   --replicas 1 \
>   --name mysql \
>  mysql
2kcq6cf72t4wu94000k3sax41
```

119

List the services; the mysql service is listed.

```
~ $ docker service ls
ID              NAME          MODE            REPLICAS      IMAGE                  PORTS
2kcq6cf72t4w    mysql         replicated      1/1           mysql:latest
```

List the service tasks. The only service task is running on a worker node.

```
~ $ docker service ps mysql
ID                    NAME            IMAGE                 NODE
DESIRED STATE         CURRENT STATE   ERROR                 PORTS
sccqv4k9r22h          mysql.1         mysql:latest          ip-172-31-33-230.ec2.internal
Running               Running 10 seconds ago
```

On inspecting the service, the container spec does not include any resources, limits, or reserves. The single service task may use all of the available resources on the node on which it's scheduled.

```
~ $ docker service inspect mysql
[
                "Resources": {
                    "Limits": {},
                    "Reservations": {}
                },
]
```

Reserving Resources

Swarm mode provides two options for resource reserves in the docker service create and docker service update commands, as listed in Table 7-1.

Table 7-1. *Options for Resource Reserves*

Option	Description	Default Value
--reserve-cpu	Reserve CPUs. A value of 0.000 implies no reserves are set.	0.000
--reserve-memory	Reserve memory. A value of 0 implies no reserves are set.	0

Setting Resource Limits

Swarm mode provides two options for resource limits in the docker service create and docker service update commands, as discussed in Table 7-2.

Table 7-2. *Options for Resource Limits*

Option	Description	Default Value
--limit-cpu	Limit CPUs	0.000
--limit-memory	Limit Memory	0

Creating a Service with Resource Specification

Next, create a service using resource specification. Set resource reserves of 0.25 CPUs and 128MB and resource limits of 1 CPU and 256MB. Remove the `mysql` service previously created before creating a new service with resources defined. The output of the command is the service ID (shown in italics).

```
~ $ docker service rm mysql
mysql
~ $ docker service create \
>    --env MYSQL_ROOT_PASSWORD='mysql'\
>    --replicas 1 \
>    --name mysql \
>    --reserve-cpu .25 --limit-cpu 1 --reserve-memory  128mb --limit-memory 256mb \
>    mysql
abwq9budo7joyd00u32z2b047
```

On inspecting the service, the resources limits and reserves are listed, which contrasts with the empty settings for resources when a service is created without the resources definition.

```
~ $ docker service inspect mysql
[
                "Resources": {
                    "Limits": {
                        "NanoCPUs": 1000000000,
                        "MemoryBytes": 268435456
                    },
                    "Reservations": {
                        "NanoCPUs": 250000000,
                        "MemoryBytes": 134217728
                    }
                },
]
```

Scaling and Resources

Before scaling up a service, it may be suitable to determine the node capacity in terms of CPU and memory resources. As all three nodes in the Swarm are identical, the node capacity on one node is the same as on the other nodes. The node capacity is 1 CPU and 1GB, as listed in the output of the `docker node inspect` command.

```
~ $ docker node inspect ip-172-31-16-11.ec2.internal
[
            "Resources": {
                "NanoCPUs": 1000000000,
                "MemoryBytes": 1039040512
            },
]
```

The CPU limit on each service task created in the preceding section is also 1 CPU. When scaling, the total of the resource limits for all service tasks on a node may exceed the node's capacity. However, the total of resource reserves must not exceed node capacity.

As an example, scale to five replicas.

```
~ $ docker service scale mysql=5
mysql scaled to 5
```

Scaling to five schedules two replicas on the manager node, two replicas on one of the worker nodes, and one replica on the other worker node. The aggregate of the resource limits on the worker nodes is exceeded but the aggregate of resource reserves are within the node's capacity.

```
~ $ docker service ps mysql
ID                   NAME              IMAGE              NODE
DESIRED STATE        CURRENT STATE            ERROR        PORTS
npc5r7xf98fg         mysql.1              mysql:latest      ip-172-31-16-11.ec2.internal
Running              Running 2 minutes ago
xokdhowntp0w         mysql.2              mysql:latest      ip-172-31-25-163.ec2.internal
Running              Running 13 seconds ago
b6h4bsf7xzdc         mysql.3              mysql:latest      ip-172-31-16-11.ec2.internal
Running              Running 12 seconds ago
j1d7ti7nb80u         mysql.4              mysql:latest      ip-172-31-33-230.ec2.internal
Running              Running 13 seconds ago
w6to9pxcdbm5         mysql.5              mysql:latest      ip-172-31-25-163.ec2.internal
Running              Running 13 seconds ago
```

Reserved Resources Must Not Be More Than Resource Limits

The resource limits are not taken into consideration when scheduling a service task, only the resource reserves are. Not setting the reserves (whether limits are set or not and whether limits exceed node capacity) schedules the service task if the resources required to run a task are within the node capacity. Resource reserves must not exceed resource limits or a service task may not get scheduled or might fail after a while. As an example, delete the mysql service and create a new service where the resource reserves exceed resource limits. The output of the command is the service ID (shown in italics).

```
~ $ docker service rm mysql
mysql
~ $ docker service create \
>    --env MYSQL_ROOT_PASSWORD='mysql'\
>    --replicas 1 \
>    --name mysql \
>    --reserve-cpu .75 --limit-cpu .5 --reserve-memory  256mb --limit-memory 128mb \
>    mysql
srot5vr8x7v7iml2awc3fxb1u
```

The service is created and even scheduled.

```
~ $ docker service ps mysql
ID                   NAME              IMAGE              NODE
DESIRED STATE        CURRENT STATE            ERROR        PORTS
pmcjrj6p3wfp         mysql.1              mysql:latest      ip-172-31-16-11.ec2.internal
Running              Running 20 seconds ago
```

The service configuration has the resource reserves exceeding the resource limits.

```
~ $ docker service inspect mysql
[
                },
                "Resources": {
                    "Limits": {
                        "NanoCPUs": 500000000,
                        "MemoryBytes": 134217728
                    },
                    "Reservations": {
                        "NanoCPUs": 750000000,
                        "MemoryBytes": 268435456
                    }
                },
]
```

The resource reserves are within the node capacity, but because the resource limits are less than the resource reserves, the newly started service task fails and is shut down. The service task keeps getting restarted and shut down.

```
~ $ docker service ps mysql
ID                   NAME             IMAGE            NODE
DESIRED STATE        CURRENT STATE              ERROR                      PORTS
vjcnjkwfdfkb         mysql.1          mysql:latest     ip-172-31-16-11.ec2.internal
Running              Running 16 seconds ago
pxdku8pxviyn         \_ mysql.1       mysql:latest     ip-172-31-16-11.ec2.internal
Shutdown             Failed 21 seconds ago      "task: non-zero exit (1)"
pmcjrj6p3wfp         \_ mysql.1       mysql:latest     ip-172-31-16-11.ec2.internal
Shutdown             Failed about a minute ago  "task: non-zero exit (1)"
```

The service task resource limits can be the same as the resource reserves. Remove the mysql service and create it again with the resource limits the same as the resource reserves. The output of the command is the service ID (shown in italics).

```
~ $ docker service rm mysql
mysql
~ $ docker service create \
>   --env MYSQL_ROOT_PASSWORD='mysql'\
>   --replicas 1 \
>   --name mysql \
>   --reserve-cpu .5 --limit-cpu .5 --reserve-memory  256mb --limit-memory 256mb \
>   mysql
81bu63v97p9rm81xfyxv9k11e
```

The service is created and the single task is scheduled. The service task does not fail as when the resource reserves exceeded the resource limit.

```
~ $ docker service ps mysql
ID                    NAME              IMAGE            NODE
DESIRED STATE         CURRENT STATE     ERROR      PORTS
4i1fpha53abs          mysql.1            mysql:latest         ip-172-31-16-11.ec2.internal
Running               Running 33 seconds ago
```

And a Docker container is started.

```
~ $ docker ps
CONTAINER ID    IMAGE          COMMAND              CREATED         STATUS
PORTS           NAMES
14d5553f0393     mysql:latest    "docker-entrypoint..."   34 seconds ago   Up 33 seconds
3306/tcp        mysql.1.4i1fpha53absl4qky9dgafo8t
```

Rolling Update to Modify Resource Limits and Reserves

This section demonstrates a rolling update to set new CPU and memory limits and reserves. The service created in the previous section is used for updating in this section. Using the docker service update command, update the CPU and memory reserves and limits. The output of the command is the service name mysql (shown in italics).

```
~ $ docker service update --reserve-cpu 1 --limit-cpu 2 --reserve-memory  256mb
--limit-memory 512mb mysql
mysql
```

The resources are updated. Updating the resource specification for a service shuts down the service replica and starts a new replica with the new resource specification.

```
~ $ docker service ls
ID              NAME          MODE            REPLICAS        IMAGE           PORTS
81bu63v97p9r    mysql         replicated      1/1             mysql:latest
~ $ docker service ps mysql
ID              NAME          IMAGE           NODE
DESIRED STATE   CURRENT STATE          ERROR      PORTS
xkis4mirgbtv    mysql.1             mysql:latest     ip-172-31-33-230.ec2.internal
Running         Running 14 seconds ago
4i1fpha53abs    \_ mysql.1          mysql:latest     ip-172-31-16-11.ec2.internal
Shutdown        Shutdown 15 seconds ago
```

The service resources configuration is updated.

```
~ $ docker service inspect mysql
[
                },
                "Resources": {
                    "Limits": {
                        "NanoCPUs": 2000000000,
                        "MemoryBytes": 536870912
                    },
```

```
            "Reservations": {
                "NanoCPUs": 1000000000,
                "MemoryBytes": 268435456
            }
        },
]
```

Resource Usage and Node Capacity

Resource usage cannot exceed node capacity. On the three-node Swarm (one manager and two worker nodes), recall that the node capacity is 1GB and 1 CPU.

Remove the mysql service that's already running and create a mysql service with three replicas that requests 4GB of memory. The service is created. The output of the command is the service ID (shown in italics).

```
~ $ docker service rm mysql
mysql
~ $ docker service create \
>    --env MYSQL_ROOT_PASSWORD='mysql'\
>    --replicas 3 \
>    --name mysql \
>    --reserve-memory=4GB\
>    mysql
cgrihwij2znn4jkfe6hswxgr7
```

None of the service replicas is scheduled, as indicated by the Replicas column value of 0/3, because the requested capacity is more than the node capacity of a single node.

```
~ $ docker service ls
ID              NAME          MODE          REPLICAS      IMAGE           PORTS
cgrihwij2znn    mysql         replicated    0/3           mysql:latest
```

The Current State of the replicas is listed as Pending.

```
~ $ docker service ps mysql
ID              NAME          IMAGE             NODE
DESIRED STATE   CURRENT STATE ERROR             PORTS
vm7z20krx3j6    mysql.1       mysql:latest
Running         Pending 19 seconds ago
exmsheo144ef    mysql.2       mysql:latest
Running         Pending 19 seconds ago
kiset9poqz2s    mysql.3       mysql:latest
Running         Pending 19 seconds ago
```

If a service that was previously running with all replicas is scaled up, some or all of the replicas could get de-scheduled. This happens if the resources required to run the new replicas exceed the available node capacity. As an example, remove the mysql service and create a new mysql service with resource settings within the provision of a node. The output of the command is the service ID (shown in italics).

```
~ $ docker service rm mysql
mysql
~ $
~ $ docker service create \
>    --env MYSQL_ROOT_PASSWORD='mysql'\
>    --replicas 1 \
>    --name mysql \
>    --reserve-cpu .5  --reserve-memory  512mb  \
>    mysql
ysef8n02mhuwa7sxerc9jwjqx
```

The service is created and the single replica is running as indicated by the Replicas column value of 1/1.

```
~ $ docker service ls
ID               NAME        MODE          REPLICAS    IMAGE             PORTS
ysef8n02mhuw     mysql       replicated    1/1         mysql:latest
```

Incrementally scale up the service to determine if all of the service replicas are scheduled. First, scale up to three replicas.

```
~ $ docker service scale mysql=3
mysql scaled to 3
```

The service description lists 3/3 Replicas as running.

```
~ $ docker service ls
ID               NAME        MODE          REPLICAS    IMAGE             PORTS
ysef8n02mhuw     mysql       replicated    3/3         mysql:latest
```

The service replicas are scheduled, one replica on each node in the Swarm, using the *spread* scheduling strategy, which is discussed in more detail in Chapter 8.

```
~ $ docker service ps mysql
ID               NAME             IMAGE             NODE
DESIRED STATE    CURRENT STATE        ERROR        PORTS
8kkkdns0l690     mysql.1          mysql:latest      ip-172-31-16-11.ec2.internal
Running          Running 51 seconds ago
k209uge36bih     mysql.2          mysql:latest      ip-172-31-25-163.ec2.internal
Running          Running 16 seconds ago
oiublpclz9eu     mysql.3          mysql:latest      ip-172-31-33-230.ec2.internal
Running          Running 16 seconds ago
```

Scale the mysql service further up to replicas.

```
~ $ docker service scale mysql=10
mysql scaled to 10
```

Only 3/10 of the replicas are listed as running.

```
~ $ docker service ls
ID               NAME        MODE          REPLICAS    IMAGE             PORTS
ysef8n02mhuw     mysql       replicated    3/10        mysql:latest
```

Some of the replicas are `Allocated` but not scheduled for running on any node due to insufficient resources. The service replicas not running are listed with `Current State` set to `Pending`.

```
~ $ docker service ps mysql
ID                  NAME                IMAGE                   NODE
DESIRED STATE       CURRENT STATE                   ERROR           PORTS
8kkkdns0l690        mysql.1                 mysql:latest        ip-172-31-16-11.ec2.internal
Running             Running about a minute ago
k209uge36bih        mysql.2                 mysql:latest        ip-172-31-25-163.ec2.internal
Running             Running 35 seconds ago
oiublpclz9eu        mysql.3                 mysql:latest        ip-172-31-33-230.ec2.internal
Running             Running 35 seconds ago
u807b7h0qvqc        mysql.4                 mysql:latest
Running             Pending 7 seconds ago
jh2ep10sonxy        mysql.5                 mysql:latest
Running             Pending 7 seconds ago
8d19osxa4fwf        mysql.6                 mysql:latest
Running             Pending 7 seconds ago
k8hba8j5o9vi        mysql.7                 mysql:latest
Running             Pending 7 seconds ago
ettk65bpin3b        mysql.8                 mysql:latest
Running             Pending 7 seconds ago
i3otbqfsfvr7        mysql.9                 mysql:latest
Running             Pending 7 seconds ago
sxdi97oo6d3b        mysql.10                mysql:latest
Running             Pending 7 seconds ago
```

Adding one or more new worker nodes could make the service reconcile its desired state and cause all the replicas to run. To demonstrate next, we scale up the CloudFormation stack to increase the number of worker nodes.

Scaling Up the Stack

To scale up the CloudFormation stack, select the Docker stack in the CloudFormation ➤ Stacks table and choose Actions ➤ Update Stack, as shown in Figure 7-8.

Figure 7-8. *Choosing Actions ➤ Update Stack*

The Update Docker Stack wizard starts. It's similar to the Create Stack wizard. In the Select Template, click on Next without modifying any settings. In Specify Details, increase Number of Swarm Worker Nodes? to 10, as shown in Figure 7-9. Click on Next.

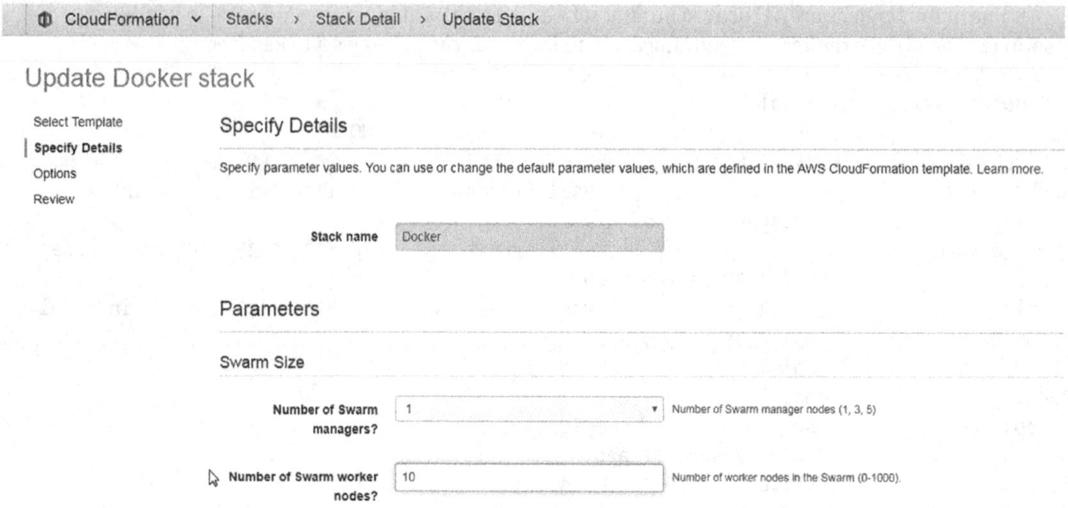

CloudFormation ∨ | Stacks › Stack Detail › Update Stack

Update Docker stack

Select Template
Specify Details
Options
Review

Specify Details

Specify parameter values. You can use or change the default parameter values, which are defined in the AWS CloudFormation template. Learn more.

Stack name Docker

Parameters

Swarm Size

Number of Swarm managers? 1 ▼ Number of Swarm manager nodes (1, 3, 5)

Number of Swarm worker nodes? 10 Number of worker nodes in the Swarm (0-1000).

Figure 7-9. *Increasing the number of worker nodes to 10*

In Preview Your Changes, click on Update, as shown in Figure 7-10.

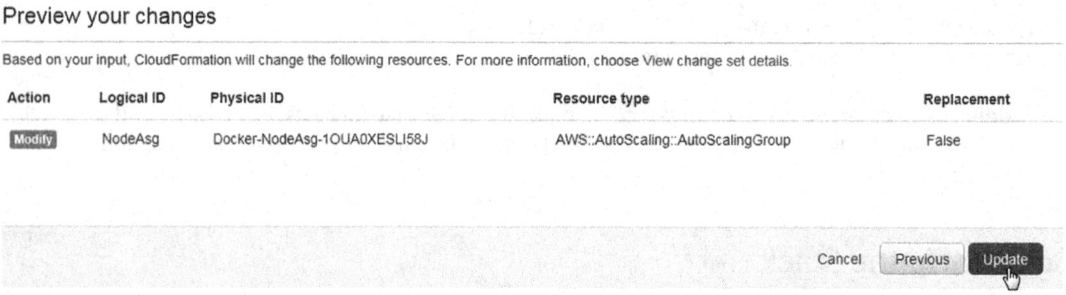

Preview your changes

Based on your input, CloudFormation will change the following resources. For more information, choose View change set details.

Action	Logical ID	Physical ID	Resource type	Replacement
Modify	NodeAsg	Docker-NodeAsg-1OUA0XESLI58J	AWS::AutoScaling::AutoScalingGroup	False

Cancel   Previous   Update

Figure 7-10. *Click Update to preview your changes*

When the update completes, the stack's status becomes UPDATE_COMPLETE, as shown in Figure 7-11.

CloudFormation ∨ | Stacks

Create Stack ▾ | Actions ▾ | Design template   C ⚙

Filter: Active ▾ By Stack Name   Showing 1 stack

Stack Name	Created Time	Status	Description
☑ Docker	2017-07-24 09:52:37 UTC-0700	UPDATE_COMPLETE	Docker CE for AWS 17.06.0-ce (17.06.0-ce-aws2)

Figure 7-11. *Stack update is complete*

The Swarm gets eight new worker nodes, for a total of 10 worker nodes. List the service description periodically (after an interval of few seconds) and, as new worker nodes are created, new replicas start to reconcile the current state with the desired state. The number of replicas in the `Replicas` column increases gradually within a few seconds. All the replicas for the `mysql` service start running, as indicated by 10/10 in the service listing.

```
~ $ docker service ls
ID              NAME          MODE          REPLICAS    IMAGE           PORTS
ysef8no2mhuw    mysql         replicated    3/10        mysql:latest
~ $ docker service ls
ID              NAME          MODE          REPLICAS    IMAGE           PORTS
ysef8no2mhuw    mysql         replicated    6/10        mysql:latest
~ $ docker service ls
ID              NAME          MODE          REPLICAS    IMAGE           PORTS
ysef8no2mhuw    mysql         replicated    9/10        mysql:latest
~ $ docker service ls
ID              NAME          MODE          REPLICAS    IMAGE           PORTS
ysef8no2mhuw    mysql         replicated    10/10       mysql:latest
```

Listing the service replicas lists all replicas as Running. The previously Pending replicas are scheduled on the new nodes.

```
~ $ docker service ps mysql
ID              NAME          IMAGE              NODE
DESIRED STATE   CURRENT STATE        ERROR         PORTS
8kkkdnso1690    mysql.1       mysql:latest       ip-172-31-16-11.ec2.internal
Running         Running 7 minutes ago
k2o9uge36bih    mysql.2       mysql:latest       ip-172-31-25-163.ec2.internal
Running         Running 6 minutes ago
oiublpclz9eu    mysql.3       mysql:latest       ip-172-31-33-230.ec2.internal
Running         Running 6 minutes ago
u807b7h0qvqc    mysql.4       mysql:latest       ip-172-31-11-105.ec2.internal
Running         Running 45 seconds ago
jh2ep10sonxy    mysql.5       mysql:latest       ip-172-31-13-141.ec2.internal
Running         Running about a minute ago
8d19osxa4fwf    mysql.6       mysql:latest       ip-172-31-24-10.ec2.internal
Running         Running about a minute ago
k8hba8j5o9vi    mysql.7       mysql:latest       ip-172-31-0-114.ec2.internal
Running         Running 55 seconds ago
ettk65bpin3b    mysql.8       mysql:latest       ip-172-31-5-127.ec2.internal
Running         Running about a minute ago
i3otbqfsfvr7    mysql.9       mysql:latest       ip-172-31-35-209.ec2.internal
Running         Running 24 seconds ago
sxdi97oo6d3b    mysql.10      mysql:latest       ip-172-31-21-57.ec2.internal
Running         Running 49 seconds ago
```

If the stack is updated again to decrease the number of worker nodes, some of the replicas shut down and are de-scheduled. After decreasing the number of worker nodes, the `Replicas` column lists only 5/10 replicas as running.

```
~ $ docker service ls
ID                  NAME                MODE                REPLICAS      IMAGE               PORTS
ysef8n02mhuw        mysql               replicated          5/10          mysql:latest
```

Some of the service tasks are listed as Shutdown because some of the worker nodes have been removed from the Swarm.

```
~ $ docker service ps mysql
ID                  NAME                IMAGE               NODE
DESIRED STATE       CURRENT STATE            ERROR              PORTS
8kkkdns0l690        mysql.1             mysql:latest        ip-172-31-16-11.ec2.internal
Running             Running 10 minutes ago
ulknt3e5zxy1        mysql.2             mysql:latest
Ready               Pending 3 seconds ago
k209uge36bih         \_ mysql.2         mysql:latest        ip-172-31-25-163.ec2.internal
Shutdown            Running 14 seconds ago
oiublpclz9eu        mysql.3             mysql:latest        ip-172-31-33-230.ec2.internal
Running             Running 9 minutes ago
mh2fpioi441k        mysql.4             mysql:latest
Running             Pending 3 seconds ago
u807b7h0qvqc         \_ mysql.4         mysql:latest        v53huw84hskqsb3e8o0a2pmun
Shutdown            Running about a minute ago
jzghd72nk0zc        mysql.5             mysql:latest
Ready               Pending 3 seconds ago
jh2ep10sonxy         \_ mysql.5         mysql:latest        ip-172-31-13-141.ec2.internal
Shutdown            Running 14 seconds ago
8d19osxa4fwf        mysql.6             mysql:latest        ip-172-31-24-10.ec2.internal
Running             Running 4 minutes ago
dlcgstxxkd9t        mysql.7             mysql:latest
Running             Pending 3 seconds ago
ziqslz7u9d9l         \_ mysql.7         mysql:latest        ip-172-31-43-179.ec2.internal
Shutdown            Assigned 57 seconds ago
k8hba8j5o9vi         \_ mysql.7         mysql:latest        op1dzvmt5eyc74l6pcl5ut64p
Shutdown            Running about a minute ago
ettk65bpin3b        mysql.8             mysql:latest        ip-172-31-5-127.ec2.internal
Running             Running 4 minutes ago
i3otbqfsfvr7        mysql.9             mysql:latest        ip-172-31-35-209.ec2.internal
Running             Running 3 minutes ago
sxdi97oo6d3b        mysql.10            mysql:latest        ip-172-31-21-57.ec2.internal
Running             Running 12 seconds ago
```

Summary

This chapter discussed the resources model of Docker Swarm mode, which is based on resource reserves and resource limits. Reserved resources cannot be more than resource limits and resource allocation to service tasks is limited by the node capacity. The next chapter discusses scheduling in Docker Swarm mode.

CHAPTER 8

■ ■ ■

Scheduling

In Chapter 2, the Docker Swarm was introduced. In Chapter 4, Docker Swarm services were introduced. A service consists of zero or more service tasks (replicas), which it schedules on the nodes in a Swarm. The desired state of a service includes the number of tasks that must be run. Scheduling is defined as the process of placing a service task that is required to be run on a node in the Swarm to keep the desired state of a service, as illustrated in Figure 8-1. A service task may only be scheduled on a worker node. A manager node is also a worker node by default.

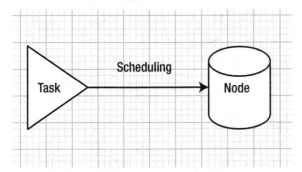

Figure 8-1. *Scheduling*

The Problem

Without a scheduling policy, the service tasks could get scheduled on a subset of nodes in a Swarm. As an example, all three tasks in a service could get scheduled on the same node in a Swarm, as illustrated in Figure 8-2.

© Deepak Vohra 2017
D. Vohra, *Docker Management Design Patterns*, https://doi.org/10.1007/978-1-4842-2973-6_8

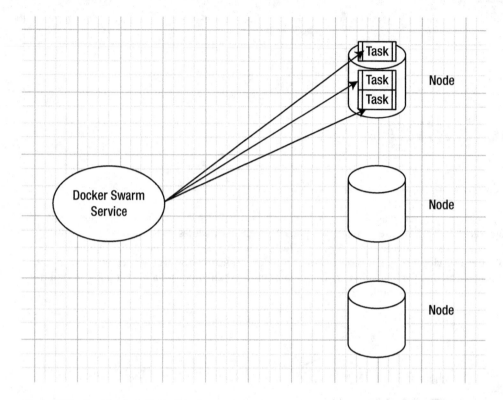

Figure 8-2. *Avoid scheduling all tasks on one node*

Not using a scheduling policy could lead to the following problems:

- *Underutilization of resources in a Swarm*—If all the tasks are scheduled on a single node or a subset of nodes, the resource capacity of the other nodes is not utilized.

- *Unbalanced utilization of resources*—If all the tasks are scheduled on a single node or a subset of nodes, the resources on the nodes on which the tasks are scheduled are over-utilized and the tasks could even use up all the resource capacity without any scope for scaling the replicas.

- *Lack of locality*—Clients access a service's tasks based on node location. If all the service tasks are scheduled on a single node, the external clients that are accessing the service on other nodes cannot access the service locally, thereby incurring a network overhead in accessing a relatively remote task.

- *Single point of failure*—If all services are running on one node and that node has a problem, it results in downtime. Increasing redundancy across nodes obviates that problem.

The Solution

To overcome the issues discussed in the preceding section, service task scheduling in a Docker Swarm is based on a built-in scheduling policy. Docker Swarm mode uses the *spread* scheduling strategy to rank nodes for placement of a service task (replica). Node ranking is computed for scheduling of each task and a task is scheduled on the node with the highest computed ranking. The *spread* scheduling strategy computes node rank based on the node's available CPU, RAM, and the number of containers already running on the node. The spread strategy optimizes for the node with the least number of containers. Load sharing is the objective of the spread strategy and results in tasks (containers) spread thinly and evenly over several machines in the Swarm. The expected outcome of the spread strategy is that if a single node or a small subset of nodes go down or become available, only a few tasks are lost and a majority of tasks in the Swarm continue to be available.

■ **Note**   Because a container consumes resources during all states, including when it is exited, the spread strategy does not take into consideration the state of a container. It is recommended that a user remove stopped containers, because a node that would otherwise be eligible and suitable for scheduling a new task becomes unsuitable if it has several stopped containers.

The spread scheduling strategy does not take into consideration for which service a task is scheduled. Only the available and requested resources are used to schedule a new task. Scheduling using the spread scheduling policy is illustrated in Figure 8-3.

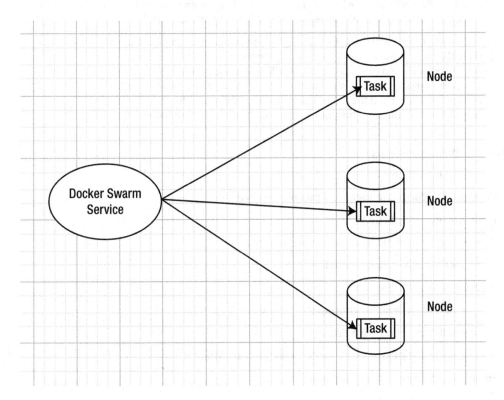

Figure 8-3. *Using the spread scheduling policy*

As a hypothetical example:

1. Start with three nodes, each with a capacity of 3GB and 3 CPUs and no containers running.

2. Create a mysql service with one replica, which requests resources of 1GB and 1 CPU. The first replica gets scheduled randomly on one of the three nodes in the Swarm as all nodes have the same ranking. If all the nodes have the same ranking, a new task gets scheduled randomly on one of the nodes.

3. Scale the mysql service to three tasks. As one of the nodes is already loaded, the two new tasks are scheduled on the other two nodes, spreading one task to each node.

4. Scale the mysql service to five tasks. Two new tasks must be started and all the nodes have the same ranking because they have the same available resource capacity and the same number of containers running. The two new tasks are scheduled randomly on two of the nodes. As a result, two nodes have two tasks each and one node has one task.

5. Create another service for the nginx server with a desired state of two tasks, with each task requesting 0.5GB and 0.5 CPU. Both the tasks are scheduled on the node that has only the task of the mysql service, as it is the least loaded. As a result, two nodes have two tasks of mysql service and an available capacity of 1GB and 1 CPU, and one node has two tasks of nginx service and one task of mysql service and also an available resource capacity of 1GB and 1 CPU.

6. Scale the nginx service to three. Even though all nodes have the same available CPU and RAM, the new task is not scheduled randomly on one of the three nodes, but is scheduled on the node with the least number of containers. As a result, the new nginx task gets scheduled randomly on one of the nodes, with two tasks of mysql each. If the nodes have the same available CPU and RAM, the node with fewer containers (running or stopped) is selected for scheduling the new task.

This chapter covers the following topics:

- Setting the environment
- Creating and scheduling a service—the spread scheduling
- Desired state reconciliation
- Scheduling tasks limited by node resource capacity
- Adding service scheduling constraints
- Scheduling on a specific node
- Adding multiple scheduling constraints
- Adding node labels for scheduling
- Adding, updating, and removing service scheduling constraints
- Spread scheduling and global services

Setting the Environment

Create a CloudFormation stack using Docker for AWS consisting of one manager node and two worker nodes. Docker for AWS was introduced in Chapter 3. The stack is shown in Figure 8-4.

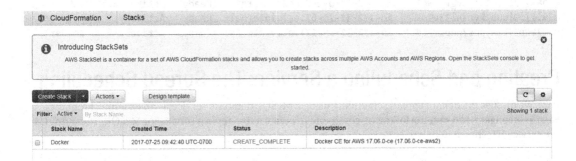

Figure 8-4. *CloudFormation stack*

The three EC2 instances in the stack are shown in Figure 8-5.

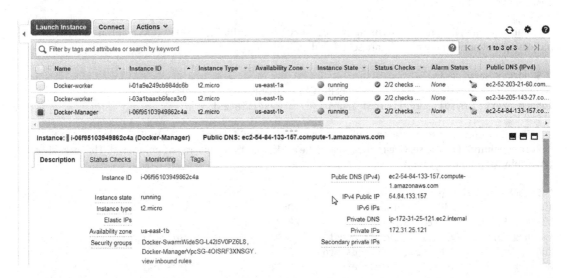

Figure 8-5. *EC2 instances for the Docker swarm*

SSH Login to the Swarm manager using the public IP address, which may be obtained from the EC2 console, as shown in Figure 8-5.

```
[root@localhost ~]# ssh -i "docker.pem" docker@54.84.133.157
Welcome to Docker!
```

List the nodes in the Swarm; three nodes should be listed.

```
~ $ docker node ls
ID                          HOSTNAME                       STATUS   AVAILABILITY  MANAGER
                                                                                  STATUS
Owaa5g3b6j641xtwsygvjvwc1   ip-172-31-0-147.ec2.internal   Ready    Active
e7vigin0luuo1kynjnl33v9pa   ip-172-31-29-67.ec2.internal   Ready    Active
ptm7e0p346zwypos7wnpcm72d * ip-172-31-25-121.ec2.internal  Ready    Active        Leader
```

Creating and Scheduling a Service: The Spread Scheduling

First, we discuss the default spread scheduling using a MySQL database service as an example. From the Swarm manager node, run the following command to create a five-replica service for MySQL. The output is the service ID (shown in italics).

```
~ $ docker service create \
>    --env MYSQL_ROOT_PASSWORD='mysql'\
>    --replicas 5 \
>    --name mysql \
>  mysql
1onpemnoz4x1lh3sv5umab8uo
```

Subsequently, list the services using docker service ls. Initially, the REPLICAS column could be 0/5, indicating that none of the replicas are scheduled and running yet.

```
~ $ docker service ls
ID          NAME    MODE        REPLICAS   IMAGE           PORTS
1onpemnoz4x1 mysql  replicated  0/5        mysql:latest
```

Run the command again after a while; all the replicas should be running as indicated by a 5/5 in the REPLICAS column. List the service replicas using the docker service ps mysql command. The tasks should be running or preparing to run.

```
~ $ docker service ps mysql
ID              NAME        IMAGE          NODE
DESIRED STATE   CURRENT STATE            ERROR      PORTS
fwjbu3gt2zn0    mysql.1     mysql:latest   ip-172-31-0-147.ec2.internal
Running         Preparing 8 seconds ago
w0521ik1awjf    mysql.2     mysql:latest   ip-172-31-29-67.ec2.internal
Running         Preparing 8 seconds ago
z9wn2nrzfzt8    mysql.3     mysql:latest   ip-172-31-0-147.ec2.internal
Running         Preparing 8 seconds ago
tm8jbque3xbb    mysql.4     mysql:latest   ip-172-31-25-121.ec2.internal
Running         Preparing 8 seconds ago
7drxfy3vbmp5    mysql.5     mysql:latest   ip-172-31-29-67.ec2.internal
Running         Preparing 8 seconds ago
```

Following the spread scheduling strategy, two of the replicas are listed as scheduled on one of the worker nodes, two on the other worker node, and one on the manager node. Because of the odd number of replicas, the placement cannot be completely evenly distributed, but a single node does not have more than two replicas.

To see how the spread scheduling strategy distributes the replicas evenly across a Swarm, scale the service to six replicas. The output of the docker service scale command is in italics.

```
~ $ docker service scale mysql=6
mysql scaled to 6
```

Subsequently, list the replicas. Each node has two replicas scheduled on it, as the spread scheduling policy is designed to schedule.

```
~ $ docker service ps mysql
ID               NAME          IMAGE            NODE
DESIRED STATE    CURRENT STATE              ERROR    PORTS
fwjbu3gt2zn0     mysql.1       mysql:latest     ip-172-31-0-147.ec2.internal
Running          Running 13 seconds ago
w0521ik1awjf     mysql.2       mysql:latest     ip-172-31-29-67.ec2.internal
Running          Running 12 seconds ago
z9wn2nrzfzt8     mysql.3       mysql:latest     ip-172-31-0-147.ec2.internal
Running          Running 13 seconds ago
tm8jbque3xbb     mysql.4       mysql:latest     ip-172-31-25-121.ec2.internal
Running          Running 8 seconds ago
7drxfy3vbmp5     mysql.5       mysql:latest     ip-172-31-29-67.ec2.internal
Running          Running 12 seconds ago
utjo8lwbtzf7     mysql.6       mysql:latest     ip-172-31-25-121.ec2.internal
Running          Running 5 seconds ago
```

As a service replica or task is nothing but a slot to run a container, each node runs two containers for the mysql service.

To further demonstrate spread scheduling, scale down the service to three tasks. The command output is in italics.

```
~ $ docker service scale mysql=3
mysql scaled to 3
```

List the service tasks. Each node has one task running on it, which again is an evenly spread scheduling of tasks.

```
~ $ docker service ps mysql
ID               NAME          IMAGE            NODE
DESIRED STATE    CURRENT STATE              ERROR    PORTS
w0521ik1awjf     mysql.2       mysql:latest     ip-172-31-29-67.ec2.internal
Running          Running 40 seconds ago
z9wn2nrzfzt8     mysql.3       mysql:latest     ip-172-31-0-147.ec2.internal
Running          Running 41 seconds ago
utjo8lwbtzf7     mysql.6       mysql:latest     ip-172-31-25-121.ec2.internal
Running          Running 33 seconds ago
```

Desired State Reconciliation

When a service is created or is scaled up or down, the service initially has a discrepancy between the *current state* and the *desired state*. The different values for the desired state are ready, running, shutdown, and accepted. Docker services are designed for desired state reconciliation, which implies that the Swarm manager continuously monitors the cluster state to reconcile any differences between the desired state of a service and the current state. The current state of a task can be assigned, preparing, ready, running, shutdown, or pending. A task that has been assigned to a node but is not currently running is in the assigned state. A task that has desired state as running and is preparing to run is in the preparing current state. A task is in the pending state if no node in the Swarm can run the task.

In the following task listing, some tasks have a desired state and current state of running. These tasks have reconciled their desired state. One task has a desired state set to running, but the current state is pending. Another task has a desired state set to shutdown and a current state set to assigned.

```
~ $ docker service ps mysql
ID                NAME            IMAGE           NODE
DESIRED STATE     CURRENT STATE                   ERROR      PORTS
opxf4ne7iyy6      mysql.1         mysql:latest    ip-172-31-25-121.ec2.internal
Running           Running 9 minutes ago
x30y3jlea047      mysql.2         mysql:latest    ip-172-31-29-67.ec2.internal
Running           Running 8 minutes ago
w4ivsbvwqqzq      mysql.3         mysql:latest    ip-172-31-2-177.ec2.internal
Running           Running 4 minutes ago
j9lp08ojofj7      mysql.4         mysql:latest
Running           Pending 28 seconds ago
ph1zpsjsvp69      \_ mysql.4      mysql:latest    ip-172-31-7-137.ec2.internal
Shutdown          Assigned 33 seconds ago
d3oxy6hxfjh3      \_ mysql.4      mysql:latest    ip-172-31-40-70.ec2.internal
Shutdown          Running 43 seconds ago
ic331aasjpdm      mysql.5         mysql:latest    ip-172-31-44-104.ec2.internal
Running           Running 8 minutes ago
```

In an earlier task listing, all tasks were in the current state preparing and the desired state running.

Swarm mode is designed to reconcile the desired state as much as feasible, implying that if node resources are available, the desired number of replicas runs. To demonstrate, update the Docker for AWS CloudFormation stack by choosing Actions ➤ Update Stack, as shown in Figure 8-6.

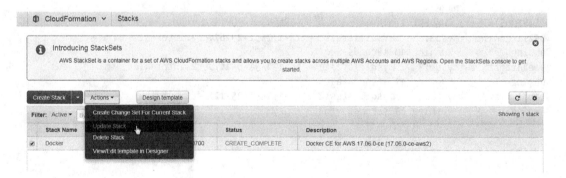

Figure 8-6. *Updating a stack*

Decrease the number of worker nodes from two to one, as shown in Figure 8-7.

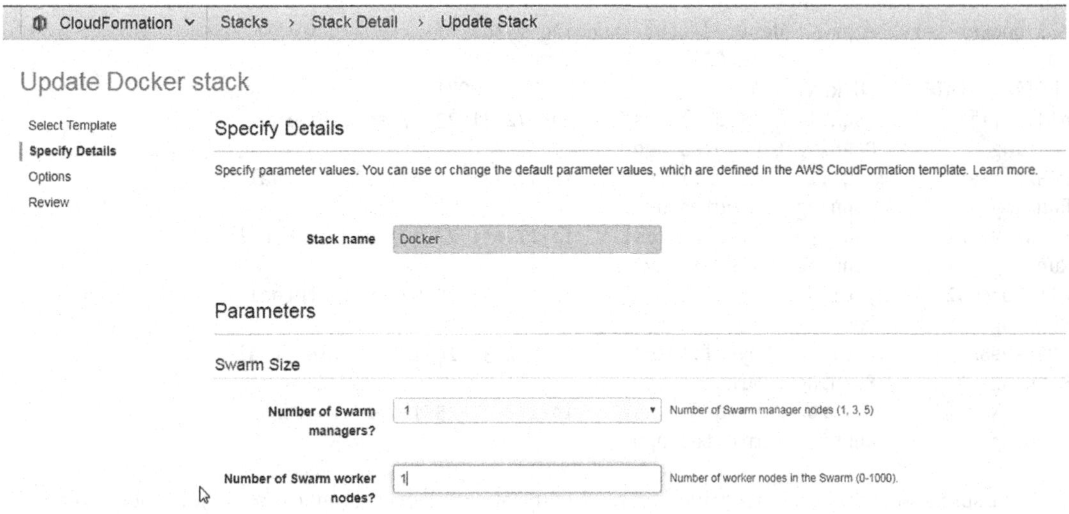

Figure 8-7. *Decreasing the number of worker nodes to one*

Subsequently, list the service replicas from the Swarm manager node.

```
docker service ps mysql
```

The service replicas running on the Swarm worker node that was made to leave the Swarm are listed as shutdown. New replicas are started on the remaining two nodes in the Swarm to reconcile the desired state.

```
~ $ docker service ps mysql
ID                NAME            IMAGE            NODE
DESIRED STATE     CURRENT STATE                   ERROR     PORTS
p14bbk7ij1mt      mysql.1         mysql:latest     ip-172-31-29-67.ec2.internal
Running           Running 5 minutes ago
w0521ik1awjf      mysql.2         mysql:latest     ip-172-31-29-67.ec2.internal
Running           Running 7 minutes ago
uatsaay7axlc      mysql.3         mysql:latest     ip-172-31-25-121.ec2.internal
Running           Running about a minute ago
z9wn2nrzfzt8      \_ mysql.3     mysql:latest     0waa5g3b6j641xtwsygvjvwc1
Shutdown          Running 2 minutes ago
w1tlw0fom42q      mysql.4         mysql:latest     ip-172-31-29-67.ec2.internal
Running           Running about a minute ago
qc75buhzzct3      \_ mysql.4     mysql:latest     0waa5g3b6j641xtwsygvjvwc1
Shutdown          Running 2 minutes ago
s09ts9s8np3d      mysql.5         mysql:latest     ip-172-31-25-121.ec2.internal
Running           Running 5 minutes ago
utjo8lwbtzf7      mysql.6         mysql:latest     ip-172-31-25-121.ec2.internal
Running           Running 7 minutes ago
```

Listing only the replicas with a desired state of running, the six replicas are listed as scheduled evenly between the two nodes—three replicas on the manager node and three replicas on the worker node.

```
~ $ docker service ps -f desired-state=running mysql
ID                NAME      IMAGE          NODE
DESIRED STATE     CURRENT STATE           ERROR     PORTS
p14bbk7ij1mt      mysql.1   mysql:latest   ip-172-31-29-67.ec2.internal
Running           Running 6 minutes ago
w0521ik1awjf      mysql.2   mysql:latest   ip-172-31-29-67.ec2.internal
Running           Running 8 minutes ago
uatsaay7axlc      mysql.3   mysql:latest   ip-172-31-25-121.ec2.internal
Running           Running 2 minutes ago
w1tlw0fom42q      mysql.4   mysql:latest   ip-172-31-29-67.ec2.internal
Running           Running 2 minutes ago
so9ts9s8np3d      mysql.5   mysql:latest   ip-172-31-25-121.ec2.internal
Running           Running 6 minutes ago
utjo8lwbtzf7      mysql.6   mysql:latest   ip-172-31-25-121.ec2.internal
Running           Running 8 minutes ago
```

The spread scheduling strategy does not reschedule already running replicas to achieve even spread across a Swarm if new nodes are added to the Swarm. To demonstrate this, we increase the number of worker nodes back to two, as shown in Figure 8-8.

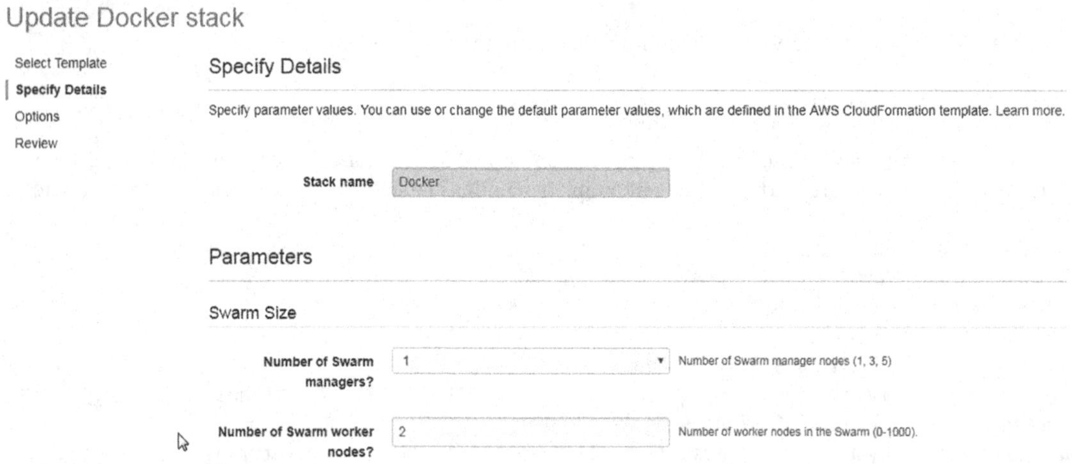

Figure 8-8. *Re-adding a worker node to Swarm*

Adding a node to a swarm does not shut down replicas on other nodes and start replicas on the new node. Listing the running replicas does not indicate a replacement of the service replicas. Service replicas continue to run on the nodes they were running on before the new node was added—three on the manager node and three on the worker node.

```
~ $ docker service ps mysql
ID                 NAME            IMAGE          NODE
DESIRED STATE      CURRENT STATE                  ERROR      PORTS
p14bbk7ij1mt       mysql.1         mysql:latest   ip-172-31-29-67.ec2.internal
Running            Running 15 minutes ago
w0521ik1awjf       mysql.2         mysql:latest   ip-172-31-29-67.ec2.internal
Running            Running 17 minutes ago
uatsaay7axlc       mysql.3         mysql:latest   ip-172-31-25-121.ec2.internal
Running            Running 12 minutes ago
z9wn2nrzfzt8       \_ mysql.3      mysql:latest   Owaa5g3b6j641xtwsygvjvwc1
Shutdown           Running 13 minutes ago
w1tlw0fom42q       mysql.4         mysql:latest   ip-172-31-29-67.ec2.internal
Running            Running 12 minutes ago
qc75buhzzct3       \_ mysql.4      mysql:latest   Owaa5g3b6j641xtwsygvjvwc1
Shutdown           Running 13 minutes ago
s09ts9s8np3d       mysql.5         mysql:latest   ip-172-31-25-121.ec2.internal
Running            Running 15 minutes ago
utjo8lwbtzf7       mysql.6         mysql:latest   ip-172-31-25-121.ec2.internal
Running            Running 17 minutes ago
```

Scheduling Tasks Limited by Node Resource Capacity

The scheduling policy is limited by the available node resources, implying that service replicas cannot be made to run if not enough node resources in terms of CPU and memory are available. Resource usage cannot exceed node capacity. The replicas are still allocated to the service to define the desired state but may not be running due to insufficient resources. To demonstrate this, we remove the service mysql and create the service again with the specified resource requests and limits. Command outputs are shown in italics.

```
~ $ docker service rm mysql
mysql

~ $ docker service create \
>    --env MYSQL_ROOT_PASSWORD='mysql'\
>    --replicas 1 \
>    --name mysql \
>    --reserve-cpu 1 --limit-cpu 2 --reserve-memory  256mb --limit-memory 512mb mysql
Oqe2thyOdlviroli6k8thist1
```

Listing the services indicates that one replica of the service is created.

```
~ $ docker service ls
ID              NAME      MODE          REPLICAS    IMAGE             PORTS
Oqe2thyOdlvi    mysql     replicated    1/1         mysql:latest
```

The single replica is scheduled on the manager node, which is chosen randomly if all nodes in a Swarm have the same node ranking.

```
~ $ docker service ps mysql
ID                 NAME          IMAGE          NODE
DESIRED STATE      CURRENT STATE                ERROR                   PORTS
opxf4ne7iyy6       mysql.1    mysql:latest      ip-172-31-25-121.ec2.internal
Running            Running 8 seconds ago
```

Next, to potentially make the service replicas consume more resources than available, scale the service to five replicas.

```
~ $ docker service scale mysql=5
mysql scaled to 5
```

Listing the services indicates that 3/5 Replicas are running.

```
~ $ docker service ls
ID                 NAME      MODE          REPLICAS     IMAGE              PORTS
0qe2thy0dlvi       mysql     replicated    3/5          mysql:latest
```

Listing the service replicas indicates that some of the replicas are pending instead of running.

```
~ $ docker service ps mysql
ID                 NAME          IMAGE          NODE
DESIRED STATE      CURRENT STATE                ERROR      PORTS
opxf4ne7iyy6       mysql.1    mysql:latest      ip-172-31-25-121.ec2.internal
Running            Running 4 minutes ago
x30y3jlea047       mysql.2    mysql:latest      ip-172-31-29-67.ec2.internal
Running            Running 3 minutes ago
w4ivsbvwqqzq       mysql.3    mysql:latest
Running            Pending 3 minutes ago
d3oxy6hxfjh3       mysql.4    mysql:latest
Running            Pending 3 minutes ago
ic331aasjpdm       mysql.5    mysql:latest      ip-172-31-44-104.ec2.internal
Running            Running 3 minutes ago
```

The pending state implies that the replicas are allocated to the service but not scheduled on any node yet. Only three replicas could run based on the requested resources and available node resources, one on each node.

Because the replicas are not scheduled due to lack of resources, we add one or more new worker nodes to potentially schedule the replicas to reconcile the desired state. Increase the number of worker nodes to five, as shown in Figure 8-9.

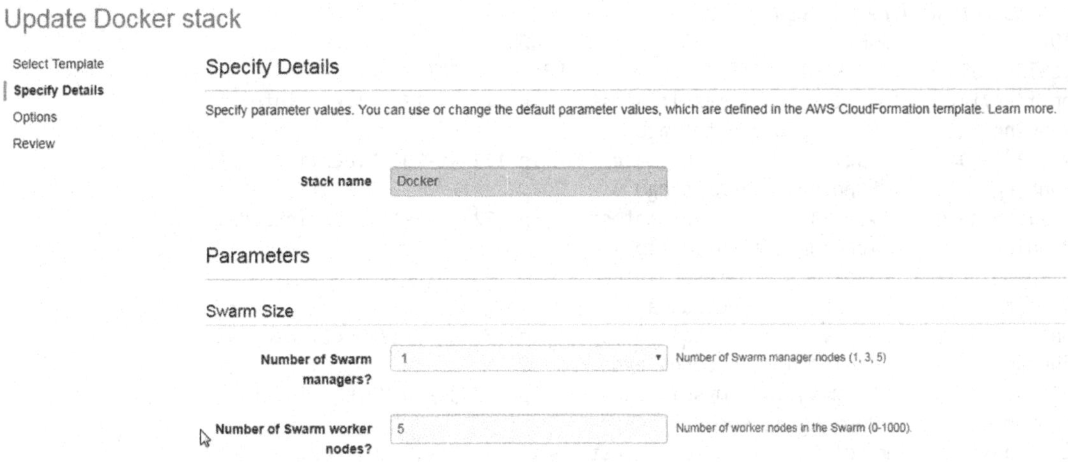

Update Docker stack

Select Template

Specify Details

Options

Review

Specify Details

Specify parameter values. You can use or change the default parameter values, which are defined in the AWS CloudFormation template. Learn more.

Stack name   Docker

Parameters

Swarm Size

Number of Swarm
managers?   1   ▾   Number of Swarm manager nodes (1, 3, 5)

Number of Swarm worker
nodes?   5   Number of worker nodes in the Swarm (0-1000).

Figure 8-9. *Increasing the number of worker nodes to five*

The Swarm should list six nodes after a new node is added. As resources became available for the pending tasks, the tasks get scheduled and start running.

```
~ $ docker service ps mysql
ID              NAME        IMAGE           NODE
DESIRED STATE       CURRENT STATE           ERROR           PORTS
opxf4ne7iyy6    mysql.1     mysql:latest    ip-172-31-25-121.ec2.internal
Running             Running 5 minutes ago
x30y3jlea047    mysql.2     mysql:latest    ip-172-31-29-67.ec2.internal
Running             Running 4 minutes ago
w4ivsbvwqqzq    mysql.3     mysql:latest    ip-172-31-2-177.ec2.internal
Running             Running 21 seconds ago
d3oxy6hxfjh3    mysql.4     mysql:latest    ip-172-31-40-70.ec2.internal
Running             Preparing 30 seconds ago
ic331aasjpdm    mysql.5     mysql:latest    ip-172-31-44-104.ec2.internal
Running             Running 4 minutes ago
```

If the number of worker nodes is decreased, some of the tasks are descheduled, as indicated by the shutdown desired state.

143

```
~ $ docker service ps mysql
ID                NAME            IMAGE          NODE
DESIRED STATE       CURRENT STATE               ERROR     PORTS
opxf4ne7iyy6      mysql.1         mysql:latest   ip-172-31-25-121.ec2.internal
Running             Running 9 minutes ago
x30y3jlea047      mysql.2         mysql:latest   ip-172-31-29-67.ec2.internal
Running             Running 8 minutes ago
w4ivsbvwqqzq      mysql.3         mysql:latest   ip-172-31-2-177.ec2.internal
Running             Running 4 minutes ago
j9lp08ojofj7      mysql.4         mysql:latest
Running             Pending 28 seconds ago
ph1zpsjsvp69      \_ mysql.4   mysql:latest     ip-172-31-7-137.ec2.internal
Shutdown            Assigned 33 seconds ago
d3oxy6hxfjh3      \_ mysql.4   mysql:latest     ip-172-31-40-70.ec2.internal
Shutdown            Running 43 seconds ago
ic331aasjpdm      mysql.5         mysql:latest   ip-172-31-44-104.ec2.internal
Running             Running 8 minutes ago
```

Updating the service to lower CPU and memory resource usage reserved only updates the UpdateConfig for the service. This does not lower the resource usage of the already running tasks or make pending or shutdown tasks run. As an example, lower the resource reserves and limits for the mysql service when some of the tasks are pending or shutdown due to lack of resources.

```
~ $ docker service update --reserve-cpu .1 --limit-cpu .5 --reserve-memory  64mb
  --limit-memory 128mb mysql
mysql
```

The UpdateConfig gets modified, but only applies to new replicas created after that point.

```
~ $ docker service inspect mysql
[
                },
                "Resources": {
                    "Limits": {
                        "NanoCPUs": 500000000,
                        "MemoryBytes": 134217728
                    },
                    "Reservations": {
                        "NanoCPUs": 100000000,
                        "MemoryBytes": 67108864
                    }
                },
]
```

Only three of the replicas in the mysql service are actually running.

```
~ $ docker service ps -f desired-state=running mysql
ID              NAME        IMAGE          NODE
DESIRED STATE   CURRENT STATE             ERROR     PORTS
opxf4ne7iyy6    mysql.1     mysql:latest   ip-172-31-25-121.ec2.internal
Running         Running 10 minutes ago
x30y3jlea047    mysql.2     mysql:latest   ip-172-31-29-67.ec2.internal
Running         Running 10 minutes ago
w4ivsbvwqqzq    mysql.3     mysql:latest   ip-172-31-2-177.ec2.internal
Running         Running 5 minutes ago
rm9uj4qevt5b    mysql.5     mysql:latest
Running         Pending 33 seconds ago
```

To force the service tasks to use the new resource settings, scale down the service to one task and then scale back up to five tasks.

```
~ $ docker service scale mysql=1
mysql scaled to 1
~ $ docker service scale mysql=5
mysql scaled to 5
```

All five tasks are now running.

```
~ $ docker service ps mysql
ID              NAME          IMAGE          NODE
DESIRED STATE   CURRENT STATE               ERROR     PORTS
anai3mptbnkp    mysql.1       mysql:latest   ip-172-31-2-177.ec2.internal
Running         Running 17 seconds ago
opxf4ne7iyy6    \_ mysql.1    mysql:latest   ip-172-31-25-121.ec2.internal
Shutdown        Shutdown 18 seconds ago
lmkn8l50t334    mysql.2       mysql:latest   ip-172-31-25-121.ec2.internal
Running         Running 10 seconds ago
7uz7q86wnzn4    mysql.3       mysql:latest   ip-172-31-2-177.ec2.internal
Running         Running 11 seconds ago
ubh4m39aw8m9    mysql.4       mysql:latest   ip-172-31-29-67.ec2.internal
Running         Running 11 seconds ago
56pnrzajogvs    mysql.5       mysql:latest   ip-172-31-25-121.ec2.internal
Running         Running 10 seconds ago
```

Adding Service Scheduling Constraints

Docker Swarm supports placement or scheduling constraints for scheduling new tasks. Service placement constraints are additional criteria for placement of service tasks and could be based on node attributes, metadata, and engine metadata. The Swarm scheduler uses the following sequence to schedule a service task.

1. Does the node satisfy all the placement constraints?

2. Does a node meet the scheduling policy requirements of an even spread?

3. Does the node have sufficient resources to schedule a task?

A placement constraint may be added using the `--constraint` option with the `docker service create` command. For an already running service, constraints may be added and removed with the `--constraint-add` and `--constraint-rm` options, respectively, with the `docker service update` command. The node attributes discussed in Table 8-1 may be used to specify constraints.

Table 8-1. *Node Attributes for Constraints*

Node Attribute	Description	Example
`node.id`	Specifies the node ID. Node IDs are listed using the `docker node ls` command.	`node.id==a3r56hj7y`
`node.hostname`	Specifies the node's hostname. The node's hostname is listed with the `docker node ls` command.	`node.hostname!=ip-10-0-0-ec2.internal`
`node.role`	Specifies the node role, which is one of `worker` or `manager`.	`node.role==manager`
`node.labels`	Specifies the node labels added by a user. A label is a key-value pair. When adding a node label, the `node.labels.` prefix is to be omitted and gets added automatically. Adding and using node labels is discussed in a subsequent section.	`node.labels.db==mysql`
`engine.labels`	Docker Engine labels such as drivers, operating system, version.	`engine.labels.os==coreos`

Next, we discuss some examples of using scheduling constraints.

Scheduling on a Specific Node

In this section we schedule service replicas on specific nodes in a Swarm. List the node IDs with the `docker node ls` command. The Swarm has the following three nodes available for scheduling.

```
~ $ docker node ls
ID                            HOSTNAME                        STATUS  AVAILABILITY  MANAGER
                                                                                    STATUS
81h6uvu8uq0emnovzkg6v7mzg     ip-172-31-2-177.ec2.internal    Ready   Active
e7vigin0luuo1kynjnl33v9pa     ip-172-31-29-67.ec2.internal    Ready   Active
ptm7e0p346zwypos7wnpcm72d *   ip-172-31-25-121.ec2.internal   Ready   Active        Leader
```

We can schedule a service by node role. Create a `mysql` service with the placement constraint that the service tasks be scheduled on worker nodes only. First, remove the `mysql` service if it's already running

```
~ $ docker service rm mysql
mysql
~ $ docker service create \
>   --env MYSQL_ROOT_PASSWORD='mysql'\
>   --replicas 3 \
>   --constraint node.role==worker \
>   --name mysql \
>   mysql
nzgte4zac1x8itx6t98y5gi42
```

The service is created and three tasks are scheduled only on the two worker nodes, as listed in the running service tasks.

```
~ $ docker service ps -f desired-state=running mysql
ID                 NAME           IMAGE            NODE
DESIRED STATE      CURRENT STATE                   ERROR      PORTS
f5t15mnrft0h       mysql.1        mysql:latest     ip-172-31-29-67.ec2.internal
Running            Running 19 seconds ago
oxvq4ljuq6yz       mysql.2        mysql:latest     ip-172-31-2-177.ec2.internal
Running            Running 19 seconds ago
k5jo862lvsxf       mysql.3        mysql:latest     ip-172-31-2-177.ec2.internal
Running            Running 19 seconds ago
```

Next, we use the node ID to schedule a service's tasks. Copy the node ID for the manager node, which is also the leader in the Swarm being the only manager node. Substitute the node ID in the following command to create a service for the MySQL database and schedule replicas only on the manager node.

```
docker service create \
  --env MYSQL_ROOT_PASSWORD='mysql'\
  --replicas 3 \
  --constraint  node.id ==<nodeid>
  --name mysql \
 mysql
```

A service is created with three tasks. Command output is shown in italics.

```
~ $ docker service create \
>    --env MYSQL_ROOT_PASSWORD='mysql'\
>    --replicas 3 \
>    --constraint  node.id==ptm7e0p346zwypos7wnpcm72d\
>    --name mysql \
>  mysql
u1qi6zqnch9hn7x6k516axg7h
```

All the three replicas of the service are scheduled on the manager node only.

```
~ $ docker service ps -f desired-state=running mysql
ID                 NAME           IMAGE            NODE
DESIRED STATE      CURRENT STATE                   ERROR      PORTS
lbttu95qdjvy       mysql.1        mysql:latest     ip-172-31-25-121.ec2.internal
Running            Running 21 seconds ago
89x0z94on0fb       mysql.2        mysql:latest     ip-172-31-25-121.ec2.internal
Running            Running 21 seconds ago
3s6508aimdaj       mysql.3        mysql:latest     ip-172-31-25-121.ec2.internal
Running            Running 22 seconds ago
```

Adding Multiple Scheduling Constraints

Multiple node constraints may also be specified and every constraint expression must be met using AND for the scheduler to schedule a replica on a node. As an example, we create a service with two roles, one that constrains the node role to worker and the other constrains the node hostname not to be a specific hostname ip-172-31-2-177.ec2.internal.

```
~ $ docker service create \
>    --env MYSQL_ROOT_PASSWORD='mysql'\
>    --replicas 3 \
>    --constraint node.role==worker \
>    --constraint   node.hostname!=ip-172-31-2-177.ec2.internal\
>    --name mysql \
>  mysql
87g0c8kauhz8yb4wv2ryc2vqr
```

A service gets created. Listing the services lists 3/3 replicas as running.

```
~ $ docker service ls
ID            NAME    MODE        REPLICAS   IMAGE          PORTS
87g0c8kauhz8  mysql   replicated  3/3        mysql:latest
```

Listing the service tasks indicates that all tasks are scheduled on a single worker node. The two constraints are met: the node is a worker node and not the worker node with hostname ip-172-31-2-177.ec2.internal.

```
~ $ docker service ps mysql
ID               NAME         IMAGE          NODE
DESIRED STATE    CURRENT STATE                 ERROR     PORTS
jlfk79mb6m6a     mysql.1      mysql:latest   ip-172-31-29-67.ec2.internal
Running          Running 13 seconds ago
if5y39ky884q     mysql.2      mysql:latest   ip-172-31-29-67.ec2.internal
Running          Running 13 seconds ago
zctm6mzbl4du     mysql.3      mysql:latest   ip-172-31-29-67.ec2.internal
Running          Running 13 seconds ago
```

If the mysql service is updated to remove the constraints, the spread scheduling strategy reschedules the tasks based on node ranking. As an example, update the service to remove the two placement constraints added. A constraint is removed with the –constraint-rm option of the docker service update command.

```
~ $ docker service update \
>    --constraint-rm node.role==worker \
>    --constraint-rm   node.hostname!=ip-172-31-2-177.ec2.internal\
>  mysql
mysql
```

When a service is updated to remove constraints, all the service tasks are shut down and new service tasks are started. The new service tasks are started, one each on the three nodes in the Swarm.

```
~ $ docker service ps mysql
ID                NAME           IMAGE          NODE
DESIRED STATE     CURRENT STATE                 ERROR       PORTS
d22bkgteivot      mysql.1        mysql:latest   ip-172-31-29-67.ec2.internal
Ready                            Ready less than a second ago
jlfk79mb6m6a      \_ mysql.1     mysql:latest   ip-172-31-29-67.ec2.internal
Shutdown                         Running 1 second ago
mp757499j3io      mysql.2        mysql:latest   ip-172-31-2-177.ec2.internal
Running                          Running 1 second ago
if5y39ky884q      \_ mysql.2     mysql:latest   ip-172-31-29-67.ec2.internal
Shutdown                         Shutdown 2 seconds ago
jtdxucteb0fl      mysql.3        mysql:latest   ip-172-31-25-121.ec2.internal
Running                          Running 4 seconds ago
zctm6mzbl4du      \_ mysql.3     mysql:latest   ip-172-31-29-67.ec2.internal
Shutdown                         Shutdown 5 seconds ago
```

List only the running tasks. One task is listed running on each node.

```
~ $ docker service ps -f desired-state=running mysql
ID                NAME          IMAGE          NODE
DESIRED STATE     CURRENT STATE                ERROR       PORTS
d22bkgteivot      mysql.1       mysql:latest   ip-172-31-29-67.ec2.internal
Running                         Running 46 seconds ago
mp757499j3io      mysql.2       mysql:latest   ip-172-31-2-177.ec2.internal
Running                         Running 49 seconds ago
jtdxucteb0fl      mysql.3       mysql:latest   ip-172-31-25-121.ec2.internal
Running                         Running 53 seconds ago
```

Similarly, multiple node constraints could be used to run replicas only on a manager node. Next, we update the mysql service to run on a specific manager node. First, promote one of the worker nodes to manager.

```
~ $ docker node promote ip-172-31-2-177.ec2.internal
Node ip-172-31-2-177.ec2.internal promoted to a manager in the swarm.
```

Subsequently, two manager nodes are listed as indicated by the Manager Status for two of the nodes.

```
~ $ docker node ls
ID                           HOSTNAME                       STATUS   AVAILABILITY   MANAGER
                                                                                    STATUS
81h6uvu8uq0emnovzkg6v7mzg    ip-172-31-2-177.ec2.internal   Ready    Active         Reachable
e7vigin0luuo1kynjnl33v9pa    ip-172-31-29-67.ec2.internal   Ready    Active
ptm7e0p346zwypos7wnpcm72d *  ip-172-31-25-121.ec2.internal  Ready    Active         Leader
```

Update the mysql service to add multiple node constraints to run replicas only on a specific manager node. Constraints are added using the --constraint-add option of the docker service update command.

```
~ $ docker service update \
>    --constraint-add node.role==manager \
>    --constraint-add  node.hostname==ip-172-31-2-177.ec2.internal\
>    mysql
mysql
```

Again, all service tasks are shut down and new tasks are started, all on the specified manager node that was promoted from the worker node.

```
~ $ docker service ps -f desired-state=running mysql
ID                NAME        IMAGE          NODE
DESIRED STATE     CURRENT STATE            ERROR       PORTS
eghm1or6yg5g      mysql.1     mysql:latest   ip-172-31-2-177.ec2.internal
Running           Running 28 seconds ago
bhfngac5ssm7      mysql.2     mysql:latest   ip-172-31-2-177.ec2.internal
Running           Running 22 seconds ago
ts3fgvq900os      mysql.3     mysql:latest   ip-172-31-2-177.ec2.internal
Running           Running 25 seconds ago
```

Adding Node Labels for Scheduling

Next, we discuss how node labels can be used to specify service placement constraints. Labels may be added to a node with the following command syntax, in which variables are <LABELKEY>, <LABELVALUE>, and <NODE>. The <NODE> is the node ID or hostname.

```
docker node update --label-add  <LABELKEY>=<LABELVALUE>  <NODE>
```

As an example, add the label db=mysql to the node with a hostname set to ip-172-31-25-121.ec2. internal, which is the leader node.

```
~ $ docker node update --label-add  db=mysql  ip-172-31-25-121.ec2.internal
ip-172-31-25-121.ec2.internal
```

A node label is added. On inspecting the node, the label is listed in the Labels field.

```
~ $ docker node inspect ip-172-31-25-121.ec2.internal
[
        "Spec": {
            "Labels": {
                "db": "mysql"
            },
            "Role": "manager",
            "Availability": "active"
        },
]
```

Next, create a service that uses the node label to add a placement constraint. The --constraint option for the label must include the prefix node.labels.

```
~ $ docker service rm mysql
mysql
~ $ docker service create \
>    --env MYSQL_ROOT_PASSWORD='mysql'\
>    --replicas 3 \
>    --constraint node.labels.db==mysql \
>    --name mysql \
>    mysql
2hhccmj9senseazbet11dekoa
```

150

The service is created. Listing the tasks lists all the tasks on the Leader manager node, which is what the node label constraint specified.

```
~ $ docker service ps -f desired-state=running mysql
ID              NAME        IMAGE          NODE
DESIRED STATE   CURRENT STATE             ERROR     PORTS
g5jz9im3fufv    mysql.1     mysql:latest   ip-172-31-25-121.ec2.internal
Running         Running 18 seconds ago
bupr27bs57h1    mysql.2     mysql:latest   ip-172-31-25-121.ec2.internal
Running         Running 18 seconds ago
5bb2yf8aehqn    mysql.3     mysql:latest   ip-172-31-25-121.ec2.internal
Running         Running 18 seconds ago
```

The label added may be removed with the --label-rm option of the docker node update command in which the only the label key is specified.

```
docker node update --label-rm db ip-172-31-25-121.ec2.internal
```

Adding, Updating, and Removing Service Scheduling Constraints

In an earlier section, we discussed adding placement constraints when creating a service with docker service create. Placement constraints may be added/removed with the docker service update command using the --constraint-add and --constraint-rm options. To discuss an example of updating placement constraints, we create a mysql service with three replicas and no placement constraints to start with.

```
~ $ docker service rm mysql
mysql
~ $ docker service create \
>    --env MYSQL_ROOT_PASSWORD='mysql'\
>    --replicas 3 \
>    --name mysql \
>    mysql
az3cq6sxwrrk4mxkksdu21i25
```

A mysql service gets created with three replicas scheduled on the three nodes in the Swarm, using the spread policy.

Next, update the service with the docker service update command to add a constraint for the service replicas to run only on the manager nodes.

```
~ $ docker service update \
>    --constraint-add node.role==manager \
>    mysql
mysql
```

In a Swarm with two manager nodes, all the service tasks are shut down and new tasks are started only on the manager nodes.

```
~ $ docker service ps mysql
ID                NAME           IMAGE            NODE
DESIRED STATE        CURRENT STATE               ERROR              PORTS
pjwseruvy4rj      mysql.1        mysql:latest     ip-172-31-2-177.ec2.internal
Running              Running 4 seconds ago
s66g9stz9af5      \_ mysql.1    mysql:latest     ip-172-31-2-177.ec2.internal
Shutdown             Shutdown 4 seconds ago
yqco9zd0vq79      mysql.2        mysql:latest     ip-172-31-25-121.ec2.internal
Running              Running 9 seconds ago
8muu6gbghhnd      \_ mysql.2    mysql:latest     ip-172-31-25-121.ec2.internal
Shutdown             Shutdown 10 seconds ago
8x7xlavcxdau      mysql.3        mysql:latest     ip-172-31-25-121.ec2.internal
Running              Running 7 seconds ago
qx95vwi2h547      \_ mysql.3    mysql:latest     ip-172-31-29-67.ec2.internal
Shutdown             Shutdown 7 seconds ago
```

Scheduling constraints may be added and removed in the same docker service update command. As an example, remove the constraint for the node to be a manager and add a constraint for the node to be a worker.

```
~ $ docker service update \
>   --constraint-rm node.role==manager \
>   --constraint-add node.role==worker \
>   mysql
mysql
```

Again. all the service tasks are shut down and new tasks are started only on the worker nodes.

```
~ $ docker service ps -f desired-state=running mysql
ID                NAME        IMAGE           NODE
DESIRED STATE        CURRENT STATE            ERROR       PORTS
6ppgmvw9lv75      mysql.1     mysql:latest    ip-172-31-29-67.ec2.internal
Running              Running 9 seconds ago
qm0loki65v9s      mysql.2     mysql:latest    ip-172-31-29-67.ec2.internal
Running              Running 17 seconds ago
ypl0tc1ft92o      mysql.3     mysql:latest    ip-172-31-29-67.ec2.internal
Running              Running
```

If the only scheduling constraint that specifies the node role as worker is removed, the spread scheduling strategy starts new tasks spread evenly across the Swarm. To demonstrate, remove the constraint for the node role to be a worker.

```
~ $ docker service update --constraint-rm node.role==worker mysql
mysql
```

Subsequently, new tasks are spread across the nodes in the Swarm.

```
~ $ docker service ps -f desired-state=running mysql
ID               NAME        IMAGE          NODE
DESIRED STATE    CURRENT STATE              ERROR    PORTS
jpx4jjw6l9d5     mysql.1     mysql:latest   ip-172-31-29-67.ec2.internal
Running          Running 5 seconds ago
ngajiik1hugb     mysql.2     mysql:latest   ip-172-31-25-121.ec2.internal
Running          Running 12 seconds ago
40eaujzlux88     mysql.3     mysql:latest   ip-172-31-2-177.ec2.internal
Running          Running 8 seconds ago
```

Spread Scheduling and Global Services

A global service runs one task on every node in a Swarm. A global service cannot be scaled to create more/fewer tasks. As a result, the spread scheduling policy concept does not apply to global services. However, node constraints may be applied to global services. As an example, we create a global service for the mysql database. Apply a placement constraint that the service should be available only on worker nodes.

```
~ $ docker service create \
>    --mode global \
>    --env MYSQL_ROOT_PASSWORD='mysql'\
>    --constraint node.role==worker \
>    --name mysql \
>    mysql
jtzcwatp001q9r26n1uubd8me
```

The global service is created. Listing the service tasks for the tasks with desired state as running lists only the tasks on the worker nodes.

```
~ $ docker service ps -f desired-state=running mysql
ID               NAME                              IMAGE          NODE
DESIRED STATE    CURRENT STATE          ERROR     PORTS
o5nskzpv27j9     mysql.e7vigin0luuo1kynjnl33v9pa  mysql:latest   ip-172-31-29-67.ec2.internal
Running          Running 17 seconds ago
```

If created without the constraint to schedule on worker nodes only, a global service schedules one task on each node, as demonstrated by the following example.

```
~ $ docker service rm mysql
mysql
~ $ docker service create \
>    --mode global \
>    --env MYSQL_ROOT_PASSWORD='mysql'\
>    --name mysql \
>    mysql
mv9yzyyntdhzz41zssbutcsvw
```

```
~ $ docker service ps -f desired-state=running mysql
ID              NAME                                IMAGE         NODE
DESIRED STATE   CURRENT STATE          ERROR  PORTS
mc87btddhmpl    mysql.e7vigin0luuo1kynjnl33v9pa    mysql:latest  ip-172-31-29-67.ec2.internal
Running          Running 19 seconds ago
o0wfdq9sd8yt    mysql.ptm7e0p346zwypos7wnpcm72d    mysql:latest  ip-172-31-25-121.ec2.internal
Running          Running 19 seconds ago
wt2q5k2dhqjt    mysql.81h6uvu8uq0emnovzkg6v7mzg    mysql:latest  ip-172-31-2-177.ec2.internal
Running          Running 19 seconds ago
```

Summary

This chapter discussed the scheduling policy of spread used in the Docker Swarm mode, whereby service replicas are spread evenly across nodes in a Swarm based on node ranking; a higher node ranking gets a service replica placement priority. We also discussed the effect of limited node resource capacity and how to alleviate it by adding new nodes to the Swarm. We discussed placement constraints for scheduling new replicas. The spread scheduling policy is not relevant for global services as they create one service task on each node by default. However, scheduling constraints may be used with global services. In the next chapter we discuss rolling updates to Docker services.

CHAPTER 9

■ ■ ■

Rolling Updates

The Docker Swarm mode provisions services consisting of replicas that run across the nodes in the Swarm. A service definition is created when a service is first created/defined. A service definition is created with the `docker service create` command. That command provides several options, including those for adding placement constraints, container labels, service labels, DNS options, environment variables, resource reserves and limits, logging driver, mounts, number of replicas, restart condition and delay, update delay, failure action, max failure ratio, and parallelism, most of which were discussed in Chapter 4.

The Problem

Once a service definition has been created, it may be required to update some of the service options such as increase/decrease the number of replicas, add/remove placement constraints, update resource reserves and limits, add/remove mounts, add/remove environment variables, add/remove container and service labels, add/remove DNS options, and modify restart and update parameters. If a service is required to be shut down as a whole to update service definition options, an interruption of service is the result.

The Solution

Docker Swarm mode includes the provision for rolling updates. In a rolling update, the service is not shut down, but individual replicas/tasks in the service are shut down one at a time and new service replicas/tasks based on the new service definition are started one at a time, as illustrated in Figure 9-1. As a result the service continues to be available during the rolling update. The service tasks that are served to a client could be from both old and new service definitions during a rolling update. As an example, if the rolling update performs an update to a more recent image tag, some of the tasks served to external clients during the rolling update could be from a mix of old image tag and new image tag.

© Deepak Vohra 2017
D. Vohra, *Docker Management Design Patterns*, https://doi.org/10.1007/978-1-4842-2973-6_9

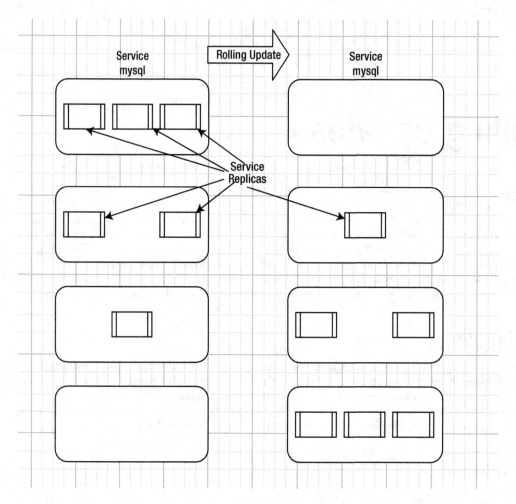

Figure 9-1. *Rolling update*

Rolling update creates a new service definition and a new desired state for a service. Rolling update involves shutting down all service replicas and starting all new service replicas and does not apply to service replicas that have not yet been scheduled, due to lack of resources for example. Even updating just the number of replicas in a rolling update shuts down or fails all the old replicas and starts all new replicas.

The following sequence is used by the scheduler during a rolling update.

1. The first task is stopped.

2. An update for the stopped task is scheduled.

3. A Docker container for the updated task is started.

4. If the update to a task returns RUNNING, wait for the duration specified in
    --update-delay and start the update to the next task.

5. If during the update, a task returns `FAILED`, perform the `--update-failure-action`, which is to pause the update by default.

6. Restart a paused update with `docker service update <SERVICE-ID>`.

7. If an update failure is repeated, find the cause of the failure and reconfigure the service by supplying other options to the docker service update.

Setting the Environment

Create a Docker Swarm consisting of a manager node and two worker nodes using Docker for AWS, as discussed in Chapter 3. Obtain the public IP address of the manager instance from the EC2 console and then SSH login to the instance.

```
[root@localhost ~]# ssh -i "docker.pem" docker@54.84.133.157
Welcome to Docker!
```

List the Swarm nodes.

```
~ $ docker node ls
ID                          HOSTNAME                      STATUS  AVAILABILITY MANAGER STATUS
81h6uvu8uq0emnovzkg6v7mzg   ip-172-31-2-177.ec2.internal  Ready   Active
e7vigin0luuo1kynjnl33v9pa   ip-172-31-29-67.ec2.internal  Ready   Active
ptm7e0p346zwypos7wnpcm72d * ip-172-31-25-121.ec2.internal Ready   Active       Leader
```

Creating a Service with a Rolling Update Policy

A rolling update policy or update config consists of the service definition options discussed in Table 9-1.

Table 9-1. Rolling Update Options

Option	Description	Default Value
`--update-delay`	Delay between updates (ns|us|ms|s|m|h).	0 seconds
`--update-failure-action`	Action on update failure. Value may be pause or continue.	pause
`--update-max-failure-ratio`		
`--update-monitor`	Duration after each task update to monitor for failure (ns|us|ms|s|m|h).	0 seconds
`--update-parallelism`	Maximum number of tasks updated simultaneously. A value of 0 updates all at once.	1

To configure the rolling update policy at service deployment time, the options to be configured must be supplied when the service is created. As an example, create a service for MySQL database and specify the update policy options --update-delay and --update-parallelism.

```
~ $ docker service create \
>    --env MYSQL_ROOT_PASSWORD='mysql'\
>    --replicas 1 \
>    --name mysql \
>    --update-delay 10s \
>    --update-parallelism 1  \
>    mysql:5.6
wr0z48v1uguk1c40pa42ywrpn
```

The service is created. Listing the services may not list all replicas as running initially, as indicated by 0/1 in the REPLICAS column.

```
~ $ docker service ls
ID             NAME       MODE          REPLICAS       IMAGE          PORTS
wr0z48v1uguk   mysql      replicated    0/1            mysql:5.6
```

Running the same command after a while should list all replicas as running, as indicated by 1/1 in REPLICAS column.

```
~ $ docker service ls
ID             NAME       MODE          REPLICAS       IMAGE          PORTS
wr0z48v1uguk   mysql      replicated    1/1            mysql:5.6
```

The single service replica is scheduled on the manager node itself and the Docker container for the replica is started.

```
~ $ docker service ps mysql
ID                NAME            IMAGE              NODE
DESIRED STATE     CURRENT STATE             ERROR          PORTS
38dm9gm6cmvk      mysql.1         mysql:5.6          ip-172-31-25-121.ec2.internal
Running           Running 13 seconds ago
```

Creating a service using rolling update options does not by itself demonstrate a rolling update. It only defines the UpdateConfig settings of the service. In the next section we perform a rolling update.

Rolling Update to Increase the Number of Replicas

A rolling update could be used to update the number of replicas with the --replicas option to the docker service update command. A rolling update updates the UpdateConfig policy applied when the service is first deployed. Next, we update the number of replicas for the mysql:5.6 image based service from the one replica created in the preceding section. Run the following command to update the service definition to five replicas from one replica. The --update-delay and --update-parallelism options modify the UpdateConfig of the service definition. The docker service update command outputs the service name if the update is successful.

```
~ $ docker service update \
>   --replicas 5 \
>   --update-delay 20s \
>   --update-parallelism 1  \
>   mysql
mysql
```

Subsequently, the services listing may list some of the replicas as not started yet in the output to the docker service ls command. But, running the command again after a while should list all replicas as running.

```
~ $ docker service ls
ID              NAME            MODE            REPLICAS        IMAGE           PORTS
wr0z48v1uguk    mysql           replicated      5/5             mysql:5.6
```

During the rolling update, all the running tasks are shut down and new tasks are started. The desired state of the mysql.1 task gets updated to shutdown and the current state is set to failed. A new task mysql.1 is started.

```
~ $ docker service ps mysql
ID              NAME            IMAGE           NODE
DESIRED STATE   CURRENT STATE           ERROR           PORTS
ydqj6vf9rsgw    mysql.1         mysql:5.6       ip-172-31-25-121.ec2.internal
Running         Running 26 seconds ago
38dm9gm6cmvk    \_ mysql.1      mysql:5.6       ip-172-31-25-121.ec2.internal
Shutdown        Failed 31 seconds ago   "task: non-zero exit (137)"
7bns96iu8ygz    mysql.2         mysql:5.6       ip-172-31-29-67.ec2.internal
Running         Running 32 seconds ago
62wfdbcv3cr4    mysql.3         mysql:5.6       ip-172-31-2-177.ec2.internal
Running         Running 33 seconds ago
ql66z5x0a2lf    mysql.4         mysql:5.6       ip-172-31-25-121.ec2.internal
Running         Running 14 seconds ago
3n3b1j7ey732    \_ mysql.4      mysql:5.6       ip-172-31-25-121.ec2.internal
Shutdown        Failed 19 seconds ago   "task: non-zero exit (137)"
bl1365y60vuu    mysql.5         mysql:5.6       ip-172-31-2-177.ec2.internal
Running             Running 33 seconds ago
```

When scaling from one to five replicas, first a few new tasks are started and then the task running initially is shut down so that the service continues to be available during the rolling update. If the only task in the service were to be shut down first before starting any new tasks, the service wouldn't have any running tasks for a short while.

The desired state of running five replicas is not immediately reconciled during a rolling update. Fewer than five tasks could be running while the rolling update is in progress. Listing the running service tasks lists only three tasks as running.

```
~ $ docker service ps -f desired-state=running mysql
ID              NAME            IMAGE           NODE
DESIRED STATE   CURRENT STATE           ERROR           PORTS
ydqj6vf9rsgw    mysql.1         mysql:5.6       ip-172-31-25-121.ec2.internal
Running             Running 35 seconds ago
7bns96iu8ygz    mysql.2         mysql:5.6       ip-172-31-29-67.ec2.internal
Running             Running 40 seconds ago
ql66z5x0a2lf    mysql.4         mysql:5.6       ip-172-31-25-121.ec2.internal
Running             Running 22 seconds ago
```

159

When the rolling update has completed, five tasks are running.

```
~ $ docker service ps -f desired-state=running mysql
ID                  NAME              IMAGE             NODE
DESIRED STATE       CURRENT STATE             ERROR       PORTS
u8falo7q95cq        mysql.1           mysql:5.6         ip-172-31-25-121.ec2.internal
Running             Running 20 seconds ago
luabknwzwqoj        mysql.2           mysql:5.6         ip-172-31-29-67.ec2.internal
Running             Running 13 seconds ago
ce4l2qvtcanv        mysql.3           mysql:5.6         ip-172-31-2-177.ec2.internal
Running             Running 25 seconds ago
iw8vwsxq3tjz        mysql.4           mysql:5.6         ip-172-31-25-121.ec2.internal
Running             Running 6 seconds ago
qfi5fionjt2v        mysql.5           mysql:5.6         ip-172-31-29-67.ec2.internal
Running             Running 25 seconds ago
```

Inspecting the service should list the updated number of replicas. The UpdateConfig is also listed with the docker service inspect command.

```
~ $ docker service inspect mysql
[
    ...
        "Spec": {
            "Name": "mysql",
    ...
            },
            "Mode": {
                "Replicated": {
                    "Replicas": 5
                }
            },
            "UpdateConfig": {
                "Parallelism": 1,
                "Delay": 20000000000,
                "FailureAction": "pause",
                "Monitor": 5000000000,
                "MaxFailureRatio": 0,
                "Order": "stop-first"
            },
            "RollbackConfig": {
                "Parallelism": 1,
                "FailureAction": "pause",
                "Monitor": 5000000000,
                "MaxFailureRatio": 0,
                "Order": "stop-first"
            },
    ...
]
```

Rolling Update to a Different Image Tag

A use case for a rolling update is to update to a newer image tag. As an example, perform a rolling update to update to Docker image mysql:latest from mysql:5.6 for the mysql service. Update parallelism is set to 2 to update two replicas at a time.

```
~ $ docker service update --image mysql:latest --update-parallelism 2  mysql
mysql
```

The service rolling update gets started. Listing the service replicas lists mysql:5.6 image-based replicas as shutting down, as indicated by the shutdown desired state and mysql:latest image-based replicas as starting, as indicated by the running desired state.

```
~ $ docker service ps mysql
ID                  NAME                IMAGE               NODE
DESIRED STATE       CURRENT STATE             ERROR                           PORTS
vqc6rhzw5uxz        mysql.1             mysql:latest        ip-172-31-2-177.ec2.internal
Ready               Ready 7 seconds ago
80kswuu4d5gc         \_ mysql.1         mysql:5.6           ip-172-31-2-177.ec2.internal
Shutdown            Running 7 seconds ago
u8falo7q95cq         \_ mysql.1         mysql:5.6           ip-172-31-25-121.ec2.internal
Shutdown            Failed 12 seconds ago       "task: non-zero exit (1)"
ydqj6vf9rsgw         \_ mysql.1         mysql:5.6           ip-172-31-25-121.ec2.internal
Shutdown            Failed 56 seconds ago       "task: non-zero exit (1)"
38dm9gm6cmvk         \_ mysql.1         mysql:5.6           ip-172-31-25-121.ec2.internal
Shutdown            Failed about a minute ago   "task: non-zero exit (137)"
tvxjmahy08uh        mysql.2             mysql:5.6           ip-172-31-29-67.ec2.internal
Running             Running 2 seconds ago
luabknwzwqoj         \_ mysql.2         mysql:5.6           ip-172-31-29-67.ec2.internal
Shutdown            Failed 8 seconds ago        "task: non-zero exit (137)"
7bns96iu8ygz         \_ mysql.2         mysql:5.6           ip-172-31-29-67.ec2.internal
Shutdown             Failed 50 seconds ago         "task: non-zero exit (137)"
u2ea4xq4yx6t        mysql.3             mysql:latest        ip-172-31-2-177.ec2.internal
Running             Running 4 seconds ago
ce4l2qvtcanv         \_ mysql.3         mysql:5.6           ip-172-31-2-177.ec2.internal
Shutdown            Shutdown 4 seconds ago
62wfdbcv3cr4         \_ mysql.3         mysql:5.6           ip-172-31-2-177.ec2.internal
Shutdown            Failed about a minute ago   "task: non-zero exit (1)"
iw8vwsxq3tjz        mysql.4             mysql:5.6           ip-172-31-25-121.ec2.internal
Running             Running 37 seconds ago
ql66z5x0a2lf         \_ mysql.4         mysql:5.6           ip-172-31-25-121.ec2.internal
Shutdown            Failed 43 seconds ago       "task: non-zero exit (137)"
3n3b1j7ey732         \_ mysql.4         mysql:5.6           ip-172-31-25-121.ec2.internal
Shutdown            Failed about a minute ago   "task: non-zero exit (137)"
f5vcf9mgluqe        mysql.5             mysql:5.6           ip-172-31-29-67.ec2.internal
Running             Running 14 seconds ago
qfi5fionjt2v         \_ mysql.5         mysql:5.6           ip-172-31-29-67.ec2.internal
Shutdown            Failed 19 seconds ago       "task: non-zero exit (1)"
bl1365y60vuu         \_ mysql.5         mysql:5.6           ip-172-31-2-177.ec2.internal
Shutdown            Failed about a minute ago   "task: non-zero exit (1)"
```

While the rolling update is in progress, some of the running tasks could be based on the previous service specification (mysql:5.6), while others are based on the new service specification (mysql:latest).

```
~ $ docker service ps -f desired-state=running mysql
ID              NAME              IMAGE             NODE
DESIRED STATE   CURRENT STATE              ERROR          PORTS
vqc6rhzw5uxz    mysql.1           mysql:latest      ip-172-31-2-177.ec2.internal
Running         Running 4 seconds ago
tvxjmahy08uh    mysql.2           mysql:5.6         ip-172-31-29-67.ec2.internal
Running         Running 11 seconds ago
u2ea4xq4yx6t    mysql.3           mysql:latest      ip-172-31-2-177.ec2.internal
Running         Running 13 seconds ago
iw8vwsxq3tjz    mysql.4           mysql:5.6         ip-172-31-25-121.ec2.internal
Running         Running 46 seconds ago
f5vcf9mgluqe    mysql.5           mysql:5.6         ip-172-31-29-67.ec2.internal
Running         Running 23 seconds ago
```

When the rolling update has completed, all running tasks are based on the new service specification.

```
~ $ docker service ps -f desired-state=running mysql
ID              NAME              IMAGE             NODE
DESIRED STATE   CURRENT STATE                    ERROR        PORTS
vqc6rhzw5uxz    mysql.1           mysql:latest      ip-172-31-2-177.ec2.internal
Running         Running 45 seconds ago
53choz0dd967    mysql.2           mysql:latest      ip-172-31-29-67.ec2.internal
Running         Running less than a second ago
u2ea4xq4yx6t    mysql.3           mysql:latest      ip-172-31-2-177.ec2.internal
Running         Running 53 seconds ago
tyo6v0yen7ev    mysql.4           mysql:latest      ip-172-31-29-67.ec2.internal
Running         Running 21 seconds ago
upt212osx7au    mysql.5           mysql:latest      ip-172-31-29-67.ec2.internal
Running         Running 25 seconds ago
```

Rolling Update to Add and Remove Environment Variables

The Docker image mysql requires one mandatory environment variable MYSQL_ROOT_PASSWORD for the root password and supports some other environment variables that may also be specified. The other environment variables are MYSQL_DATABASE for the MySQL database, MYSQL_USER for the MYSQL user, MYSQL_PASSWORD for the MySQL password, and MYSQL_ALLOW_EMPTY_PASSWORD for whether to allow the root password to be empty. The MYSQL_ROOT_PASSWORD was already set when the mysql service was created. Using the --env-add option to the docker service update command, we can add the other environment variables.

```
~ $ docker service update --env-add MYSQL_DATABASE='mysqldb' --env-add MYSQL_USER='mysql'
--env-add MYSQL_PASSWORD='mysql'  --env-add MYSQL_ALLOW_EMPTY_PASSWORD='no' --update-
parallelism 1 mysql
mysql
```

An output of mysql implies the command ran successfully.

The rolling update status is found with the docker service inspect command, which in addition to listing the env variables added in the Env JSON object, lists the UpdateStatus. The State of the update status is updating and the message is "update in progress".

```
~ $ docker service inspect mysql
[
    {...
        "Spec": {
            "Name": "mysql",
                "ContainerSpec": {
...
                    "Env": [
                        "MYSQL_ROOT_PASSWORD=mysql",
                        "MYSQL_DATABASE=mysqldb",
                        "MYSQL_USER=mysql",
                        "MYSQL_PASSWORD=mysql",
                        "MYSQL_ALLOW_EMPTY_PASSWORD=no"
                    ],
...
            },
        "UpdateStatus": {
            "State": "updating",
            "StartedAt": "2017-07-25T19:18:11.44139778Z",
            "Message": "update in progress"
        }
    }
}
]
```

When the update has completed, the UpdateStatus state becomes "completed" and the Message becomes "update completed".

```
~ $ docker service inspect mysql
[
...
        },
        "UpdateStatus": {
            "State": "completed",
            "StartedAt": "2017-07-25T19:18:11.44139778Z",
            "CompletedAt": "2017-07-25T19:20:37.9129934312",
            "Message": "update completed"
        }
    }
}
]
```

As indicated by the StartedAt and CompletedAt timestamp, the rolling update takes about two minutes. Listing only tasks with desired state of running indicates that one task has been running for 21 seconds and another task has been running for two minutes.

```
~ $ docker service ps -f desired-state=running mysql
ID                   NAME            IMAGE               NODE
DESIRED STATE        CURRENT STATE            ERROR           PORTS
3zhf94kklu6r         mysql.1             mysql:latest        ip-172-31-29-67.ec2.internal
Running              Running 21 seconds ago
ta16ch5kjlr9         mysql.2             mysql:latest        ip-172-31-29-67.ec2.internal
Running              Running 2 minutes ago
fc7uxvwvcmk3         mysql.3             mysql:latest        ip-172-31-2-177.ec2.internal
Running              Running about a minute ago
```

```
jir97p344kol        mysql.4              mysql:latest         ip-172-31-29-67.ec2.internal
Running             Running about a minute ago
5rly53mcc8yq        mysql.5              mysql:latest         ip-172-31-2-177.ec2.internal
Running             Running 45 seconds ago
```

The environment variables added may be removed with another docker service update command and the --env-rm options for each environment variable to remove. Only the env variable name is to be specified in --env-rm, not the env value.

```
~ $ docker service update --env-rm MYSQL_DATABASE --env-rm MYSQL_USER  --env-rm
MYSQL_PASSWORD  --env-rm MYSQL_ALLOW_EMPTY_PASSWORD mysql
mysql
```

Another rolling update gets performed. All service tasks get shut down and new service tasks based on the new service specification are started. The service definition lists only the mandatory environment variable MYSQL_ROOT_PASSWORD.

```
~ $ docker service inspect mysql
[...
                "Env": [
                    "MYSQL_ROOT_PASSWORD=mysql"
                ],
        },
        "UpdateStatus": {
            "State": "completed",
            "StartedAt": "2017-07-25T19:20:57.9686686604Z",
            "CompletedAt": "2017-07-25T19:22:59.18517919Z",
            "Message": "update completed"
        }
    }
]
```

Rolling Update to Set CPU and Memory Limits and Reserve

A rolling update may be used to set new resource limits and reserves.

```
~ $ docker service update --reserve-cpu 1 --limit-cpu 2 --reserve-memory 256mb -
-limit-memory 512mb mysql
mysql
```

New resource limits and reserves are configured, as listed in the service specification. The PreviousSpec indicates that no Resources Limits and Reservations are configured to start with.

```
~ $ docker service inspect mysql
[
  ...
        "Spec": {
            "Name": "mysql",
  ...
                "ContainerSpec": {
  ...
                },
```

```
              "Resources": {
                  "Limits": {
                      "NanoCPUs": 2000000000,
                      "MemoryBytes": 536870912
                  },
                  "Reservations": {
                      "NanoCPUs": 1000000000,
                      "MemoryBytes": 268435456
                  }
              },
...       },
      "PreviousSpec": {
...
          "Name": "mysql",
              "Resources": {
                  "Limits": {},
                  "Reservations": {}
              },
      "UpdateStatus": {
          "State": "updating",
          "StartedAt": "2017-07-25T19:23:44.004458295Z",
          "Message": "update in progress"
      }
  }
]
```

Setting new resource limits and reserves are subject to node capacity limits. If requested resources exceed the node capacity the rolling update may continue to run and not get completed, with some tasks in the pending current state.

```
~ $ docker service ps -f desired-state=running mysql
ID                   NAME                 IMAGE            NODE
DESIRED STATE        CURRENT STATE            ERROR            PORTS
5u7zifw15n7t         mysql.1              mysql:latest     ip-172-31-25-121.ec2.internal
Running              Running about an hour ago
2kgsb16c8m8u         mysql.2              mysql:latest
Running              Pending about an hour ago
mu08iu9qzqlh         mysql.3              mysql:latest     ip-172-31-29-67.ec2.internal
Running              Running about an hour ago
aakxr8dw5s15         mysql.4              mysql:latest     ip-172-31-2-177.ec2.internal
Running              Running about an hour ago
z6045639f20p         mysql.5              mysql:latest     ip-172-31-25-121.ec2.internal
Running              Running about an hour ago
```

If some tasks are pending, adding resources to the Swarm could make the pending tasks run. We can update the CloudFormation stack to increase the number of worker nodes from 2 to 3, as shown in Figure 9-2.

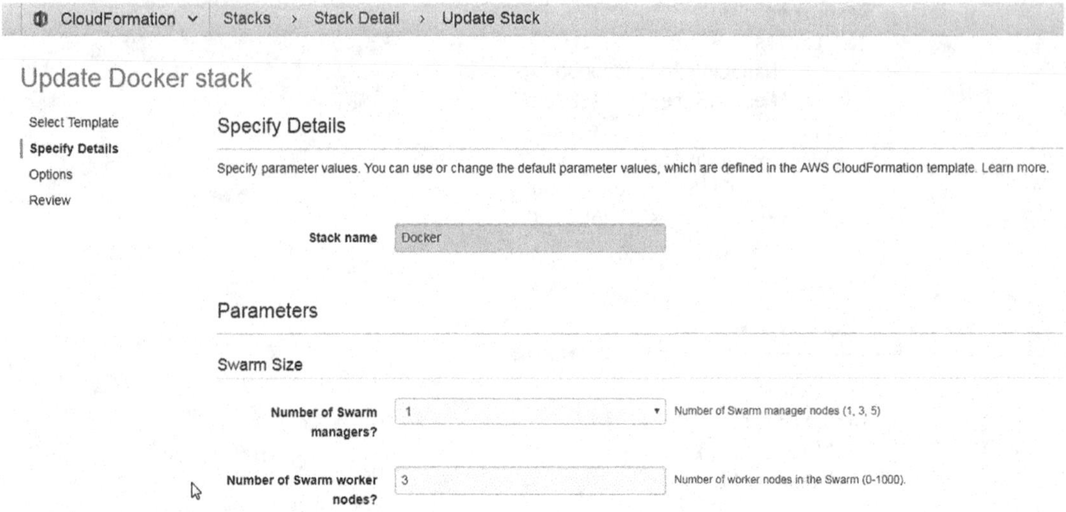

CloudFormation ∨ › Stacks › Stack Detail › Update Stack

Update Docker stack

Select Template
Specify Details
Options
Review

Specify Details

Specify parameter values. You can use or change the default parameter values, which are defined in the AWS CloudFormation template. Learn more.

Stack name   Docker

Parameters

Swarm Size

Number of Swarm managers?   1   Number of Swarm manager nodes (1, 3, 5)

Number of Swarm worker nodes?   3   Number of worker nodes in the Swarm (0-1000).

Figure 9-2. Increasing the number of worker nodes in the Swarm

Subsequently, the Swarm should list four nodes.

```
~ $ docker node ls
ID                          HOSTNAME                     STATUS AVAILABILITY  MANAGER STATUS
81h6uvu8uq0emnovzkg6v7mzg   ip-172-31-2-177.ec2.internal  Ready  Active
e7vigin0luuo1kynjnl33v9pa   ip-172-31-29-67.ec2.internal  Ready  Active
ptm7e0p346zwypos7wnpcm72d * ip-172-31-25-121.ec2.internal Ready  Active        Leader
t4d0aq9w2a6avjx94zgkwc557   ip-172-31-42-198.ec2.internal Ready  Active
```

With increased resources in the Swarm, the pending tasks also start to run.

```
~ $ docker service ps -f desired-state=running mysql
ID               NAME              IMAGE               NODE
DESIRED STATE    CURRENT STATE          ERROR          PORTS
5u7zifw15n7t     mysql.1                mysql:latest   ip-172-31-25-121.ec2.internal
Running          Running about an hour ago
2kgsb16c8m8u     mysql.2                mysql:latest   ip-172-31-2-177.ec2.internal
Running          Running 7 minutes ago
mu08iu9qzqlh     mysql.3                mysql:latest   ip-172-31-29-67.ec2.internal
Running          Running about an hour ago
i5j2drlcm75f     mysql.4                mysql:latest   ip-172-31-42-198.ec2.internal
Running          Running 4 seconds ago
z6045639f20p     mysql.5                mysql:latest   ip-172-31-25-121.ec2.internal
Running          Running about an hour ago
```

Rolling Update to a Different Image

Rolling update may also be used to update to a completely different Docker image. As an example, perform a rolling update to the mysql service to use Docker image postgres instead of the mysql image it is using. Other options such as --update-parallelism may also be set.

```
~ $ docker service update --image postgres --update-parallelism 1  mysql
mysql
```

The mysql:latest image-based tasks start to get shut down and postgres image-based replacement tasks begin to get started one task at a time. The rolling update does not get completed immediately and listing the service tasks with the desired state as running lists some tasks based on the postgres:latest image, while other tasks are still using the mysql:latest image.

```
~ $ docker service ps -f desired-state=running mysql
ID                   NAME              IMAGE                 NODE
DESIRED STATE        CURRENT STATE              ERROR        PORTS
9tzm5pa6pcyx         mysql.1                postgres:latest  ip-172-31-2-177.ec2.internal
Running              Running 39 seconds ago
xj23fu5svv9d         mysql.2                postgres:latest  ip-172-31-42-198.ec2.internal
Running              Running about a minute ago
mu08iu9qzqlh         mysql.3                mysql:latest     ip-172-31-29-67.ec2.internal
Running              Running about an hour ago
skzxi33c606o         mysql.4                postgres:latest  ip-172-31-2-177.ec2.internal
Running              Running 13 seconds ago
z6045639f20p         mysql.5                mysql:latest     ip-172-31-25-121.ec2.internal
Running              Running about an hour ago
```

One replica at a time, the mysql image-based replicas are shut down and postgres image-based replicas are started. After about two minutes, all tasks have updated to the postgres:latest image.

```
~ $ docker service ps -f desired-state=running mysql
ID                   NAME              IMAGE                 NODE
DESIRED STATE        CURRENT STATE              ERROR        PORTS
9tzm5pa6pcyx         mysql.1                postgres:latest  ip-172-31-2-177.ec2.internal
Running              Running about a minute ago
xj23fu5svv9d         mysql.2                postgres:latest  ip-172-31-42-198.ec2.internal
Running              Running about a minute ago
kd9pk31vpof2         mysql.3                postgres:latest  ip-172-31-42-198.ec2.internal
Running              Running 35 seconds ago
skzxi33c606o         mysql.4                postgres:latest  ip-172-31-2-177.ec2.internal
Running              Running 59 seconds ago
umtitiuvt5gg         mysql.5                postgres:latest  ip-172-31-25-121.ec2.internal
Running              Running 8 seconds ago
```

The service name continues to be the same and the replica names also include the mysql prefix. The mysql service definition ContainerSpec lists the image as postgres. Updating the image to postgres does not imply that all other service definition settings are updated for the new image. The postgres image does not use the MYSQL_ROOT_PASSWORD, but the environment variable continues to be in the service specification.

```
~ $ docker service inspect mysql
[
        "Spec": {
            "Name": "mysql",
                "ContainerSpec": {
                    "Image": "postgres:latest@sha256:e92fe21f695d27be7050284229a1c8c63ac10d8
                    8cba58d779c243566e125aa34",
                    "Env": [
                        "MYSQL_ROOT_PASSWORD=mysql"
                    ],
            "PreviousSpec": {
                "Name": "mysql",
                    "ContainerSpec": {
                        "Image": "mysql:latest@sha256:75c563c474f1adc149978011fedfe2e6670483d133
                        b22b07ee32789b626f8de3",
                        "Env": [
                            "MYSQL_ROOT_PASSWORD=mysql"
...         },
        "UpdateStatus": {
            "State": "completed",
            "StartedAt": "2017-07-25T20:39:45.230997671Z",
            "CompletedAt": "2017-07-25T20:42:04.186537673Z",
            "Message": "update completed"
        }
    }
}
]
```

The MYSQL_ROOT_PASSWORD environment variable may be removed with another update command.

```
~ $ docker service update    --env-rm MYSQL_ROOT_PASSWORD     mysql
mysql
```

Subsequently, the ContainerSpec does not include the MYSQL_ROOT_PASSWORD environment variable.

```
~ $ docker service inspect mysql
[
...
        "Spec": {
            "Name": "mysql",
            ...
                "ContainerSpec": {
                    "Image": "postgres:latest@sha256:e92fe21f695d27be7050284229a1c8c63ac10d8
                    8cba58d779c243566e125aa34",
                    "StopGracePeriod": 10000000000,
                    "DNSConfig": {}
                },
...         },
        "PreviousSpec": {
                "ContainerSpec": {
                    "Image": "postgres:latest@sha256:e92fe21f695d27be7050284229a1c8c63ac10d8
                    8cba58d779c243566e125aa34",
```

```
                  "Env": [
                      "MYSQL_ROOT_PASSWORD=mysql"
                  ],
...          },
          "UpdateStatus": {
              "State": "updating",
              "StartedAt": "2017-07-25T20:42:56.6510258162Z",
              "Message": "update in progress"
          }
      }
]
```

A rolling update to remove an environment variable involves shutting down all service tasks and starting all new tasks. The update takes about two minutes to complete.

```
~ $ docker service inspect mysql
[
          },
          "UpdateStatus": {
              "State": "completed",
              "StartedAt": "2017-07-25T20:42:56.6510258162Z",
              "CompletedAt": "2017-07-25T20:44:55.0789063592Z",
              "Message": "update completed"
          }
      }
]
```

Listing the running tasks indicates that tasks have only been running two minutes at the maximum.

```
~ $ docker service ps -f desired-state=running mysql
ID                    NAME                  IMAGE                NODE
DESIRED STATE         CURRENT STATE         ERROR        PORTS
menpo2zgit5u          mysql.1               postgres:latest      ip-172-31-2-177.ec2.internal
Running               Running about a minute ago
adnid3t69sue          mysql.2               postgres:latest      ip-172-31-25-121.ec2.internal
Running               Running about a minute ago
we92apfuivil          mysql.3               postgres:latest      ip-172-31-42-198.ec2.internal
Running               Running 46 seconds ago
ed7vh4ozefm5          mysql.4               postgres:latest      ip-172-31-29-67.ec2.internal
Running               Running 2 minutes ago
i2x2377ad7u0          mysql.5               postgres:latest      ip-172-31-25-121.ec2.internal
Running               Running about a minute ago
```

By removing the env variable MYSQL_ROOT_PASSWORD the mysql service gets updated to use Docker image postgres. The service name itself cannot be updated. The service may be updated back to the mysql image and the mandatory environment variable MYSQL_ROOT_PASSWORD added with another rolling update.

```
~ $ docker service update --image mysql --env-add MYSQL_ROOT_PASSWORD='mysql'  mysql
mysql
```

Again, listing the replicas with a desired state as running lists the postgres image-based replicas being replaced by mysql image-based replicas. One replica at a time, the postgres image-based replicas are replaced by mysql image-based replicas.

```
~ $ docker service ps -f desired-state=running mysql
ID                   NAME            IMAGE              NODE
DESIRED STATE        CURRENT STATE            ERROR          PORTS
menpo2zgit5u         mysql.1         postgres:latest    ip-172-31-2-177.ec2.internal
Running              Running 2 minutes ago
adnid3t69sue         mysql.2         postgres:latest    ip-172-31-25-121.ec2.internal
Running              Running 2 minutes ago
we92apfuivil         mysql.3         postgres:latest    ip-172-31-42-198.ec2.internal
Running              Running about a minute ago
pjvj50j822xr         mysql.4         mysql:latest       ip-172-31-29-67.ec2.internal
Running              Running 12 seconds ago
i2x2377ad7u0         mysql.5         postgres:latest    ip-172-31-25-121.ec2.internal
Running              Running 2 minutes ago
```

Within a minute or two, all the postgres image replicas are replaced by mysql image-based replicas.

```
~ $ docker service ps -f desired-state=running mysql
ID                   NAME            IMAGE              NODE
DESIRED STATE        CURRENT STATE            ERROR          PORTS
sobd90v7gbmz         mysql.1         mysql:latest       ip-172-31-25-121.ec2.internal
Running              Running about a minute ago
st5t7y8rdgg1         mysql.2         mysql:latest       ip-172-31-29-67.ec2.internal
Running              Running 57 seconds ago
upekevrlbmgo         mysql.3         mysql:latest       ip-172-31-42-198.ec2.internal
Running              Running about a minute ago
pjvj50j822xr         mysql.4         mysql:latest       ip-172-31-29-67.ec2.internal
Running              Running 2 minutes ago
nmrmdug87cy0         mysql.5         mysql:latest       ip-172-31-2-177.ec2.internal
Running              Running 2 minutes ago
```

The service specification is updated to the mysql image and the mandatory environment variable MYSQL_ROOT_PASSWORD is added. When the update has completed, the UpdateStatus State becomes completed.

```
~ $ docker service inspect mysql
[
        "Spec": {
            "Name": "mysql",
 ...
                    "Image": "mysql:latest@sha256:75c563c474f1adc149978011fedfe2e6670483d133
                    b22b07ee32789b626f8de3",
                    "Env": [
                        "MYSQL_ROOT_PASSWORD=mysql"
                    ],

 ...        },
        "PreviousSpec": {
            "Name": "mysql",
                "ContainerSpec": {
```

```
                "Image": "postgres:latest@sha256:e92fe21f695d27be7050284229a1c8c63ac10d8
                8cba58d779c243566e125aa34",
...            },
        "UpdateStatus": {
            "State": "completed",
            "StartedAt": "2017-07-25T20:45:54.104241339Z",
            "CompletedAt": "2017-07-25T20:47:47.996420791Z",
            "Message": "update completed"
        }
    }
]
```

Rolling Restart

Docker 1.13 added a new option to perform a rolling restart even when no update is required based on the update options. As an example starting with the `mysql` service with update config as `--update-parallelism 1` and `--update-delay 20s`, the following update command won't perform any rolling update, as no changes are being made to the service.

```
~ $ docker service update  --update-parallelism 1 --update-delay 20s mysql
mysql
```

To force a rolling restart, include the `--force` option.

```
~ $ docker service update --force --update-parallelism 1 --update-delay 20s mysql
mysql
```

Service tasks begin to get shut down and new service tasks are started even though no update is made to the service specification. Some tasks are listed as having started a few seconds ago.

```
~ $ docker service ps -f desired-state=running mysql
ID                NAME            IMAGE                 NODE
DESIRED STATE     CURRENT STATE                  ERROR          PORTS
sobd90v7gbmz      mysql.1         mysql:latest          ip-172-31-25-121.ec2.internal
Running           Running 3 minutes ago
trye9chir91l      mysql.2         mysql:latest          ip-172-31-25-121.ec2.internal
Running           Running 23 seconds ago
uu7sfp147xnu      mysql.3         mysql:latest          ip-172-31-42-198.ec2.internal
Running           Running less than a second ago
pjvj50j822xr      mysql.4         mysql:latest          ip-172-31-29-67.ec2.internal
Running           Running 4 minutes ago
nmrmdug87cy0      mysql.5         mysql:latest          ip-172-31-2-177.ec2.internal
Running           Running 3 minutes ago
```

A rolling restart could take 1-2 minutes to complete.

```
~ $ docker service inspect mysql
[
    ...
    },
```

```
        "UpdateStatus": {
            "State": "completed",
            "StartedAt": "2017-07-25T20:49:34.716535081Z",
            "CompletedAt": "2017-07-25T20:51:36.880045931Z",
            "Message": "update completed"
        }
    }
}
]
```

After the rolling restart has completed, the service has all new service tasks as shown.

```
~ $ docker service ps -f desired-state=running mysql
ID                NAME                 IMAGE              NODE
DESIRED STATE     CURRENT STATE                 ERROR              PORTS
z2n2qcgfsbke      mysql.1              mysql:latest       ip-172-31-29-67.ec2.internal
Running           Running 6 seconds ago
trye9chir91l      mysql.2              mysql:latest       ip-172-31-25-121.ec2.internal
Running           Running about a minute ago
uu7sfp147xnu      mysql.3              mysql:latest       ip-172-31-42-198.ec2.internal
Running           Running about a minute ago
1aovurxkteq1      mysql.4              mysql:latest       ip-172-31-29-67.ec2.internal
Running           Running 29 seconds ago
r0lslq6jibvp      mysql.5              mysql:latest       ip-172-31-2-177.ec2.internal
Running           Running 52 seconds ago
```

Rolling Update to Add and Remove Mounts

Rolling update can also be used to add and remove mounts. As an example, we add a mount of type volume with the source volume specified with src and the destination directory specified with dst.

```
~ $ docker service update \
>     --mount-add type=volume,src=mysql-scripts,dst=/etc/mysql/scripts \
>     mysql
mysql
```

A mount is added to the service and is listed in the service definition. Adding a mount involves shutting down all service tasks and starting new tasks. The rolling update could take 1-2 minutes.

```
~ $ docker service inspect mysql
[
        "Spec": {
                "ContainerSpec": {
...
                    "Mounts": [
                        {
                            "Type": "volume",
                            "Source": "mysql-scripts",
                            "Target": "/etc/mysql/scripts"
                        }
                    ],
...
```

```
        "UpdateStatus": {
            "State": "completed",
            "StartedAt": "2017-07-25T20:51:55.205456644Z",
            "CompletedAt": "2017-07-25T20:53:56.451313826Z",
            "Message": "update completed"
        }
    }
]
```

The mount added may be removed with the --mount-rm option of the docker service update command and by supplying only the mount destination directory as an argument.

```
~ $ docker service update \
>    --mount-rm /etc/mysql/scripts \
>    mysql
mysql
```

Another rolling update is performed and the mount is removed. It does not get listed in the service definition. The PreviousSpec lists the mount. The UpdateStatus indicates the status of the rolling update.

```
~ $ docker service inspect mysql
[
        "Spec": {
            "Name": "mysql",
                "ContainerSpec": {
...
        "PreviousSpec": {
            "Name": "mysql",
...
                    "Mounts": [
                        {
                            "Type": "volume",
                            "Source": "mysql-scripts",
                            "Target": "/etc/mysql/scripts"
                        }
        "UpdateStatus": {
            "State": "completed",
            "StartedAt": "2017-07-25T20:55:56.30844324Z",
            "CompletedAt": "2017-07-25T20:57:58.489349432Z",
            "Message": "update completed"
        }
    }
]
```

Rolling Update Failure Action

The --update-failure-action option of the docker service create and docker service update commands specifies the follow-up action to take if the update to a task fails and returns FAILED. We set the UpdateConfig for the mysql service to include a --update-failure-action of pause (the default). The other option setting is continue, which does not pause a rolling update but continues with the update of the next task. To demonstrate a update failure action, specify a Docker image that does not exist, such as mysql:5.9.

```
~ $ docker service update \
>    --replicas 10 \
>    --image mysql:5.9  \
>    --update-delay 10s \
>    --update-failure-action pause \
>  mysql
image mysql:5.9 could not be accessed on a registry to record
its digest. Each node will access mysql:5.9 independently,
possibly leading to different nodes running different
versions of the image.
mysql
```

The rolling update is still started and the update status indicates that the update is paused. The update status message indicates "update paused due to failure or early termination of task".

```
~ $ docker service inspect mysql
[
        "Spec": {
            "Name": "mysql",
            },
            "UpdateConfig": {
                "Parallelism": 1,
                "Delay": 10000000000,
                "FailureAction": "pause",
                "Monitor": 5000000000,
                "MaxFailureRatio": 0,
                "Order": "stop-first"
            },
            "RollbackConfig": {
                "Parallelism": 1,
                "FailureAction": "pause",
                "Monitor": 5000000000,
                "MaxFailureRatio": 0,
                "Order": "stop-first"
            },
...         },
        "UpdateStatus": {
            "State": "paused",
            "StartedAt": "2017-07-25T20:58:51.695333064Z",
            "Message": "update paused due to failure or early termination of task
            s1p1n0x3k67uwpoj7qxg13747"
        }
    }
]
```

Two options are available if a rolling update is paused due to update to a task having failed.

- Restart a paused update using docker service update <SERVICE-ID>.

- If an update failure is repeated, find the cause of the failure and reconfigure the service by supplying other options to the docker service update <SERVICE-ID> command.

Roll Back to Previous Specification

Docker 1.13 Swarm mode added the feature to roll back to the previous service definition. As an example, perform a rolling update to update the image of the mysql service to postgres. The mysql-based replicas begin to be shut down and postgres-based replicas are started. At any time during the rolling update from the mysql image to the postgres image or after the update to the postgres image has completed, if it is ascertained that the rolling update should not have been started or performed, the rolling update may be rolled back with the following command. To demonstrate a rollback, we first start a mysql service.

```
~ $ docker service rm mysql
mysql
~ $ docker service create \
>    --env MYSQL_ROOT_PASSWORD='mysql'\
>    --replicas 5 \
>    --name mysql \
>    --update-delay 10s \
>    --update-parallelism 1  \
>    mysql:5.6
xkmrhnk0a444zambp9yh1mk9h
```

We start a rolling update to the postgres image from the mysql image.

```
~ $ docker service update --image postgres  mysql
mysql
```

Subsequently, some of the tasks are based on the postgres image and some on the mysql image.

```
~ $ docker service ps mysql
ID                 NAME             IMAGE              NODE
DESIRED STATE      CURRENT STATE             ERROR          PORTS
mnm5pg9ha61u       mysql.1          mysql:5.6          ip-172-31-25-121.ec2.internal
Running            Running 58 seconds ago
9y0fzn4sgiv0       mysql.2          postgres:latest    ip-172-31-2-177.ec2.internal
Ready              Ready 2 seconds ago
ewl7zxwi07gc       \_ mysql.2       mysql:5.6          ip-172-31-2-177.ec2.internal
Shutdown           Running 2 seconds ago
l3ock28cmtzx       mysql.3          mysql:5.6          ip-172-31-42-198.ec2.internal
Running            Running 22 seconds ago
1vqs3lcqvbt5       mysql.4          postgres:latest    ip-172-31-29-67.ec2.internal
Running            Running 12 seconds ago
wu11jjbszesy       \_ mysql.4       mysql:5.6          ip-172-31-29-67.ec2.internal
Shutdown           Shutdown 13 seconds ago
g3tr6z9l5vzx       mysql.5          mysql:5.6          ip-172-31-42-198.ec2.internal
Running            Running 22 seconds ago
```

Start a rollback to revert to the mysql image.

```
~ $ docker service update --rollback mysql
mysql
```

The `postgres` image-based tasks start to get shut down and the `mysql` image-based tasks are started.

```
~ $ docker service ps mysql
ID                NAME                IMAGE                NODE
DESIRED STATE     CURRENT STATE              ERROR                        PORTS
mnm5pg9ha61u      mysql.1             mysql:5.6            ip-172-31-25-121.ec2.internal
Running           Running about a minute ago
gyqgtoc4ix3y      mysql.2             mysql:5.6            ip-172-31-2-177.ec2.internal
Running           Running 14 seconds ago
9y0fzn4sgiv0      \_ mysql.2          postgres:latest      ip-172-31-2-177.ec2.internal
Shutdown          Shutdown 15 seconds ago
ewl7zxwi07gc      \_ mysql.2          mysql:5.6            ip-172-31-2-177.ec2.internal
Shutdown          Shutdown 23 seconds ago
l3ock28cmtzx      mysql.3             mysql:5.6            ip-172-31-42-198.ec2.internal
Running           Running 46 seconds ago
ecvh8fd5308k      mysql.4             mysql:5.6            ip-172-31-29-67.ec2.internal
Running           Running 16 seconds ago
1vqs3lcqvbt5      \_ mysql.4          postgres:latest      ip-172-31-29-67.ec2.internal
Shutdown          Shutdown 16 seconds ago
wu11jjbszesy      \_ mysql.4          mysql:5.6            ip-172-31-29-67.ec2.internal
Shutdown          Shutdown 37 seconds ago
m27d3gz4g6dy      mysql.5             mysql:5.6            ip-172-31-25-121.ec2.internal
Running           Running 1 second ago
g3tr6z9l5vzx      \_ mysql.5          mysql:5.6            ip-172-31-42-198.ec2.internal
Shutdown          Failed 6 seconds ago       "task: non-zero exit (1)"
```

The rolling update from `mysql` to `postgres` is rolled back. When the rollback has completed, all replicas are `mysql` image-based, which is the desired state of the service to start with.

```
~ $ docker service ps -f desired-state=running mysql
ID                NAME                IMAGE                NODE
DESIRED STATE     CURRENT STATE              ERROR                        PORTS
xamxi29okj74      mysql.1             mysql:5.6            ip-172-31-25-121.ec2.internal
Running           Running 30 seconds ago
gyqgtoc4ix3y      mysql.2             mysql:5.6            ip-172-31-2-177.ec2.internal
Running           Running 56 seconds ago
l3ock28cmtzx      mysql.3             mysql:5.6            ip-172-31-42-198.ec2.internal
Running           Running about a minute ago
ecvh8fd5308k      mysql.4             mysql:5.6            ip-172-31-29-67.ec2.internal
Running           Running 58 seconds ago
```

Rolling Update on a Global Service

A rolling update may also be performed on a global service. To demonstrate, we create a global service for the `mysql:latest` image.

```
~ $ docker service rm mysql
mysql
~ $ docker service create \
>    --mode global \
>    --env MYSQL_ROOT_PASSWORD='mysql'\
```

```
>    --name mysql \
>    mysql
7nokncnti3izud08gfdovwxwa
```

Start a rolling update to Docker image mysql:5.6. ~ $ docker service update \
```
>    --image mysql:5.6 \
>    --update-delay 10s \
>    mysql
mysql
```

The service is updated. The Spec>ContainerSpec>Image is updated to mysql:5.6 from the PreviousSpec> ContainerSpec>Image of mysql:latest.

```
~ $ docker service inspect mysql
[
        "Spec": {
            "Name": "mysql",
                "ContainerSpec": {
                    "Image": "mysql:5.6@sha256:6ad5bd392c9190fa92e65fd21f6debc8b2a76fc54f139
                    49f9b5bc6a0096a5285",
                },
            "PreviousSpec": {
                "Name": "mysql",
                    "ContainerSpec": {
                        "Image": "mysql:latest@sha256:75c563c474f1adc149978011fedfe2e6670483d133
                        b22b07ee32789b626f8de3",
            "UpdateStatus": {
                "State": "completed",
                "StartedAt": "2017-07-25T21:06:46.973666693Z",
                "CompletedAt": "2017-07-25T21:07:46.656023733Z",
                "Message": "update completed"
            }
        }
]
```

Within a minute, all the new service tasks based on mysql:5.6 are started.

```
~ $ docker service ps -f desired-state=running mysql
ID                   NAME                               IMAGE           NODE
DESIRED STATE        CURRENT STATE           ERROR          PORTS
ybf4xpofte8l         mysql.81h6uvu8uq0emnovzkg6v7mzg     mysql:5.6       ip-172-31-2-177.ec2.internal
Running              Running 46 seconds ago
7nq99jeil9n0         mysql.t4d0aq9w2a6avjx94zgkwc557     mysql:5.6       ip-172-31-42-198.ec2.internal
Running              Running about a minute ago
wcng24mq7e8m         mysql.e7viginoluuo1kynjnl33v9pa     mysql:5.6       ip-172-31-29-67.ec2.internal
Running              Running about a minute ago
q14t2pyhra3w         mysql.ptm7e0p346zwypos7wnpcm72d     mysql:5.6       ip-172-31-25-121.ec2.internal
Running              Running about a minute ago
```

A rolling update cannot be performed on a global service to set replicas with the `--replicas` option, as indicated by the message in the following `docker service update` command.

```
~ $ docker service update \
>    --image mysql \
>    --replicas 1 \
>    mysql
replicas can only be used with replicated mode
```

As the output indicates, while replicas are set on a replicated service `mysql`, replicas are not set on the global service.

Summary

This chapter discussed rolling updates on a service. A rolling update on a service involves shutting down previous service tasks and updating the service definition to start new tasks. In the next chapter, we discuss configuring networking in Swarm mode.

■ ■ ■

CHAPTER 10

Networking

Networking on a Docker Engine is provided by a *bridge* network, the docker0 bridge. The docker0 bridge is local in scope to a Docker host and is installed by default when Docker is installed. All Docker containers run on a Docker host and are connected to the docker0 bridge network. They communicate with each other over the network.

The Problem

The default docker0 bridge network has the following limitations:

- The bridge network is limited in scope to the local Docker host to provide container-to-container networking and not for multi-host networking.

- The bridge network isolates the Docker containers on the host from external access. A Docker container may expose a port or multiple ports and the ports may be published on the host for an external client host access, as illustrated in Figure 10-1, but by default the docker0 bridge does not provide any external client access outside the network.

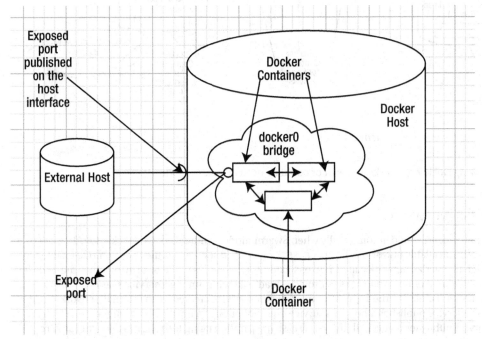

Figure 10-1. *The default docker0 bridge network*

© Deepak Vohra 2017
D. Vohra, *Docker Management Design Patterns*, https://doi.org/10.1007/978-1-4842-2973-6_10

The Solution

The Swarm mode (Docker Engine >=1.12) creates an overlay network called *ingress* for the nodes in the Swarm. The ingress overlay network is a multi-host network to route ingress traffic to the Swarm; external clients use it to access Swarm services. Services are added to the ingress network if they publish a port. The ingress overlay network has a default gateway and a subnet and all services in the ingress network are exposed on all nodes in the Swarm, whether a service has a task scheduled on each node or not. In addition to the ingress network, custom overlay networks may be created using the overlay driver. Custom overlay networks provide network connectivity between the Docker daemons in the Swarm and are used for service-to-service communication. Ingress is a special type of overlay network and is not for network traffic between services or tasks. Swarm mode networking is illustrated in Figure 10-2.

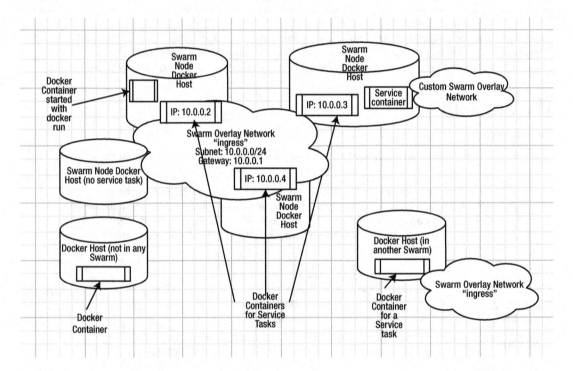

Figure 10-2. *The Swarm overlay networks*

The following Docker networks are used or could be used in Swarm mode.

The Ingress Network

The *ingress* network is created automatically when Swarm mode is initialized. On Docker for AWS, the ingress network is available out-of-the-box because the managed service has the Swarm mode enabled by default. The default overlay network called ingress extends to all nodes in the Swarm, whether the node has a service task scheduled or not. The ingress provides load balancing among a service's tasks. All services that publish a port are added to the ingress network. Even a service created in an internal network is added to ingress if the service publishes a port. If a service does not publish a port, it is not added to the ingress network. A service publishes a port with the --publish or –p option using the following docker service create command syntax.

```
docker service create \
  --name <SERVICE-NAME> \
  --publish <PUBLISHED-PORT>:<TARGET-PORT> \
  <IMAGE>
```

If the `<PUBLISHED-PORT>` is omitted, the Swarm manager selects a port in the range 30000-32767 to publish the service.

The following ports must be open between the Swarm nodes to use the `ingress` network.

- Port 7946 TCP/UDP is used for the container network discovery

- Port 4789 UDP is used for the container `ingress` network

Custom Overlay Networks

Custom overlay networks are created using the overlay driver and services may be created in the overlay networks. A service is created in an overlay network using the `--network` option of the `docker service create` command. Overlay networks provide service-to-service communication. One Docker container in the overlay network can communicate directly with another Docker container in the network, whether the container is on the same node or a different node. Only Docker containers for Swarm service tasks can connect with each using the overlay network and not just any Docker containers running on the hosts in a Swarm. Docker containers started with the `docker run <img>` command, for instance, cannot connect to a Swarm overlay network, using `docker network connect <overlay network> <container>` for instance. Nor are Docker containers on Docker hosts that are not in a Swarm able to connect and communicate with Docker containers in the Swarm directly. Docker containers in different Swarm overlay networks cannot communicate with each other directly, as each Swarm overlay network is isolated from other networks.

While the default overlay network in a Swarm, `ingress`, extends to all nodes in the Swarm whether a service task is running on it or not, a custom overlay network whose scope is also the Swarm does not extend to all nodes in the Swarm by default. A custom Swarm overlay network extends to only those nodes in the Swarm on which a service task created with the custom Swarm overlay network is running.

An "overlay" network overlays the underlay network of the hosts and the scope of the overlay network is the Swarm. Service containers in an overlay network have different IP addresses and each overlay network has a different range of IP addresses assigned. On modern kernels, the overlay networks are allowed to overlap with the underlay network, and as a result, multiple networks can have the same IP addresses.

The docker_gwbridge Network

Another network that is created automatically (in addition to the `ingress` network) when the Swarm mode is initialized is the `docker_gwbridge` network. The `docker_gwbridge` network is a bridge network that connects all the overlay networks, including the `ingress` network, to a Docker daemon's host network. Each service container is connected to the local Docker daemon host's `docker_gwbridge` network.

The Bridge Network

A *bridge* network is a network on a host that is managed by Docker. Docker containers on the host communicate with each other over the bridge network. A Swarm mode service that does not publish a port is also created in the bridge network. So are the Docker containers started with the `docker run` command. This implies that a Swarm mode Docker service that does not publish a port is in the same network as Docker containers started with the `docker run` command.

This chapter covers the following topics:

- Setting the environment
- Networking in Swarm mode
- Using the default overlay network ingress to create a service
- Creating a custom overlay network
- Using a custom overlay network to create a service
- Connecting to another Docker container in the same overlay network
- Creating an internal network
- Deleting a network

Setting the Environment

Create a three-node Docker Swarm on Docker for AWS, as discussed in Chapter 3. An AWS CloudFormation stack, shown in Figure 10-3, is used to create a Swarm.

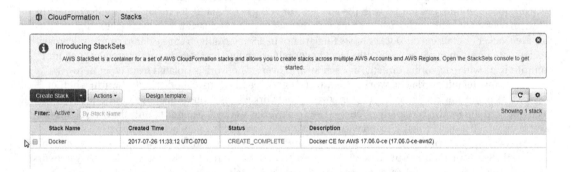

Figure 10-3. *AWS CloudFormation stack*

Obtain the public IP address of the Swarm manager node, as shown in Figure 10-4.

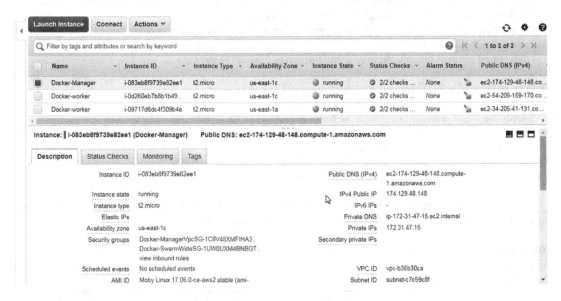

Figure 10-4. *Obtaining the public IP address of a Swarm manager node instance*

SSH login into the Swarm manager instance.

```
[root@localhost ~]# ssh -i "docker.pem" docker@174.129.48.148
Welcome to Docker!
```

List the Swarm nodes—one manager and two worker nodes.

```
~ $ docker node ls
ID                           HOSTNAME                    STATUS  AVAILABILITY  MANAGER STATUS
npz2akark8etv4ib9biob5yyk    ip-172-31-47-123.ec2.internal  Ready  Active
p6wat4lxq6a1o3h4fp2ikgw6r    ip-172-31-3-168.ec2.internal   Ready  Active
tb5agvzbi0rupq7b83tk00cx3 *  ip-172-31-47-15.ec2.internal   Ready  Active        Leader
```

Networking in Swarm Mode

The Swarm mode provides some default networks, which may be listed with the docker network ls command. These networks are available not just on Docker for AWS but on any platform (such as CoreOS) in Swarm mode.

```
~ $ docker network ls
NETWORK ID      NAME             DRIVER    SCOPE
34a5f77de8cf    bridge           bridge    local
0e06b811a613    docker_gwbridge  bridge    local
6763ebad69cf    host             host      local
e41an60iwval    ingress          overlay   swarm
eb7399d3ffdd    none             null      local
```

We discussed most of these networks in a preceding section. The "host" network is the networking stack of the host. The "none" network provides no networking between a Docker container and the host networking stack and creates a container without network access.

The default networks are available on a Swarm manager node and Swarm worker nodes even before any service task is scheduled.

The listed networks may be filtered using the driver filter set to overlay.

```
docker network ls --filter driver=overlay
```

Only the ingress network is listed. No other overlay network is provisioned by default.

```
~ $ docker network ls --filter driver=overlay
NETWORK ID          NAME            DRIVER          SCOPE
e41an60iwval        ingress         overlay         swarm
```

The network of interest is the overlay network called ingress, but all the default networks are discussed in Table 10-1 in addition to being discussed in the chapter introduction.

Table 10-1. *Docker Networks*

Network	Description
bridge	The bridge network is the docker0 network created on all Docker hosts. The Docker daemon connects containers to the docker0 network by default. Any Docker container started with the docker run command, even on a Swarm node, connects to the docker0 bridge network.
docker_gwbridge	Used for communication among Swarm nodes on different hosts. The network is used to provide external connectivity to a container that lacks an alternative network for connectivity to external networks and other Swarm nodes. When a container is connected to multiple networks, its external connectivity is provided via the first non-internal network, in lexical order.
host	Adds a container to the host's network stack. The network configuration inside the container is the same as the host's.
ingress	The overlay network used by the Swarm for ingress, which is external access. The ingress network is only for the routing mesh/ingress traffic.
none	Adds a container to a container specific network stack and the container lacks a network interface.

The default networks cannot be removed and, other than the ingress network, a user does not need to connect directly or use the other networks. To find detailed information about the ingress network, run the following command.

```
docker network inspect ingress
```

The ingress network's scope is the Swarm and the driver used is overlay. The subnet and gateway are 10.255.0.0/16 and 10.255.0.1, respectively. The ingress network is not an internal network as indicated by the internal setting of false, which implies that the network is connected to external networks. The ingress network has an IPv4 address and the network is not IPv6 enabled.

```
~ $ docker network inspect ingress
[
    {
        "Name": "ingress",
        "Id": "e41an60iwvalbeq5y3stdfem9",
        "Created": "2017-07-26T18:38:29.753424199Z",
        "Scope": "swarm",
        "Driver": "overlay",
        "EnableIPv6": false,
        "IPAM": {
            "Driver": "default",
            "Options": null,
            "Config": [
                {
                    "Subnet": "10.255.0.0/16",
                    "Gateway": "10.255.0.1"
                }
            ]
        },
        "Internal": false,
        "Attachable": false,
        "Ingress": true,
        "ConfigFrom": {
            "Network": ""
        },
        "ConfigOnly": false,
        "Containers": {
            "ingress-sbox": {
                "Name": "ingress-endpoint",
                "EndpointID": "f646b5cc4316994b8f9e5041ae7c82550bc7ce733db70df3f
                              66b8d771d0f53c4",
                "MacAddress": "02:42:0a:ff:00:02",
                "IPv4Address": "10.255.0.2/16",
                "IPv6Address": ""
            }
        },
        "Options": {
            "com.docker.network.driver.overlay.vxlanid_list": "4096"
        },
        "Labels": {},
        "Peers": [
            {
                "Name": "ip-172-31-47-15.ec2.internal-17c7f752fb1a",
                "IP": "172.31.47.15"
            },
            {
```

```
                "Name": "ip-172-31-47-123.ec2.internal-d6ebe8111adf",
                "IP": "172.31.47.123"
            },
            {
                "Name": "ip-172-31-3-168.ec2.internal-99510f4855ce",
                "IP": "172.31.3.168"
            }
        ]
    }
]
```

Using the Default Bridge Network to Create a Service

To create a service in Swarm mode using the default bridge network, no special option needs to be specified. The --publish or –p option must not be specified. Create a service for the mysql database.

```
~ $ docker service create \
>   --env MYSQL_ROOT_PASSWORD='mysql'\
>   --replicas 1 \
>   --name mysql \
>   mysql
likujs72e46ti5go1xjtksnky
```

The service is created and the service task is scheduled on one of the nodes.

```
~ $ docker service ls
ID              NAME    MODE         REPLICAS     IMAGE          PORTS
likujs72e46t    mysql   replicated   1/1          mysql:latest
```

The service may be scaled to run tasks across the Swarm.

```
~ $ docker service scale mysql=3
mysql scaled to 3
~ $ docker service ps mysql
ID                  NAME            IMAGE            NODE
DESIRED STATE       CURRENT STATE        ERROR           PORTS
v4bn24seygc6        mysql.1              mysql:latest     ip-172-31-47-15.ec2.internal
Running             Running 2 minutes ago
29702ebj52gs        mysql.2              mysql:latest     ip-172-31-47-123.ec2.internal
Running             Running 3 seconds ago
c7b8v16msudl        mysql.3              mysql:latest     ip-172-31-3-168.ec2.internal
Running             Running 3 seconds ago
```

The mysql service created is not added to the ingress network, as it does not publish a port.

Creating a Service in the Ingress Network

In this section, we create a Docker service in the `ingress` network. The `ingress` network is not to be specified using the `--network` option of `docker service create`. A service must publish a port to be created in the `ingress` network. Create a Hello World service published (exposed) on port 8080.

```
~ $ docker service rm hello-world
hello-world
~ $ docker service create \
>   --name hello-world \
>   -p 8080:80\
>   --replicas 3 \
>   tutum/hello-world
l76ukzrctq22mn97dmg0oatup
```

The service creates three tasks, one on each node in the Swarm.

```
~ $ docker service ls
ID            NAME          MODE         REPLICAS    IMAGE                       PORTS
l76ukzrctq22  hello-world   replicated   3/3         tutum/hello-world:latest    *:8080->80/tcp
~ $ docker service ps hello-world
ID            NAME              IMAGE                    NODE
DESIRED STATE   CURRENT STATE                           ERROR          PORTS
5ownzdjdt1yu  hello-world.1    tutum/hello-world: latest   ip-172-31-14-234.ec2.internal
Running         Running 33 seconds ago
csgofrbrznhq  hello-world.2    tutum/hello-world:latest    ip-172-31-47-203.ec2.internal
Running         Running 33 seconds ago
sctlt9rvn571  hello-world.3    tutum/hello-world:latest    ip-172-31-35-44.ec2.internal
Running         Running 32 seconds ago
```

The service may be accessed on any node instance in the Swarm on port 8080 using the `<Public DNS>`: `<8080>` URL. If an elastic load balancer is created, as for Docker for AWS, the service may be accessed at `<LoadBalancer DNS>`:`<8080>`, as shown in Figure 10-5.

Figure 10-5. *Invoking a Docker service in the ingress network using EC2 elastic load balancer public DNS*

The `<PublishedPort>` 8080 may be omitted in the `docker service create` command.

```
~ $ docker service create \
>   --name hello-world \
>   -p 80\
>   --replicas 3 \
>   tutum/hello-world
pbjcjhx163wm37d5cc5au2fog
```

Three service tasks are started across the Swarm.

```
~ $ docker service ls
ID            NAME          MODE         REPLICAS  IMAGE                      PORTS
pbjcjhx163wm  hello-world   replicated   3/3       tutum/hello-world:latest   *:0->80/tcp
```

```
~ $ docker service ps hello-world
ID               NAME            IMAGE                    NODE
DESIRED STATE    CURRENT STATE             ERROR    PORTS
xotbpvl0508n     hello-world.1   tutum/hello-world:latest   ip-172-31-37-130.ec2.internal
Running          Running 13 seconds ago
nvdn3j5pzuqi     hello-world.2   tutum/hello-world:latest   ip-172-31-44-205.ec2.internal
Running          Running 13 seconds ago
uuveltc5izpl     hello-world.3   tutum/hello-world:latest   ip-172-31-15-233.ec2.internal
Running          Running 14 seconds ago
```

The Swarm manager automatically assigns a published port (30000), as listed in the docker service inspect command.

```
~ $ docker service inspect hello-world
[
        "Spec": {
            "Name": "hello-world",
...

            "EndpointSpec": {
                "Mode": "vip",
                "Ports": [
                    {
                        "Protocol": "tcp",
                        "TargetPort": 80,
                        "PublishMode": "ingress"
                    }
                ]
            }
        },
        "Endpoint": {
            "Spec": {
                "Mode": "vip",
                "Ports": [
                    {
                        "Protocol": "tcp",
                        "TargetPort": 80,
                        "PublishMode": "ingress"
                    }
                ]
            },
            "Ports": [
                {
                    "Protocol": "tcp",
                    "TargetPort": 80,
                    "PublishedPort": 30000,
                    "PublishMode": "ingress"
                }
            ],
```

```
        "VirtualIPs": [
            {
                "NetworkID": "bllwwocjw5xejffmy6n8nhgm8",
                "Addr": "10.255.0.5/16"
            }
        ]
    }
}
]
```

Even though the service publishes a port (30000 or other available port in the range 30000-32767), the AWS elastic load balancer for the Docker for AWS Swarm does not add a listener for the published port (30000 or other available port in the range 30000-32767). We add a listener with <Load Balancer Port:Instance Port> mapping of 30000:30000, as shown in Figure 10-6.

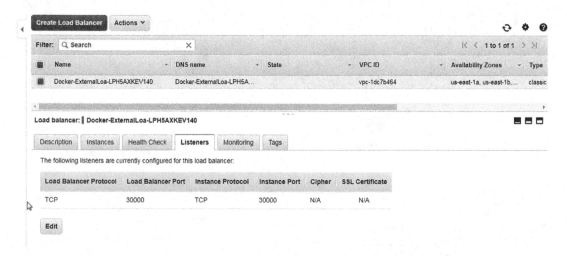

Figure 10-6. *Adding a load balancer listener*

Invoke the service at the <Load Balancer DNS>:<30000> URL, as shown in Figure 10-7.

Figure 10-7. Invoking a Hello World service on port 30000

Creating a Custom Overlay Network

We used the default overlay network ingress provisioned in Swarm mode. The ingress network is only for the Swarm mode routing mesh in which all nodes are included. The Swarm routing mesh is provided so that each node in the Swarm may accept connections on published ports for services in the Swarm even if a service does not run a task on a node. The ingress network is not for service-to-service communication.

A custom overlay network may be used in Swarm mode for service-to-service communication. Next, create an overlay network using some advanced options, including setting subnets with the --subnet option and the default gateway with the --gateway option, as well as the IP range with the --ip-range option. The --driver option must be set to overlay and the network must be created in Swarm mode. A matching subnet for the specified IP range must be available. A subnet is a logical subdivision of an IP network. The gateway is a router that links a host's subnet to other networks. The following command must be run from a manager node.

```
~ $ docker network create \
>    --subnet=192.168.0.0/16 \
>    --subnet=192.170.0.0/16 \
>    --gateway=192.168.0.100 \
>    --gateway=192.170.0.100 \
>    --ip-range=192.168.1.0/24 \
```

```
>    --driver overlay \
>    mysql-network
mkileuo6ve329jx5xbd1m6r1o
```

The custom overlay network is created and listed in networks as an overlay network with Swarm scope.

```
~ $ docker network ls
NETWORK ID          NAME                DRIVER              SCOPE
34a5f77de8cf        bridge              bridge              local
0e06b811a613        docker_gwbridge     bridge              local
6763ebad69cf        host                host                local
e41an60iwval        ingress             overlay             swarm
mkileuo6ve32        mysql-network       overlay             swarm
eb7399d3ffdd        none                null                local
```

Listing only the overlay networks should list the ingress network and the custom mysql-network.

```
~ $ docker network ls --filter driver=overlay
NETWORK ID          NAME                DRIVER              SCOPE
e41an60iwval        ingress             overlay             swarm
mkileuo6ve32        mysql-network       overlay             swarm
```

The detailed information about the custom overlay network mysql-network lists the subnets and gateways.

```
~ $ docker network inspect mysql-network
[
    {
        "Name": "mysql-network",
        "Id": "mkileuo6ve329jx5xbd1m6r1o",
        "Created": "0001-01-01T00:00:00Z",
        "Scope": "swarm",
        "Driver": "overlay",
        "EnableIPv6": false,
        "IPAM": {
            "Driver": "default",
            "Options": null,
            "Config": [
                {
                    "Subnet": "192.168.0.0/16",
                    "IPRange": "192.168.1.0/24",
                    "Gateway": "192.168.0.100"
                },
                {
                    "Subnet": "192.170.0.0/16",
                    "Gateway": "192.170.0.100"
                }
            ]
        },
        "Internal": false,
        "Attachable": false,
        "Ingress": false,
```

```
        "ConfigFrom": {
            "Network": ""
        },
        "ConfigOnly": false,
        "Containers": null,
        "Options": {
            "com.docker.network.driver.overlay.vxlanid_list": "4097,4098"
        },
        "Labels": null
    }
]
```

Only a single overlay network can be created for specific subnets, gateways, and IP ranges. Using a different subnet, gateway, or IP range, a different overlay network may be created.

```
~ $ docker network create \
>    --subnet=10.0.0.0/16 \
>    --gateway=10.0.0.100 \
>    --ip-range=10.0.1.0/24 \
>    --driver overlay \
>    mysql-network-2
qwgb1lwycgvogoq9t62ea4ny1
```

The mysql-network-2 is created and added to the list of networks.

```
~ $ docker network ls
NETWORK ID          NAME                DRIVER              SCOPE
34a5f77de8cf        bridge              bridge              local
0e06b811a613        docker_gwbridge     bridge              local
6763ebad69cf        host                host                local
e41an6Oiwval        ingress             overlay             swarm
mkileuo6ve32        mysql-network       overlay             swarm
qwgb1lwycgvo        mysql-network-2     overlay             swarm
eb7399d3ffdd        none                null                local
```

New overlay networks are only made available to worker nodes that have containers using the overlay. While the new overlay networks mysql-network and mysql-network-2 are available on the manager node, the network is not extended to the two worker nodes. SSH login to a worker node.

```
[root@localhost ~]# ssh -i "docker.pem" docker@54.209.159.170
Welcome to Docker!
```

The mysql-network and mysql-network-2 networks are not listed on the worker node.

```
~ $ docker network ls
NETWORK ID          NAME                DRIVER              SCOPE
255542d86c1b        bridge              bridge              local
3a4436c0fb00        docker_gwbridge     bridge              local
bdd0be4885e9        host                host                local
e41an6Oiwval        ingress             overlay             swarm
5c5f44ec3933        none                null                local
```

To extend the custom overlay network to worker nodes, create a service in the network that runs a task on the worker nodes, as we discuss in the next section.

The Swarm mode overlay networking is secure by default. The `gossip` protocol is used to exchange overlay network information between Swarm nodes. The nodes encrypt and authenticate the information exchanged using the AES algorithm in GCM mode. Manager nodes rotate the encryption key for gossip data every 12 hours by default. Data exchanged between containers on different nodes on the overlay network may also be encrypted using the `--opt encrypted` option, which creates IPSEC tunnels between all the nodes on which tasks are scheduled. The IPSEC tunnels also use the AES algorithm in GCM mode and rotate the encryption key for gossip data every 12 hours. The following command creates an encrypted network.

```
~ $ docker network create \
>   --driver overlay \
>   --opt encrypted \
>   overlay-network-2
aqppoe3qpy6mzln46g5tunecr
```

A Swarm scoped network that is encrypted is created.

```
~ $ docker network ls
NETWORK ID          NAME                  DRIVER          SCOPE
34a5f77de8cf        bridge                bridge          local
0e06b811a613        docker_gwbridge       bridge          local
6763ebad69cf        host                  host            local
e41an60iwval        ingress               overlay         swarm
mkileuo6ve32        mysql-network         overlay         swarm
qwgb1lwycgvo        mysql-network-2       overlay         swarm
eb7399d3ffdd        none                  null            local
aqppoe3qpy6m        overlay-network-2     overlay         swarm
```

Using a Custom Overlay Network to Create a Service

If a custom overlay network is used to create a service, the `--network` must be specified. The following command creates a MySQL database service in Swarm mode using the custom Swarm scoped overlay network `mysql-network`.

```
~ $ docker service create \
>   --env MYSQL_ROOT_PASSWORD='mysql'\
>   --replicas 1 \
>   --network mysql-network \
>   --name mysql-2\
>   mysql
ocd9sz8qqp2becf0ww2rj5p5n
```

The `mysql-2` service is created. Scale the `mysql-2` service to three replicas and lists the service tasks for the service.

```
~ $ docker service scale mysql-2=3
mysql-2 scaled to 3
```

Docker containers in two different networks for the two services—mysql (bridge network) and mysql-2 (mysql-network overlay network)—are running simultaneously on the same node.

A custom overlay network is not extended to all nodes in the Swarm until the nodes have service tasks that use the custom network. The mysql-network does not get extended to and get listed on a worker node until after a service task for mysql-2 has been scheduled on the node.

A Docker container managed by the default Docker Engine bridge network docker0 cannot connect with a Docker container in a Swarm scoped overlay network. Using a Swarm overlay network in a docker run command, connecting with a Swarm overlay network with a docker network connect command, or linking a Docker container with a Swarm overlay network using the --link option of the docker network connect command is not supported. The overlay networks in Swarm scope can only be used by a Docker service in the Swarm.

For connecting between service containers:

- Docker containers for the same or different services in the same Swarm scoped overlay network are able to connect with each other.

- Docker containers for the same or different services in different Swarm scoped overlay networks are not able to connect with each other.

In the next section, we discuss an internal network, but before we do so, the external network should be introduced. The Docker containers we have created as of yet are external network containers. The ingress network and the custom overlay network mysql-network are external networks. External networks provide a default route to the gateway. The host and the wider Internet network may connect to a Docker container in the ingress or custom overlay networks. As an example, run the following command to ping google.com from a Docker container's bash shell; the Docker container should be in the ingress overlay network or a custom Swarm overlay network.

```
docker exec -it  <containerid> ping -c 1 google.com
```

A connection is established and data is exchanged. The command output is shown in italics.

```
~ $ docker exec -it  3762d7c4ea68  ping -c 1 google.com
PING google.com (172.217.7.142): 56 data bytes
64 bytes from 172.217.7.142: icmp_seq=0 ttl=47 time=0.703 ms
--- google.com ping statistics ---
1 packets transmitted, 1 packets received, 0% packet loss
round-trip min/avg/max/stddev = 0.703/0.703/0.703/0.000 ms
```

Creating an Internal Overlay Network

In this section, we discuss creating and using an internal overlay network. An internal network does not provide external connectivity. What makes a network internal is that a default route to a gateway is not provided for external connectivity from the host or the wider Internet.

First, create an internal overlay network using the --internal option of the docker network create command. Add some other options, such as --label, which have no bearing on the internal network. It's configured with the --internal option of the docker network create command.

```
~ $ docker network create \
>    --subnet=10.0.0.0/16 \
>    --gateway=10.0.0.100 \
>    --internal  \
>    --label HelloWorldService \
>    --ip-range=10.0.1.0/24 \
```

```
>    --driver overlay \
>    hello-world-network
pfwsrjeakomplo5zm6t4p19a9
```

The internal network is created and listed just the same as an external network would be.

```
~ $ docker network ls
NETWORK ID        NAME                    DRIVER        SCOPE
194d51d460e6      bridge                  bridge        local
a0674c5f1a4d      docker_gwbridge         bridge        local
pfwsrjeakomp      hello-world-network     overlay       swarm
03a68475552f      host                    host          local
tozyadp06rxr      ingress                 overlay       swarm
3dbd3c3ef439      none                    null          local
```

In the network description, the internal is set to true.

```
core@ip-172-30-2-7 ~ $ docker network inspect hello-world-network
[
    {
        "Name": "hello-world-network",
        "Id": "58fzvj4arudk2053q6k2t8rrk",
        "Scope": "swarm",
        "Driver": "overlay",
        "EnableIPv6": false,
        "IPAM": {
            "Driver": "default",
            "Options": null,
            "Config": [
                {
                    "Subnet": "10.0.0.0/16",
                    "IPRange": "10.0.1.0/24",
                    "Gateway": "10.0.0.100"
                }
            ]
        },
        "Internal": true,
        "Containers": null,
        "Options": {
            "com.docker.network.driver.overlay.vxlanid_list": "257"
        },
        "Labels": {
            "HelloWorldService": ""
        }
    }
]
```

Create a service that uses the internal network with the --network option.

```
~ $ docker service create \
>   --name hello-world \
>   --network  hello-world-network \
>   --replicas 3 \
>   tutum/hello-world
hm5pf6ftcvphdrd2zm3pp4lpj
```

The service is created and the replicas are scheduled.
Obtain the container ID for one of the service tasks, d365d4a5ff4c.

```
~ $ docker ps
CONTAINER ID    IMAGE                        COMMAND                CREATED
STATUS                   PORTS    NAMES
d365d4a5ff4c    tutum/hello-world:latest    "/bin/sh -c 'php-f..."  About a minute ago
Up About a minute                 hello-world.3.r759ddnl1de11spo0zdi7xj4z
```

As before, ping google.com from the Docker container.

```
docker exec -it  <containerid> ping -c 1 google.com
```

A connection is not established, which is because the container is in an internal overlay network.

```
~ $ docker exec -it  d365d4a5ff4c ping -c 1 google.com
ping: bad address 'google.com'
```

Connection is established between containers in the same internal network, as the limitation is only on external connectivity. To demonstrate, obtain the container ID for another container in the same internal network.

```
~ $ docker ps
CONTAINER ID    IMAGE                        COMMAND                CREATED
STATUS           PORTS        NAMES
b7b505f5eb8d    tutum/hello-world:latest    "/bin/sh -c 'php-f..."  3 seconds ago
Up 2 seconds                   hello-world.6.i60ezt6da2t1odwdjvecb75fx
57e612f35a38    tutum/hello-world:latest    "/bin/sh -c 'php-f..."  3 seconds ago
Up 2 seconds                   hello-world.7.6ltqnybn8twhtblpqjtvulkup
d365d4a5ff4c    tutum/hello-world:latest    "/bin/sh -c 'php-f..."  7 minutes ago
Up 7 minutes                   hello-world.3.r759ddnl1de11spo0zdi7xj4z
```

Connect between two containers in the same internal network. A connection is established.

```
~ $ docker exec -it  d365d4a5ff4c ping -c 1 57e612f35a38
PING 57e612f35a38 (10.0.1.7): 56 data bytes
64 bytes from 10.0.1.7: seq=0 ttl=64 time=0.288 ms

--- 57e612f35a38 ping statistics ---
1 packets transmitted, 1 packets received, 0% packet loss
round-trip min/avg/max = 0.288/0.288/0.288 ms
```

If a service created in an internal network publishes (exposes) a port, the service gets added to the ingress network and, even though the service is in an internal network, external connectivity is provisioned. As an example, we add the --publish option of the docker service create command to publish the service on port 8080.

```
~ $ docker service create \
>   --name hello-world \
>   --network hello-world-network \
>   --publish 8080:80 \
>   --replicas 3 \
>   tutum/hello-world
mqgek4umisgycagy4qa206f9c
```

Find a Docker container ID for a service task.

```
~ $ docker ps
CONTAINER ID    IMAGE                      COMMAND                CREATED
STATUS          PORTS      NAMES
1c52804dc256    tutum/hello-world:latest   "/bin/sh -c 'php-f..."  28 seconds ago
Up 27 seconds   80/tcp     hello-world.1.20152n01ng3t6uaiahpex9n4f
```

Connect from the container in the internal network to the wider external network at google.com, as an example. A connection is established. Command output is shown in italics.

```
~ $ docker exec -it  1c52804dc256  ping -c 1 google.com
PING google.com (172.217.7.238): 56 data bytes
64 bytes from 172.217.7.238: seq=0 ttl=47 time=1.076 ms

--- google.com ping statistics ---
1 packets transmitted, 1 packets received, 0% packet loss
round-trip min/avg/max = 1.076/1.076/1.076 ms
```

Deleting a Network

A network that is not in use may be removed with the docker network rm <networkid> command. Multiple networks may be removed in the same command. As an example, we can list and remove multiple networks.

```
~ $ docker network ls
NETWORK ID      NAME                 DRIVER     SCOPE
34a5f77de8cf    bridge               bridge     local
0e06b811a613    docker_gwbridge      bridge     local
wozpfgo8vbmh    hello-world-network             swarm
6763ebad69cf    host                 host       local
e41an60iwval    ingress              overlay    swarm
mkileuo6ve32    mysql-network        overlay    swarm
qwgb1lwycgvo    mysql-network-2      overlay    swarm
eb7399d3ffdd    none                 null       local
aqppoe3qpy6m    overlay-network-2    overlay    swarm
```

Networks that are being used by a service are not removed. The command output is shown in italics.

```
~ $ docker network rm hello-world-network mkileuo6ve32 qwgb1lwycgvo overlay-network-2
hello-world-network
Error response from daemon: rpc error: code = 9 desc = network mkileuo6ve329jx5xbd1m6r1o is
in use by service ocd9sz8qqp2becf0ww2rj5p5nqwgb1lwycgvo
overlay-network-2
```

Summary

This chapter discussed the networking used by the Docker Swarm mode. The default networking used in Swarm mode is the overlay network ingress, which is a multi-host network spanning all Docker nodes in the same Swarm to provide a routing mesh for each node to be able to accept ingress connections for services on published ports. Custom overlay network may be used to create a Docker service with the difference that a custom overlay network provides service-to-service communication instead of ingress communication and extends to a Swarm worker node only if a service task using the network is scheduled on the node. The chapter also discussed the difference between an internal and an external network. In the next chapter, we discuss logging and monitoring in Docker Swarm mode.

CHAPTER 11

■ ■ ■

Logging and Monitoring

Docker includes several built-in logging drivers for containers, such as `json-file`, syslog, journald, gelf, fluentd, and awslogs. Docker also provides the `docker logs` command to get the logs for a container. Docker 1.13 includes an experimental feature for getting a Docker service log using the `docker service logs` command.

The Problem

Docker Swarm mode does not include a native monitoring service for Docker services and containers. Also the experimental feature to get service logs is a command-line feature and required to be run per service. A logging service with which all the services' logs and metrics could be collected and viewed in a dashboard is lacking.

The Solution

Sematext is an integrated data analytics platform that provides SPM performance monitoring for metrics and events collection, and Logsene for log collection, including correlation between performance metrics, logs, and events. Logsene is a hosted ELK (Elasticsearch, Logtash, Kibana) stack. Sematext Docker Agent is required to be installed on each Swarm node in the Swarm for continuously collecting logs, metrics, and events, as illustrated in Figure 11-1.

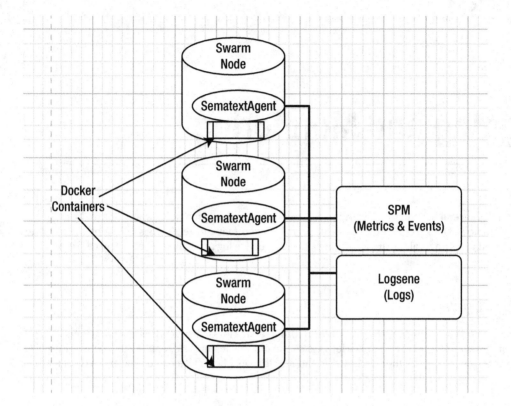

Figure 11-1. *Sematext Docker agent on each Swarm node*

This chapter covers the following topics:

- Setting the environment
- Creating a SPM application
- Creating a Logsene application
- Deploying the Sematext Docker agent as a service
- Creating a MySQL database deployment on Docker Swarm
- Monitoring the Docker Swarm metrics
- Getting Docker Swarm logs in Logsene

Setting the Environment

Start a three-node Swarm consisting of one manager and two worker nodes using Docker for AWS. (This is discussed in Chapter 3.) Obtain the public IP address of the manager node instance from the EC2 console and SSH login into the instance.

```
[root@localhost ~]# ssh -i "docker.pem" docker@54.227.123.67
Welcome to Docker!
```

The procedure to use Sematext SPM and Logsene for logging and monitoring with a Docker Swarm is as follows.

1. Create an account at https://apps.sematext.com/ui/registration.

2. Log in to the user account at https://apps.sematext.com/ui/login.

3. Select the integrations (Logsene app and SPM Docker app) from https://apps. sematext.com/ui/integrations?newUser, as listed in Steps 4 and 5.

4. Create a SPM (a performance monitoring app). An app is like a namespace for data. A SPM token is generated that is to be used to install a Sematext agent on each Swarm node.

5. Create a Logsene app. A Logsene token is generated that is also used to install a Sematext agent on each Swarm node.

6. Install a Sematext agent on each Swarm node. Docker Swarm metrics, logs, and events start getting collected in the SPM dashboard and the Logsene dashboard.

Creating a SPM Application

Log in to a Sematext account at https://apps.sematext.com/ui/integrations?newUser to display the Integrations page. For a SPM Docker app, select Docker from Infrastructure and Application Performance Monitoring. In the Add SPM Docker App dialog, specify an application name (DockerSwarmSPM), as shown in Figure 11-2. Click on Create App.

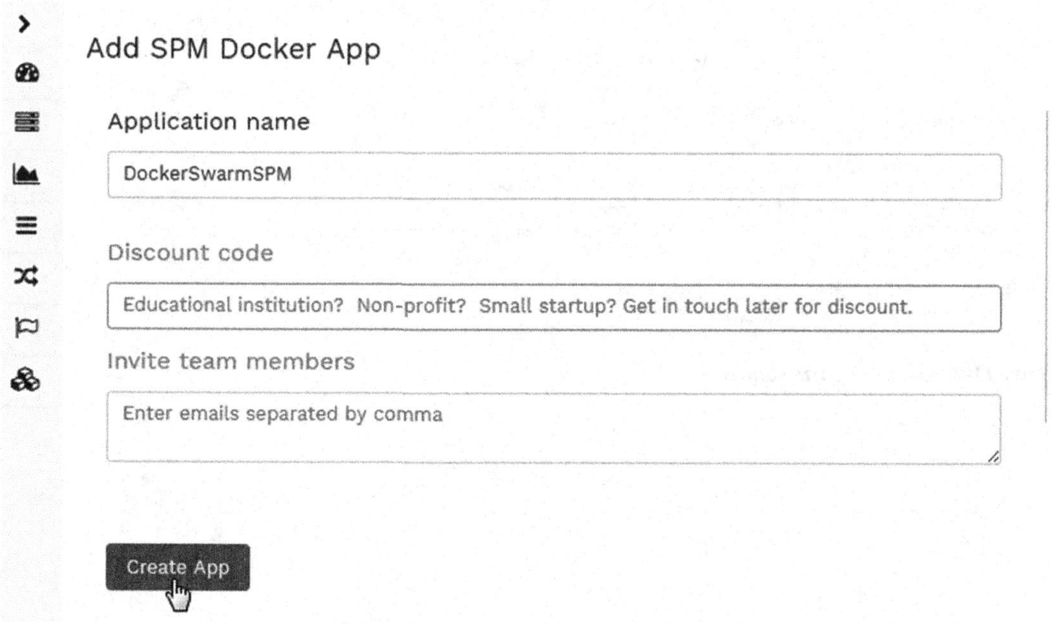

Figure 11-2. *Adding a SPM Docker app*

An SPM App is created, as shown in Figure 11-3. Several client configurations are listed.

Figure 11-3. *SPM app is created*

Click on the Client Configuration tab for Docker Swarm, as shown in Figure 11-4. The Docker Swarm tab displays the docker service create command to create a service for a Sematext Docker agent; copy the command. The command includes a SPM_TOKEN, which is unique for each SPM app.

Client Configuration

Requirement: Docker v1.6 or newer installed (or v1.12 in case of Docker Swarm).

| Linux / Mac OS X / Windows | CoreOS | Kubernetes | RancherOS | Mesos | Docker Swarm |

1. The following configuration will activate Sematext Docker Agent on every node in the Swarm Cluster cluster

```
docker service create --mode global \
--restart-condition any \
--name sematext-agent-docker \
--mount type=bind,src=/var/run/docker.sock,dst=/var/run/docker.sock \
--mount type=bind,src=/,dst=/rootfs,readonly=true \
-e SPM_TOKEN=9b5552fd-001d-44f0-9452-76046d4a3413  sematext/sematext-agent-docker
```

⟲ Waiting for data. Configure monitoring agent.

Figure 11-4. *Docker Swarm configuration*

The SPM app is added to the dashboard, as shown in Figure 11-5. Click on the App link to navigate to App Reports, which shows the monitoring data, metrics, and events collected by the SPM app and the charts generated from the data.

Figure 11-5. *DockerSwarmSPM app on the dashboard*

As the message in Figure 11-6 indicates, the app has not received any data yet. All the metrics graphs are empty initially, but they will display the graphs when data starts getting received.

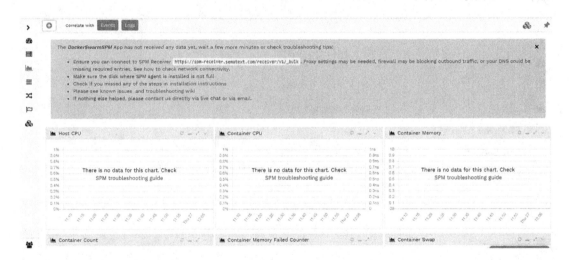

Figure 11-6. *The DockerSwarmSPM app has not received any data*

Creating a Logsene Application

To create a Logsene app, select Logs App from the integrations page at `https://apps.sematext.com/ui/integrations?newUser`, as shown in Figure 11-7.

Figure 11-7. *Selecting the Logs app*

In the Add Logsene App dialog, specify an application name (`DockerSwarmLogsene`) and click on Create App, as shown in Figure 11-8.

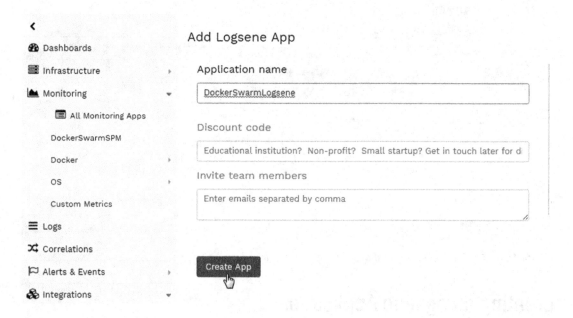

Figure 11-8. *Adding the Logsene app*

A new Logsene application called `DockerSwarmLogsene` is created, as shown in Figure 11-9. Copy the `LOGSENE_TOKEN` that's generated, which we will use to create a Sematext Docker agent service in a Docker Swarm.

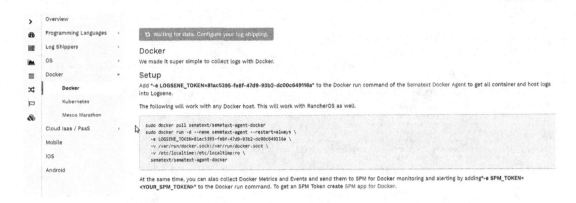

Figure 11-9. *The Logsene app is added and LOGSENE_TOKEN is generated*

A new Logsene application called `DockerSwarmLogsene` is added to the dashboard, as shown in Figure 11-10.

Figure 11-10. *The DockerSwarmLogsene app*

Click on the DockerSwarmLogsene app link to display the log data collected by the app. Initially, the app does not receive any data, as indicated by a message in Figure 11-11, because we have not yet configured a Sematext Docker agent service on the Docker Swarm. The Logsene UI is integrated with the Kibana dashboard.

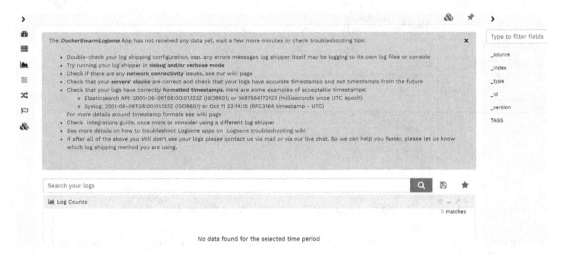

Figure 11-11. *The app does not receive any data at first*

Connecting the SPM and Logsene Apps

Next, connect the SPM and Logsene apps so that the metrics and events collected by the SPM are integrated with the Logsene app. Choose Integrations ➤ Connected Apps, as shown in Figure 11-12.

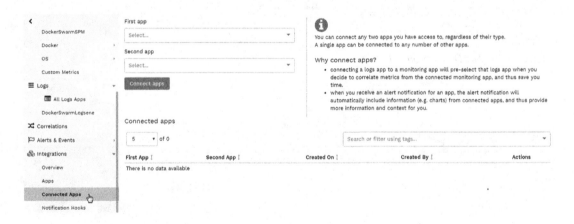

Figure 11-12. *Choosing Integrations ➤ Connected Apps*

Select DockerSwarmSPM as the first app and DockerSwarmLogsene as the second app, as shown in Figure 11-13. Then click on Connect Apps.

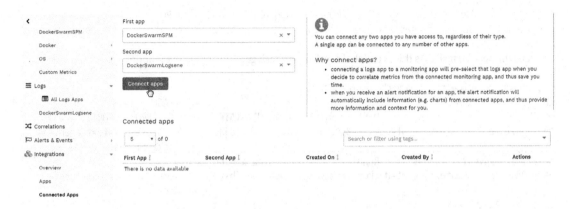

Figure 11-13. *DockerSwarmLogsene*

The connected apps are listed, as shown in Figure 11-14.

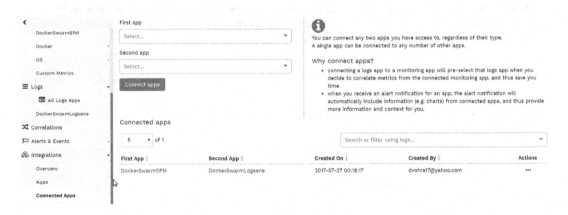

Figure 11-14. *The connected apps*

Deploying the Sematext Docker Agent as a Service

The docker service create command copied earlier includes just the SPM_TOKEN token. Add -e LOGSENE_TOKEN obtained from the Logsene app. Run the docker service create command on the Swarm manager node.

```
~ $ docker service create --mode global \
> --restart-condition any \
> --name sematext-agent-docker \
> --mount type=bind,src=/var/run/docker.sock,dst=/var/run/docker.sock \
> --mount type=bind,src=/,dst=/rootfs,readonly=true \
> -e SPM_TOKEN=9b5552fd-001d-44f0-9452-76046d4a3413 \
> -e LOGSENE_TOKEN=81ac5395-fe8f-47d9-93b2-dc00c649116a \
>   sematext/sematext-agent-docker
oubjk53mpdnjgak5dgfdxs4ft
```

A service for the Sematext Docker agent is created; it's listed using docker service ls.

```
~ $ docker service ls
ID            NAME                  MODE     REPLICAS  IMAGE       PORTS
oubjk53mpdnj  sematext-agent-docker  global   3/3       sematext/sematext-agent-docker:latest
```

List the service tasks. As this is a global service, one task gets started on each node.

```
~ $ docker service ps sematext-agent-docker
ID            NAME                                                 IMAGE
NODE                          DESIRED STATE   CURRENT STATE        ERROR   PORTS
5jvl7gnvl0te  sematext-agent-docker.8d0qv1epqu8xop4o2f94i8j40      sematext/sematext-agent-
                                                                   docker:latest
ip-172-31-8-4.ec2.internal    Running         Running 2 minutes ago
y53f20d3kknh  sematext-agent-docker.xks3sw6qgwbcuacyypemfbxyj      sematext/sematext-agent-
                                                                   docker:latest
ip-172-31-31-117.ec2.internal  Running        Running 2 minutes ago
t5w2pxy4fc9l  sematext-agent-docker.r02ftwtp3n4m0cl7v2llw4gi8      sematext/sematext-agent-
                                                                   docker:latest
ip-172-31-44-8.ec2.internal   Running         Running 2 minutes ago
```

If additional nodes are added to the Swarm, the Sematext Docker agent starts a service task on the new nodes. As an example, update the CloudFormation stack to increase the number of manager nodes to three and worker nodes to five, as shown in Figure 11-15.

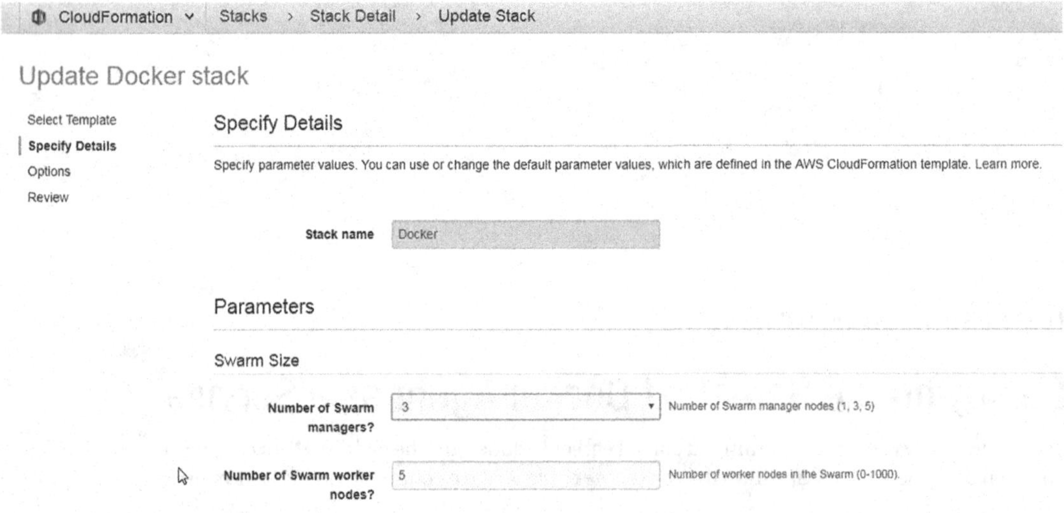

Figure 11-15. *Increasing the number of worker nodes*

The Swarm nodes are increased to three manager nodes and five worker nodes when the Stack update is complete.

```
~ $ docker node ls
ID                          HOSTNAME                          STATUS AVAILABILITY MANAGER STATUS
8d0qv1epqu8xop4o2f94i8j40   ip-172-31-8-4.ec2.internal        Ready  Active
9rvieyqnndgecagbuf73r9gs5   ip-172-31-35-125.ec2.internal     Ready  Active       Reachable
j4mg3fyzjtsdcnmr7rkiytltj   ip-172-31-18-156.ec2.internal     Ready  Active
mhbbunhl358chah1dmr0y6i71   ip-172-31-7-78.ec2.internal       Ready  Active       Reachable
r02ftwtp3n4m0cl7v2llw4gi8   ip-172-31-44-8.ec2.internal       Ready  Active
vdamjjjrz7a3ri3prv9fjngvy   ip-172-31-6-92.ec2.internal       Ready  Active
xks3sw6qgwbcuacyypemfbxyj * ip-172-31-31-117.ec2.internal     Ready  Active       Leader
xxyy4ys4oo30bb4l5daoicsr2   ip-172-31-21-138.ec2.internal     Ready  Active
```

Adding nodes to the Swarm starts a Sematext agent on the nodes that were added.

```
~ $ docker service ps sematext-agent-docker
ID                  NAME
IMAGE                                   NODE                            DESIRED STATE
CURRENT STATE       ERROR               PORTS
cgaturw05p59        sematext-agent-docker.xxyy4ys4oo30bb4l5daoicsr2
sematext/sematext-agent-docker:latest   ip-172-31-21-138.ec2.internal   Running
Running 2 minutes ago
lj4f46q3ydv1        sematext-agent-docker.j4mg3fyzjtsdcnmr7rkiytltj
sematext/sematext-agent-docker:latest   ip-172-31-18-156.ec2.internal   Running
Running 2 minutes ago
v54bjs3c8u5r        sematext-agent-docker.vdamjjjrz7a3ri3prv9fjngvy
sematext/sematext-agent-docker:latest   ip-172-31-6-92.ec2.internal     Running
Running 2 minutes ago
s7arohbeoake        sematext-agent-docker.9rvieyqnndgecagbuf73r9gs5
sematext/sematext-agent-docker:latest   ip-172-31-35-125.ec2.internal   Running
Running 3 minutes ago
ixpri65xwpds        sematext-agent-docker.mhbbunhl358chah1dmr0y6i71
sematext/sematext-agent-docker:latest   ip-172-31-7-78.ec2.internal     Running
Running 4 minutes ago
5jvl7gnvl0te        sematext-agent-docker.8d0qv1epqu8xop4o2f94i8j40
sematext/sematext-agent-docker:latest   ip-172-31-8-4.ec2.internal      Running
Running 15 minutes ago
y53f20d3kknh        sematext-agent-docker.xks3sw6qgwbcuacyypemfbxyj
sematext/sematext-agent-docker:latest   ip-172-31-31-117.ec2.internal   Running
Running 15 minutes ago
t5w2pxy4fc9l        sematext-agent-docker.r02ftwtp3n4m0cl7v2llw4gi8
sematext/sematext-agent-docker:latest   ip-172-31-44-8.ec2.internal     Running
Running 15 minutes ago
```

211

Creating a MySQL Database Service on a Docker Swarm

In this section, we create a MySQL database service from which metrics, logs, and events can be collected with Sematext SCM and Logsene using the Sematext Docker Agent, which we installed. To start, run the following command to create a mysql service with 10 replicas.

```
~ $ docker service create \
>    --env MYSQL_ROOT_PASSWORD='mysql'\
>    --replicas 10 \
>    --name mysql \
>    mysql
rmy45fpa31twkyb3dowzpc74a
```

The service is created and listed in addition to the Sematext Docker agent service.

```
~ $ docker service ls
ID              NAME                   MODE        REPLICAS  IMAGE                       PORTS
oubjk53mpdnj    sematext-agent-docker  global      8/8       sematext/sematext-agent-
                                                             docker:latest
rmy45fpa31tw    mysql                  replicated  10/10     mysql:latest
```

The service tasks for the mysql service are also listed.

```
~ $ docker service ps mysql
ID              NAME       IMAGE         NODE                          DESIRED STATE
CURRENT STATE        ERROR     PORTS
x8j221ws4kx2    mysql.1    mysql:latest  ip-172-31-21-138.ec2.internal Running
Running 13 seconds ago
98rbd6nwspqz    mysql.2    mysql:latest  ip-172-31-44-8.ec2.internal   Running
Running 11 seconds ago
vmq0lylni8or    mysql.3    mysql:latest  ip-172-31-8-4.ec2.internal    Running
Running 24 seconds ago
0vb6oda3yh3d    mysql.4    mysql:latest  ip-172-31-7-78.ec2.internal   Running
Running 23 seconds ago
vdpplkyxy1uy    mysql.5    mysql:latest  ip-172-31-6-92.ec2.internal   Running
Running 23 seconds ago
9ser7fwz6998    mysql.6    mysql:latest  ip-172-31-18-156.ec2.internal Running
Running 17 seconds ago
vfsfvanghns0    mysql.7    mysql:latest  ip-172-31-18-156.ec2.internal Running
Running 17 seconds ago
v71qwpvjhhzn    mysql.8    mysql:latest  ip-172-31-6-92.ec2.internal   Running
Running 23 seconds ago
j7172i5ml43d    mysql.9    mysql:latest  ip-172-31-31-117.ec2.internal Running
Running 24 seconds ago
5p5mg2wnbb0o    mysql.10   mysql:latest  ip-172-31-35-125.ec2.internal Running
Running 20 seconds ago
```

After the Sematext Docker agent service has been started on the Swarm and a MySQL database service has been started, both the SPM and Logsene apps start receiving data, as indicated by the Data Received column in the dashboard. See Figure 11-16.

Figure 11-16. *DockerSwarmSPM overview*

Monitoring the Docker Swarm Metrics

After the `mysql` service is started on the Swarm, the metrics for the service start getting loaded into the SPM – Performance Monitoring dashboard. This happens as soon as the Sematext Docker agent is installed and new metrics from a deployment become available. Graphs for different metrics—including Host CPU, Container CPU, Container Memory, Container Count, Container Memory Failed Counter, Container Swap, Container I/O Throughput, Container Network Traffic, and Container Network Errors—are displayed, as shown in Figure 11-17.

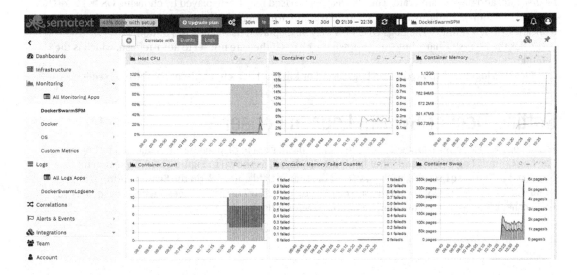

Figure 11-17. *Docker Swarm SPM overview*

The Docker container metrics—including Container Count, Container CPU, Container Disk, Container Memory, and Container Network—may be displayed by selecting Docker in the navigation. The Docker Container Count metrics are shown in Figure 11-18.

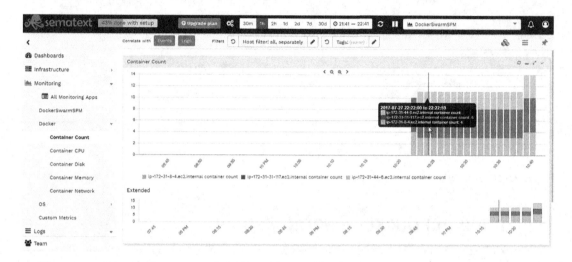

Figure 11-18. *Docker metrics*

The Docker ➤ Container Network selection displays the network traffic received and transmitted, the receive rate, and the transmit rate. The OS Disk Space Used may be displayed by choosing OS ➤ Disk. The metrics collection granularity may be set to auto granularity (default), by month, by week, by day, by hour, by 5 minutes, or by 1 minute. The Logs Overview may be displayed using the Logs button.

Click the Refresh Charts button to refresh the charts if they are not set to auto-refresh, which is the default.

Detailed logs are displayed using Logsene UI or Kibana 4, which we discuss in the next section.

Getting Docker Swarm Logs in Logsene

Select Logs ➤ DockerSwarmLogsene in the margin navigation to display the logs collected by Logsene. The Log Counts, Log Events, and Filter fields are displayed, as shown in Figure 11-19. To search for logs generated by the mysql service, add "mysql" to the search field and click on the Search button. The logs generated by the mysql Docker service are displayed, including status messages such as "mysqld ready for connections". Click on the Refresh button to refresh the logs.

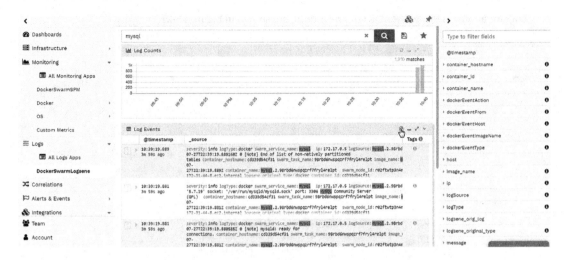

Figure 11-19. *Logs generated by the mysql Docker Service*

The Logsene collects all the Docker events, such as the Docker pull event for the mysql:latest image, as shown in Figure 11-20.

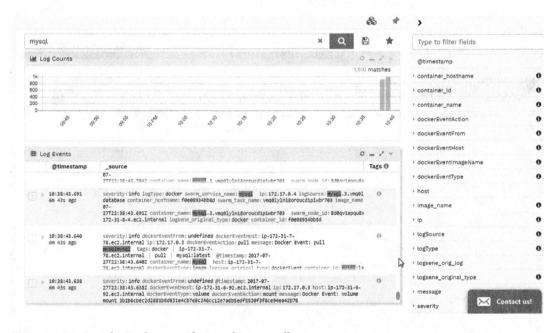

Figure 11-20. *Logs for Docker event for mysql image pull*

Logs for another Docker event, a volume mount, are shown in Figure 11-21.

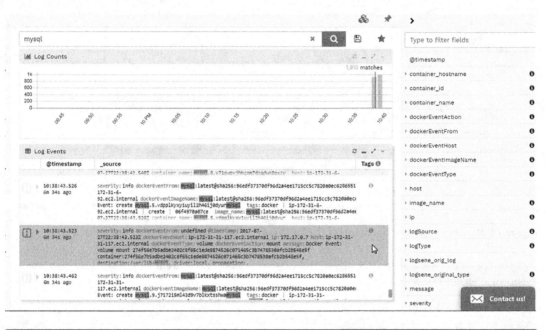

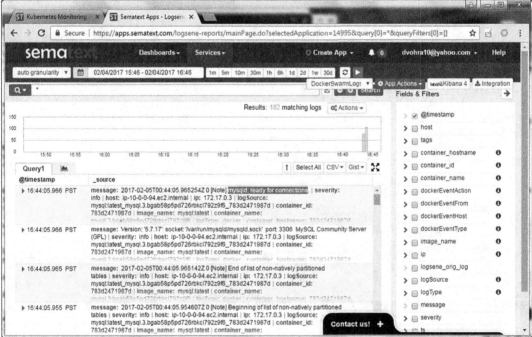

Figure 11-21. *Logs for Docker event volume mount*

Summary

This chapter discussed continuous logging and monitoring of a Docker Swarm with Sematext SPM performance monitoring and Logsene log management. First, you learned how to create a SPM app and a Logsene app. Then you installed a Sematext agent service on each of the Swarm nodes and monitored the metrics and events in a SPM dashboard. You also learned how to monitor the logs in the Logsene UI or a Kibana 4 dashboard. The next chapter discusses load balancing in a Docker Swarm.

CHAPTER 12

■ ■ ■

Load Balancing

A Docker Swarm mode service provides a distributed application that may be scaled across a cluster of nodes. Swarm mode provides internal load balancing among the different services in the Swarm based on the DNS name of a service. Swarm mode also provides ingress load balancing among a service's different tasks if the service is published on a host port. Additionally, service tasks may be scheduled on specific nodes using placement constraints.

Service Discovery

A Swarm has a DNS server embedded in it. Service discovery is based on the DNS name. Swarm manager assigns each service in the Swarm a unique DNS name entry. Swarm manager uses internal load balancing to distribute requests for the different services in the Swarm based on the DNS name for a service.

Custom Scheduling

Service replicas are scheduled on the nodes in a Swarm using the *spread* scheduling strategy by default. A user may configure placement constraints for a service so that replicas are scheduled on specific nodes. Scheduling using constraints is discussed in Chapter 6.

Ingress Load Balancing

By default, each service that's exposed on a published port for external access is added to the ingress overlay network. A user may specify any available port to expose a service by using the --publish, or -p, option. The syntax for the --publish (-p) option is --publish <PublishedPort>:<TargetPort> in which the <PublishedPort> variable is for the published port on the host and the <TargetPort> variable is for the container port. If the --publish, -p option does not specify a <PublishedPort> port to publish the service on the Swarm, the manager automatically exposes the service on a published port chosen from the range 30000-32767.

The Problem

Ingress load balancing is for distributing the load among the service tasks and is used even if a Swarm consists of a single node. Ingress load balancing for a multi-node Swarm is illustrated in Figure 12-1. A client may access any node in the Swarm, whether the node has a service task scheduled or not, and the client request is forwarded to one of the service tasks using ingress load balancing.

© Deepak Vohra 2017

D. Vohra, *Docker Management Design Patterns*, https://doi.org/10.1007/978-1-4842-2973-6_12

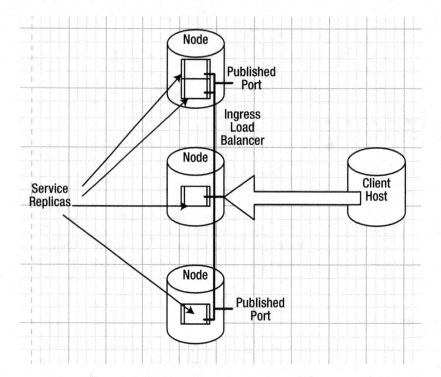

Figure 12-1. *Ingress load balancing*

A single client accesses a single node and, as a result, the Swarm is under-utilized in terms of distributing external client load across the Swarm nodes. The client load is not balanced across the Swarm nodes. A single node does not provide any fault tolerance. If the node fails, the service becomes unavailable to an external client accessing the service at the node.

The Solution

An AWS Elastic Load Balancer (ELB) is used to distribute client load across multiple EC2 instances. When used for Docker Swarm mode an AWS Elastic Load Balancer distributes client load across the different EC2 instances, which are hosting the Swarm nodes. The external load balancer accesses (listens to) the Swarm on each EC2 instance at the published ports for the services running in the Swarm using LB listeners. Each LB listener has an LB port mapped to an instance port (a published port for a service) on each EC2 instance. An ELB on a Swarm is illustrated in Figure 12-2.

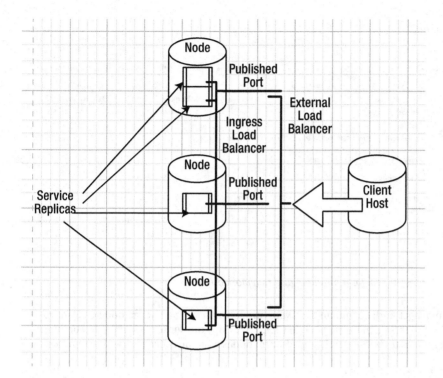

Figure 12-2. *External load balancer*

As a client is not accessing the service at a single host even if a single node goes down or becomes unavailable, the Swarm does not become unavailable as the external load balancer directs the client request to a different node in the Swarm. Even when all the nodes are available, the client traffic is distributed among the different nodes. As an example, a client could be being served from one node at a particular time and from a different node shortly thereafter. Thus, an external load balancer serves two functions: load balancing and fault tolerance. Additionally the cloud provider on which a Swarm is hosted may provide additional features such as a secure and elastic external load balancing. Elastic load balancing, as provided by AWS Elastic Load Balancer, scales the request handling capacity based on the client traffic.

This chapter discusses load balancing with a user-created Swarm on CoreOS. It also discusses the automatically provisioned elastic load balancer on Docker for AWS managed services.

Setting the Environment

Start three CoreOS instances—one for the manager node and two for the worker nodes—as shown in Figure 12-3. Obtain the public IP address of the manager instance from the EC2 dashboard, as shown in Figure 12-3.

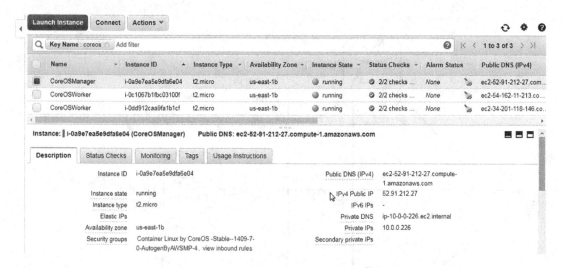

Figure 12-3. *CoreOS instances on EC2 for a manager and two worker nodes*

SSH login into the manager node to initiate the Swarm mode. Initializing a Swarm mode on CoreOS and joining worker nodes to the Swarm is discussed in Chapter 2. Copy the docker swarm join command output to join the worker nodes to the Swarm. List the Swarm nodes with the docker node ls command.

```
core@ip-10-0-0-226 ~ $ docker node ls
ID                        HOSTNAME                 STATUS  AVAILABILITY  MANAGER STATUS
9iqh5tg7hxy8u43tlifd1ri0q  ip-10-0-0-203.ec2.internal  Ready   Active
aoe1b2623qj03852mrc5cax97  ip-10-0-0-198.ec2.internal  Ready   Active
dsyo3b6553ueishozhfb1apad * ip-10-0-0-226.ec2.internal  Ready   Active        Leader
```

Creating a Hello World Service

Next, create a hello world service with the docker service create command. Expose the service at port 8080 using the --publish option. The syntax to publish a service using --publish or -p is as follows.

```
docker service create \
  --name <SERVICE-NAME> \
  --publish <PUBLISHED-PORT>:<TARGET-PORT> \
  <IMAGE>
```

The <PUBLISHED-PORT> is the port exposed on the hosts and the <TARGET-PORT> is the port on which the Docker container exposes the service. Using the tutum/hello-world Docker image, <PUBLISHED-PORT> as 8080, <TARGET-PORT> as 80, and <SERVICE-NAME> as hello-world, run the following command to create the service.

```
core@ip-10-0-0-226 ~ $ docker service create \
>   --name hello-world \
>   --publish 8080:80 \
>   --replicas 3 \
>   tutum/hello-world
0gk3wom7z91fpm5o9e6optmb5
```

The service is added to the ingress overlay network and the service is exposed at each node on the Swarm, whether a service task is running on the node or not. The `hello-world` service lists 3/3 replicas.

```
core@ip-10-0-0-226 ~ $ docker service ls
ID            NAME          REPLICAS  IMAGE              COMMAND
0gk3wom7z91f  hello-world   3/3       tutum/hello-world
```

List the service tasks using the `docker service ps hello-world` command and the three tasks are listed as scheduled, one on each node.

```
core@ip-10-0-0-226 ~ $ docker service ps hello-world
ID                         NAME           IMAGE              NODE
DESIRED STATE  CURRENT STATE          ERROR
di5oilh96jmr6fd5haevkkkt2  hello-world.1  tutum/hello-world  ip-10-0-0-198.ec2.internal
Running        Running 24 seconds ago
5g5d075yib2td8466mh7c01cz  hello-world.2  tutum/hello-world  ip-10-0-0-226.ec2.internal
Running        Running 24 seconds ago
5saarf4ngju3xr7uh7ninho0o  hello-world.3  tutum/hello-world  ip-10-0-0-203.ec2.internal
Running        Running 23 seconds ago
```

One Docker container is running on the manager node.

```
core@ip-10-0-0-226 ~ $ docker ps
CONTAINER ID   IMAGE                      COMMAND             CREATED
STATUS             PORTS        NAMES
b73cbcd0c37e   tutum/hello-world:latest   "/bin/sh -c 'php-fpm "   34 seconds ago
Up 32 seconds      80/tcp       hello-world.2.5g5d075yib2td8466mh7c01cz
```

One Docker container is running on one of the worker nodes.

```
core@ip-10-0-0-198 ~ $ docker ps
CONTAINER ID   IMAGE                      COMMAND             CREATED
STATUS             PORTS        NAMES
8bf11f2df213   tutum/hello-world:latest   "/bin/sh -c 'php-fpm "   38 seconds ago
Up 36 seconds      80/tcp       hello-world.1.di5oilh96jmr6fd5haevkkkt2
```

And the third Docker container is running on the other worker node.

```
core@ip-10-0-0-203 ~ $ docker ps
CONTAINER ID   IMAGE                      COMMAND             CREATED
STATUS             PORTS        NAMES
a461bfc8d4f9   tutum/hello-world:latest   "/bin/sh -c 'php-fpm "   40 seconds ago
Up 38 seconds      80/tcp       hello-world.3.5saarf4ngju3xr7uh7ninho0o
```

Invoking the Hello World Service

Without an external load balancer, an ingress connection may be made at each of the nodes at the published port. To invoke the service at the manager node, obtain the public DNS of the Swarm manager instance from the EC2 console, as shown in Figure 12-3.

Invoke the service in a web browser at the `<PublicDNS>:<PublishedPort>` URL, as shown in Figure 12-4.

Figure 12-4. *Invoking the service in a browser*

Similarly, to invoke the service at a worker node, obtain the public DNS of the worker instance from the EC2 console and invoke the service in a web browser at the `<PublicDNS>:<PublishedPort>` URL, as shown in Figure 12-5.

Figure 12-5. Invoking the service at a worker node

Similarly, to invoke the service at the other worker node, obtain the public DNS of the worker instance from the EC2 console and invoke the service in a web browser at the `<PublicDNS>:<PublishedPort>` URL, as shown in Figure 12-6.

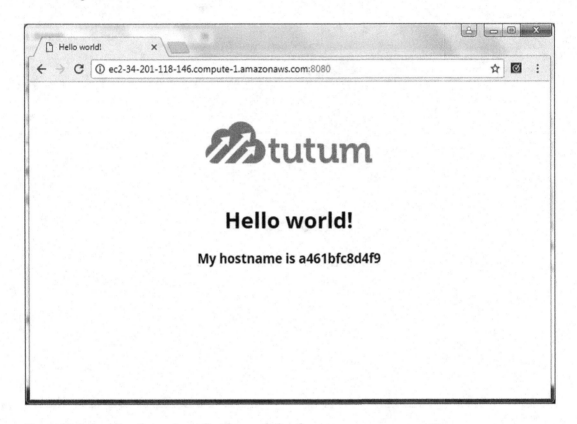

Figure 12-6. *Invoking the service at the other worker node*

While the external AWS Elastic Load Balancer distributes the load among the EC2 instances, the ingress load balancer distributes the load among the service tasks. In the preceding example, the same service task is invoked when the service is invoked at the Swarm manager instance and at a Swarm worker instance, as indicated by the same hostname (Figures 12-4 and 12-6). This demonstrates the ingress load balancing.

A different service task could get invoked if the service is invoked at the same host. As an example, invoke the service at the Swarm manager instance again. A different service task is served, as indicated by a different hostname in Figure 12-7. This is in comparison to the hostname served earlier in Figure 12-4, again demonstrating the ingress load balancing.

Figure 12-7. Different hostname served when invoking the service at the manager node again

Creating an External Elastic Load Balancer

In this section, we create an external elastic load balancer on the AWS cloud. Click on Load Balancers in the EC2 dashboard. Then click on Create Load Balancer to create a new load balancer, as shown in Figure 12-8.

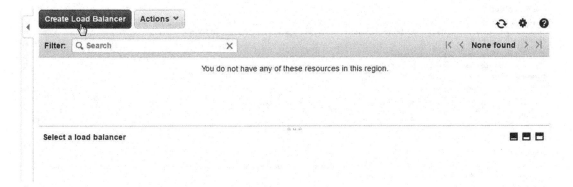

Figure 12-8. Creating a new load balancer

AWS Elastic Load Balancing offers two types of load balancers—classic load balancers and application load balancers. The classic load balancer routes traffic based on either application or network level information whereas the application load balancer routes traffic based on advanced application-level information. The classic load balancer should suffice for most simple load balancing of traffic to multiple EC2 instances and is the one we use for Docker Swarm instances. Select the Classic Load Balancer and then click on Continue, as shown in Figure 12-9.

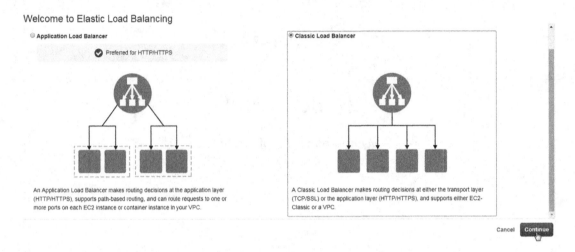

Figure 12-9. *Selecting the classic load balancer option*

In the Define Load Balancer dialog, specify a load balancer name (`HelloWorldLoadBalancer`) and select a VPC to create the load balancer in, as shown in Figure 12-10. The VPC must exist prior to creating the load balancer and must be where the EC2 instances to be load balanced are created. The load balancer protocol is HTTP and so is the instance protocol, by default. Keeping the default setting of HTTP protocol, specify the load balancer port and the instance port as 8080, because the Hello World service is exposed at port 8080.

| 1. Define Load Balancer | 2. Assign Security Groups | 3. Configure Security Settings | 4. Configure Health Check | 5. Add EC2 Instances | 6. Add Tags | 7. Review |

Step 1: Define Load Balancer

Basic Configuration

This wizard will walk you through setting up a new load balancer. Begin by giving your new load balancer a unique name so that you can identify it from other load balancers you might create. You will also need to configure ports and protocols for your load balancer. Traffic from your clients can be routed from any load balancer port to any port on your EC2 instances. By default, we've configured your load balancer with a standard web server on port 80.

Load Balancer name: HelloWorldLoadBalancer

Create LB Inside: vpc-18c6a261 (10.0.0.0/24) | redshift-vpc

Create an internal load balancer: ☐ (what's this?)

Listener Configuration:

Load Balancer Protocol	Load Balancer Port	Instance Protocol	Instance Port	
HTTP	8080	HTTP	8080	✖

Add

Select Subnets

You will need to select a Subnet for each Availability Zone where you wish traffic to be routed by your load balancer. If you have instances in only one Availability Zone, please select at least two Subnets in different Availability Zones to provide higher availability for your load balancer.

Cancel   **Next: Assign Security Groups**

Figure 12-10. *Selecting the load balancer protocol*

In the Select Subnets tab, click on one or more subnets listed in the Available Subnets table. The subnets are added to the selected subnets, as shown in Figure 12-11. Click on Next. To provide high availability, select at least two subnets in different availability zones.

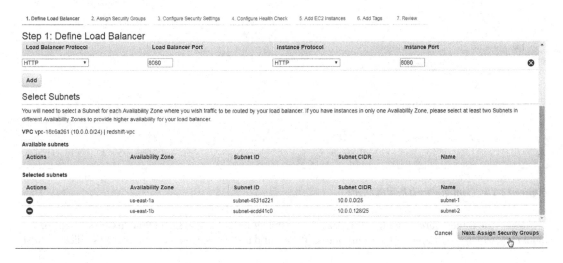

Figure 12-11. *Selecting subnets*

In the Assign Security Groups tab, select Create a New Security Group, as shown in Figure 12-12. In Type, select Custom TCP Rule. Choose the TCP protocol and the port range as 8080. Select Anywhere for the source and its value as 0.0.0.0/0. Click on Next.

Figure 12-12. *Assigning security groups*

Click on Next in Configure Security Settings, as we have not used the HTTPS or the SSL protocol. In the Configure Health Check tab, select HTTP for the ping protocol and 8080 for the ping port. Specify the ping path as /, as shown in Figure 12-13. Keep the defaults as is in the Advanced Details area and then click on Next.

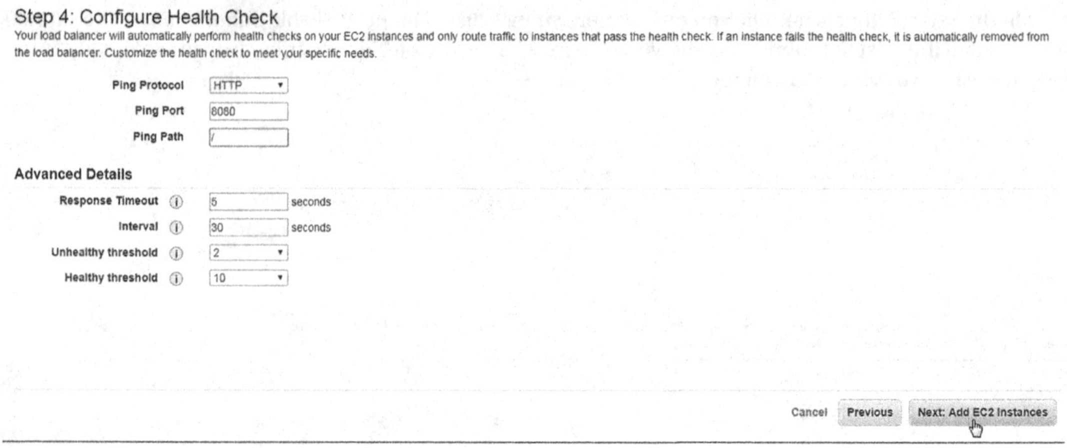

Step 4: Configure Health Check

Your load balancer will automatically perform health checks on your EC2 instances and only route traffic to instances that pass the health check. If an instance fails the health check, it is automatically removed from the load balancer. Customize the health check to meet your specific needs.

Ping Protocol	HTTP ▼
Ping Port	8080
Ping Path	/

Advanced Details

Response Timeout ⓘ	5	seconds
Interval ⓘ	30	seconds
Unhealthy threshold ⓘ	2 ▼	
Healthy threshold ⓘ	10 ▼	

Cancel Previous Next: Add EC2 Instances

Figure 12-13. *Configuring a health check*

Select the three Swarm instances listed, as shown in Figure 12-14. Also select Enable Cross-Zone Load Balancing, which distributes traffic evenly across all backend instances in all availability zones. Click on Next.

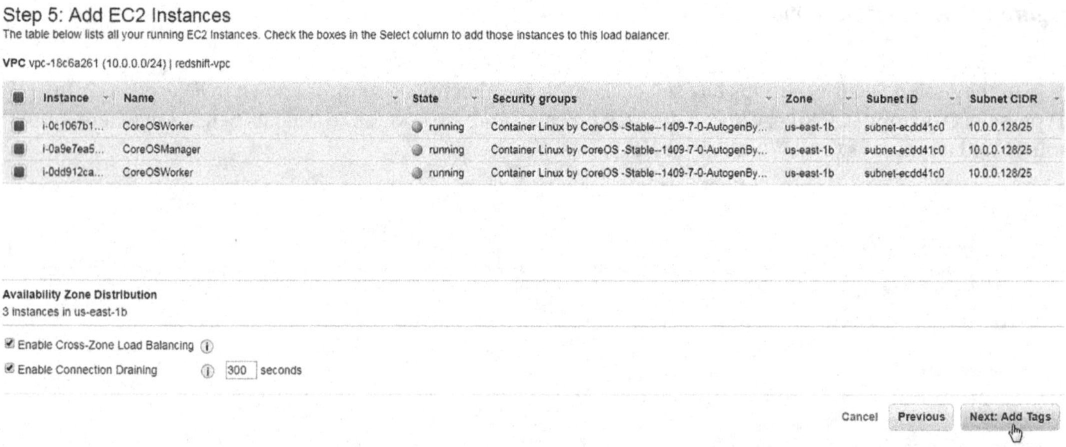

Step 5: Add EC2 Instances

The table below lists all your running EC2 instances. Check the boxes in the Select column to add those instances to this load balancer.

VPC vpc-18c6a261 (10.0.0.0/24) | redshift-vpc

■	Instance	Name	State	Security groups	Zone	Subnet ID	Subnet CIDR
■	i-0c1067b1...	CoreOSWorker	● running	Container Linux by CoreOS -Stable--1409-7-0-AutogenBy...	us-east-1b	subnet-ecdd41c0	10.0.0.128/25
■	i-0a9e7ea5...	CoreOSManager	● running	Container Linux by CoreOS -Stable--1409-7-0-AutogenBy...	us-east-1b	subnet-ecdd41c0	10.0.0.128/25
■	i-0dd912ca...	CoreOSWorker	● running	Container Linux by CoreOS -Stable--1409-7-0-AutogenBy...	us-east-1b	subnet-ecdd41c0	10.0.0.128/25

Availability Zone Distribution
3 instances in us-east-1b

☑ Enable Cross-Zone Load Balancing ⓘ
☑ Enable Connection Draining ⓘ 300 seconds

Cancel Previous Next: Add Tags

Figure 12-14. *Adding EC2 instances*

In the Add Tags tab, no tags need to be added. In the Review tab, click on Create, as shown in Figure 12-15. As indicated, the load balancer is an Internet-facing type.

Figure 12-15. *Review your settings then create the load balancer*

A load balancer is created, as shown in Figure 12-16.

Figure 12-16. *The load balancer has been created*

231

Obtain the DNS name of the load balancer from the EC2 console, as shown in Figure 12-17. Initially, the status will be "0 of 3 instances in service" because the registration is still in progress.

Figure 12-17. *Obtaining the DNS name of the load balancer*

After a while, the status should become "3 of 3 instances in service" and all the instance should be InService, as shown in Figure 12-18.

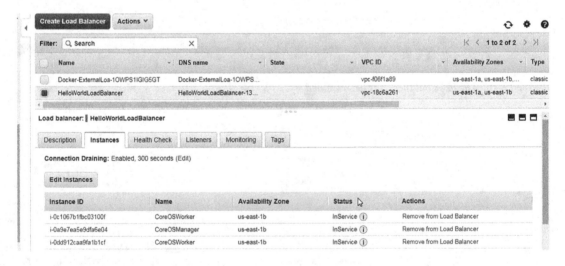

Figure 12-18. *Status indicates three of three instances InService*

The Hello World service may be invoked from the `<DNSname>:<LoadBalancerPort>` URL in a web browser, as shown in Figure 12-19.

Figure 12-19. *Invoking the Hello World service*

The external elastic load balancer balances the load among the EC2 instances in the Swarm. Because the ingress load balancer balances the load among the different service tasks, a different service task could get invoked if the service is invoked at the ELB DNS name again, as shown in Figure 12-20.

Figure 12-20. Different service task served

Load Balancing in Docker for AWS

While an external elastic load balancer had to be created when creating a Docker Swarm using the command line (by first initiating the Swarm mode and subsequently joining the worker nodes to the Swarm), the Docker for AWS managed service, which was introduced in Chapter 3, automatically creates an elastic load balancer.

Create a Swarm (a Swarm created earlier may be updated) with three manager nodes and five worker nodes using Docker for AWS, as shown in Figure 12-21. An external elastic load balancer is created as one of the Swarm resources, as listed in the Resources tab in Figure 12-21.

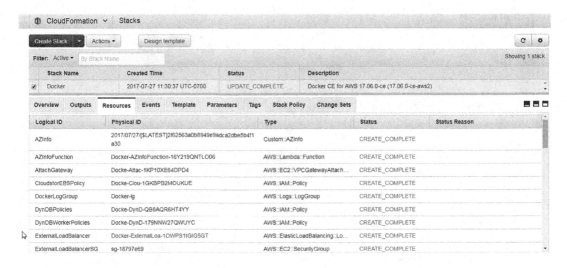

Figure 12-21. *CloudFormation stack for a Docker Swarm*

An Internet-facing Elastic Load Balancer is created, as shown in Figure 12-22. The public DNS for the load balancer may be used to access the Swarm, as discussed later.

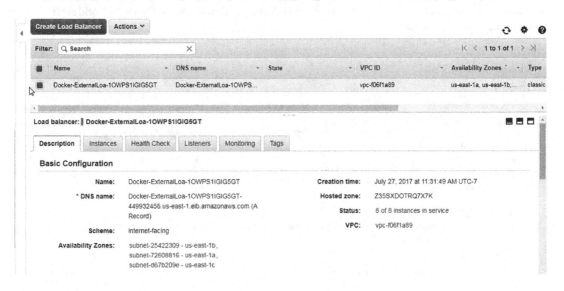

Figure 12-22. *Load balancer for the Swarm created with Docker for AWS*

Select the Instances tab. All the instances in the Swarm, manager or worker, are listed. All the instances should be InService, as shown in Figure 12-23.

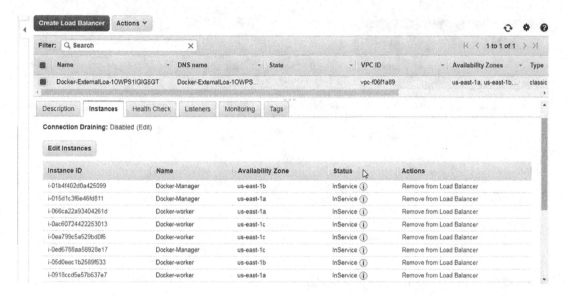

Figure 12-23. *Instances status is InService*

Update the load balancer listeners in the Listeners tab to add/modify a listener with a load balancer port set to 8080 and an instance port set to 8080, which is the published port for the Hello World service we create, as shown in Figure 12-24.

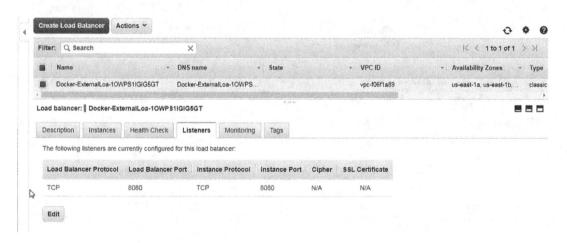

Figure 12-24. *The Listeners tab*

Obtain the public IP address of one of the manager nodes from the EC2 console.
SSH login to the manager node.

```
[root@localhost ~]# ssh -i "docker.pem" docker@34.205.43.53
Welcome to Docker!
```

List the Swarm nodes.

```
~ $ docker node ls
ID                          HOSTNAME                          STATUS AVAILABILITY MANAGER STATUS
8d0qv1epqu8xop4o2f94i8j40   ip-172-31-8-4.ec2.internal        Ready  Active
8eckb0twpbuoslfr58lbibplh   ip-172-31-32-133.ec2.internal     Ready  Active
b6f18h4f3o44gkf5dhkzavoy3   ip-172-31-2-148.ec2.internal      Ready  Active
k9nl2zcmjzobbqu5c5bkd829g   ip-172-31-21-41.ec2.internal      Ready  Active
pod70jwh5vpjwximc1cpjfjkp * ip-172-31-1-130.ec2.internal      Ready  Active       Leader
r02ftwtp3n4m0cl7v2llw4gi8   ip-172-31-44-8.ec2.internal       Ready  Active
rd8d0kksuts3aa07orhgkri3i   ip-172-31-41-86.ec2.internal      Ready  Active       Reachable
xks3sw6qgwbcuacyypemfbxyj   ip-172-31-31-117.ec2.internal     Ready  Active       Reachable
```

Create a Hello World service and expose the service at port 8080 (published port).

```
~ $ docker service create \
>    --name hello-world \
>    --publish 8080:80 \
>    --replicas 10 \
>    tutum/hello-world
n4hmfognhjrasf5nhukr55krb
```

Service tasks are scheduled across the Swarm.

```
~ $ docker service ps hello-world
ID              NAME            IMAGE                      NODE
DESIRED STATE         CURRENT STATE         ERROR         PORTS
y1fetn3kpwwn    hello-world.1   tutum/hello-world:latest   ip-172-31-2-148.ec2.internal
Running               Running 15 seconds ago
5i15zl9dickd    hello-world.2   tutum/hello-world:latest   ip-172-31-44-8.ec2.internal
Running               Running 17 seconds ago
k9glaavn0gzg    hello-world.3   tutum/hello-world:latest   ip-172-31-8-4.ec2.internal
Running               Running 17 seconds ago
n83f89ijlokn    hello-world.4   tutum/hello-world:latest   ip-172-31-41-86.ec2.internal
Running               Running 17 seconds ago
nelf275h9tp1    hello-world.5   tutum/hello-world:latest   ip-172-31-8-4.ec2.internal
Running               Running 16 seconds ago
w4c8zcvlq5v7    hello-world.6   tutum/hello-world:latest   ip-172-31-32-133.ec2.internal
Running               Running 17 seconds ago
b5qvbbgkrpd5    hello-world.7   tutum/hello-world:latest   ip-172-31-21-41.ec2.internal
Running               Running 16 seconds ago
qlm8dt9fuv92    hello-world.8   tutum/hello-world:latest   ip-172-31-31-117.ec2.internal
Running               Running 17 seconds ago
t3tenhpahh7g    hello-world.9   tutum/hello-world:latest   ip-172-31-44-8.ec2.internal
Running               Running 17 seconds ago
up64ekxqeftk    hello-world.10  tutum/hello-world:latest   ip-172-31-1-130.ec2.internal
Running               Running 17 seconds ago
```

The hello-world service may be created without explicitly specifying a published port.

```
~ $ docker service create \
>   --name hello-world \
>   --publish 80 \
>   --replicas 3 \
>   tutum/hello-world
```

The Swarm manager automatically assigns a published port in the range 30000-32767; the default being port 30000 if it's available. The listener in the load balancer for the Docker for AWS Swarm may need to be modified to add a mapping for the LoadBalancerPort:ServiceInstancePort, such as 30000:30000.

Obtain the public DNS for the elastic load balancer, which gets created automatically, as shown in Figure 12-25.

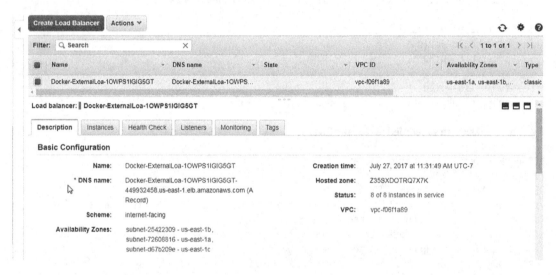

Figure 12-25. *Obtaining the public DNS of the ELB*

Access the service at <PublicDNS>:<PublishedPort> in a web browser, as shown in Figure 12-26. The request is forwarded to the ingress load balancer on one of the instances in the Swarm. The instance that the external request is forwarded to does not have to be hosting a service task. Finding a service task is what the ingress load balancer does.

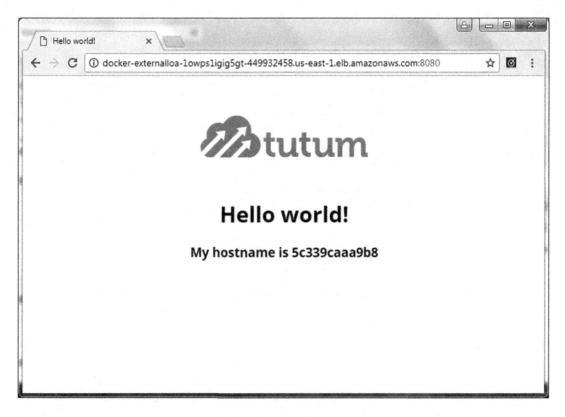

Figure 12-26. Accessing a Docker service at the elastic load balancer DNS

Summary

This chapter discussed load balancing in Swarm mode. An ingress load balancer is used to distribute the load among a service's tasks. Each service in a Swarm is assigned a DNS name and an internal load balancer balances service requests among the services based on DNS name. We also created an external load balancer for AWS EC2 instances to distribute load among the EC2 instances. Docker for AWS creates an external load balancer automatically on AWS. In the next chapter we discuss developing a Docker Swarm based highly available website.

CHAPTER 13

Developing a Highly Available Website

High availability of a website refers to a website being available continuously without service interruption. A website is made highly available by provisioning fault tolerance into the Docker Swarm application. High availability is provided at various levels. The ingress load balancer balances incoming client requests across the multiple service tasks and provides fault tolerance at the tasks level. If one service task fails, client traffic is routed to another service task. Using an external load balancer for a Docker Swarm hosted across multiple availability zones is another method for providing high availability. An external load balancer provides fault tolerance at the node level. If one node fails, client traffic is routed to Swarm nodes on another node.

The Problem

Using an external load balancer such as an AWS Elastic Load Balancer provides fault tolerance across multiple availability zones in an AWS region. The elastic load balancer may be accessed at its DNS name by a client host, as illustrated in Figure 13-1. The Swarm is not highly available, as failure of a single AWS region would cause a website to become unavailable.

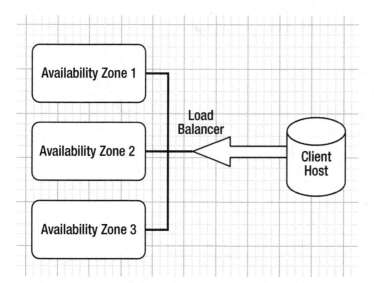

Figure 13-1. *The elastic load balancer may be accessed at its DNS name by a client host*

© Deepak Vohra 2017

D. Vohra, *Docker Management Design Patterns*, https://doi.org/10.1007/978-1-4842-2973-6_13

The Solution

Amazon Route 53 provides high availability with various DNS failover options, including active-active and active-passive failover using alias resource record sets. Amazon Route 53 provides DNS failover across AWS regions that are geographically spread, as illustrated in Figure 13-2. We use the Amazon Route 53 active-passive failover configuration based on the primary-secondary architectural patter for load balancer DNSes.

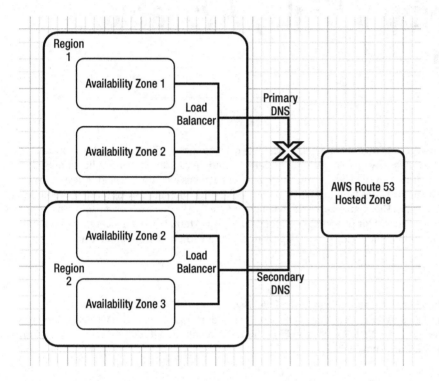

Figure 13-2. *Amazon Route 53 provides DNS failover across AWS regions*

This chapter covers the following topics:

- Setting the environment
- Creating multiple Docker swarms
- Deploying a Docker Swarm service
- Creating a AWS Route 53
- Creating a hosted zone
- Configuring name servers
- Creating record sets
- Testing high availability
- Deleting a hosted zone

Setting the Environment

We use two Docker for AWS managed Swarms for providing two DNS for active-passive DNS failover configuration. A Route 53 provides the primary-secondary architectural pattern for the two DNSes. The only prerequisite is an AWS account, which may be created at https://aws.amazon.com/resources/create-account/. Create a key pair (Swarm) that is to be used for SSH login to Swarm manager nodes, as shown in Figure 13-3. Set the permissions on the key pair to read-only by the owner only with the chmod 400 swarm.pem command.

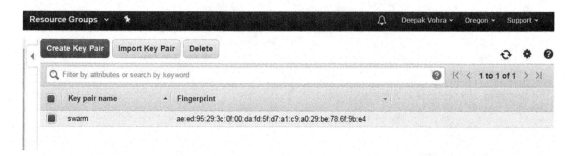

Figure 13-3. *Key pair*

A domain name must be registered to be used for creating an Amazon Route 53 hosted zone.

Creating Multiple Docker Swarms

Create two Docker Swarms using the Docker for AWS managed service at https://docs.docker.com/docker-for-aws/. The two Docker Swarms must be in two different AWS regions to use the high availability provided by geographically distributed AWS regions. Create one Docker Swarm Oregon region as an example, as shown in Figure 13-4.

Figure 13-4. *CloudFormation stack for Docker Swarm*

Each Docker Swarm has manager and worker nodes spread across the AWS availability zones in an AWS region. The public IP of a manager node may be obtained from the EC2 console, as shown in Figure 13-5.

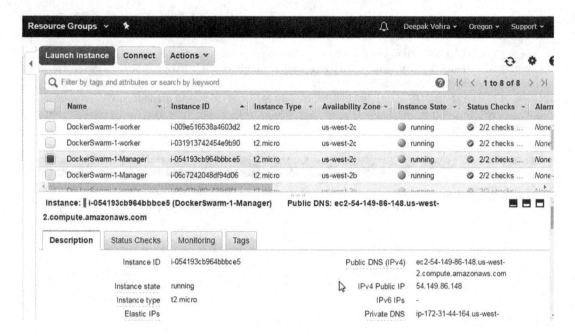

Figure 13-5. Obtaining the public IP of the Swarm manager node

Using the public IP address for a manager node in the first Docker Swarm, SSH login to the manager node EC2 instance.

```
[root@localhost ~]# ssh -i "swarm.pem" docker@54. 149.86.148

Welcome to Docker!

~$
```

Create the other Docker Swarm in the Ohio AWS region as an example, as shown in Figure 13-6. The regions may be different for different users.

Figure 13-6. CloudFormation stack for the Docker Swarm in one region

The Swarm node EC2 instances for the second Docker Swarm are also spread across the AWS availability zones in the second AWS region, as shown in Figure 13-7. Obtain the public IP for a manager node.

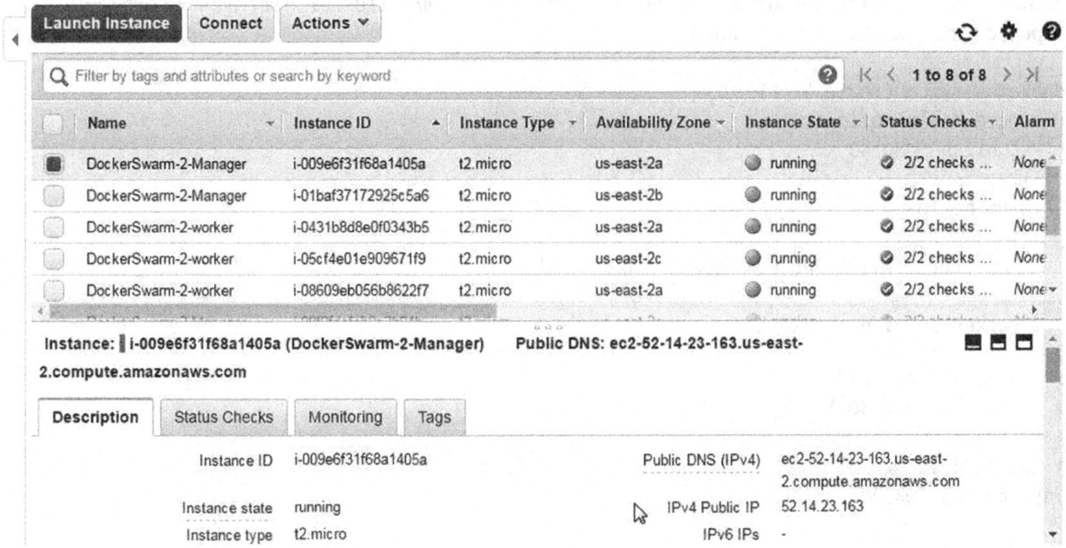

Figure 13-7. The Availability Zone column lists multiple zones

SSH login to the instance.

```
[root@1oca1.host ~]# ssh -i "docker.pem" docker@52.14.23.163
Welcome to Docker!
~$
```

List the Swarm nodes in a Docker Swarm with the Docker node.

```
~ $ docker node ls
```

```
ID HOSTNAME STATUS AVAILABILITY MANAGER STATUS

fncv7ducej3ind4u2sy9xtwi7 ip-172-31-34-223.us-east-2.compute.internal. Ready Active
Reachable
grdeu2x49yi2fmvuy9lmoogqg ip-172-31-43-174.us-east-2.compute.internal Ready Active
ke0d75qef9bg8t22eqv9spdpm ip-172-31-30-180.us-east-2.compute.internal. Ready Active
Reachable
m2mmifbrnjbdriub5r36zxyjc * ip-172-31-8-11.us-east-2.compute.internal Ready Active Leader
qenbfrms0xv7wom6wpw9yspw4 ip-172-31-27-178.us-east-2.compute.internal Ready Active
tipzy29hgh3m6og5bzkgsego8 ip-172-31-12-37.us-east-2.compute.internal Ready Active
v4xdl4jvthovrzsamujoxy3ju ip-172-31-7-219.us-east-2.compute.internal Ready Active
vuq68yex58vzgx3audj3sm23a ip-172-31-28-182.us-east-2.compute.internal Ready Active
```

Deploying a Docker Swarm Service

Next, we deploy a Hello World service that will be hosted on a website. Run the following command on a manager instance for the DockerSwarm-1 Swarm to create a tutum/hello-world service with two replicas exposed at port 8080 on the host nodes.

```
docker service create \
  --name hello-world \
  --publish 8080:80 \
  --replicas 2 \
  tutum/hello-world
```

A Docker service with two service tasks is created.

```
~ $ docker service create \

> --name hello-world \
> --publish 8080:80 \
> -- replicas 2 \
> tutum/hello-world
vn5fl8h7t65sjwk54dwcoklhu

~ $ docker service 1s

ID NAME MODE REPLICAS IMAGE

vn5tl8h7t65s hello-world replicated 2/2 tutum/hello-world:latest

~ $ docker service ps hello-world

ID NAME IMAGE NODE DESIRED STATE CURRENT STATE ERROR PORTS

ac9ks5y9duni2 hello-world.1 tutum/hello-wor1d:latest ip-172-31-19-220.us-west-2.compute.
internal Running Running 13 seconds ago
8s6r48wUui9 hello-world.2 tutum/hello-world:latest ip-172-31-24-250.us-west-2.compute.
internal Running Running 13 seconds ago
```

Scale the service to 10 replicas to provide load distribution. Subsequently, list the services to list 10/10 replicas as running.~ $ docker service scale hello-world=10

```
hello-world scaled to 10
~ $ docker service ls

ID NAME MODE REPLICAS IMAGE

vn5U8h7t65s hello-world replicated 10/10 tutum/hello-world:latest
~ $
```

The 10 service task replicas are scheduled across the Swarm nodes, as shown in Figure 13-8.

```
~ $ docker service ps hello-world
ID              NAME              IMAGE                          NODE
                        DESIRED STATE  CURRENT STATE                    ERROR  PORTS
ac9ks5y9dum2  hello-world.1    tutum/hello-world:latest  ip-172-31-19-220.us-west
-2.compute.internal   Running         Running about a minute ago
8s6r48wltui9  hello-world.2    tutum/hello-world:latest  ip-172-31-24-250.us-west
-2.compute.internal   Running         Running about a minute ago
k4r20unv1xxs  hello-world.3    tutum/hello-world:latest  ip-172-31-19-220.us-west
-2.compute.internal   Running         Running 49 seconds ago
imz825y6j5ya  hello-world.4    tutum/hello-world:latest  ip-172-31-6-109.us-west-
2.compute.internal    Running         Running 46 seconds ago
m2lz9wpsbtea  hello-world.5    tutum/hello-world:latest  ip-172-31-44-164.us-west
-2.compute.internal   Running         Running 45 seconds ago
4kxqmmc3ux1w  hello-world.6    tutum/hello-world:latest  ip-172-31-42-245.us-west
-2.compute.internal   Running         Running 46 seconds ago
o3ychxa9p1y8  hello-world.7    tutum/hello-world:latest  ip-172-31-36-249.us-west
-2.compute.internal   Running         Running 46 seconds ago
uriyh6hh9o26  hello-world.8    tutum/hello-world:latest  ip-172-31-20-251.us-west
-2.compute.internal   Running         Running 46 seconds ago
nmrlnzv17yj5  hello-world.9    tutum/hello-world:latest  ip-172-31-3-209.us-west-
2.compute.internal    Running         Running 46 seconds ago
ghfduagrtgqg  hello-world.10   tutum/hello-world:latest  ip-172-31-3-209.us-west-
2.compute.internal    Running         Running 45 seconds ago
~ $ █
```

Figure 13-8. *Service tasks scheduled across the Swarm nodes*

Obtain the load balancer DNS for the first Docker Swarm from the EC2 dashboard, as shown in Figure 13-9.

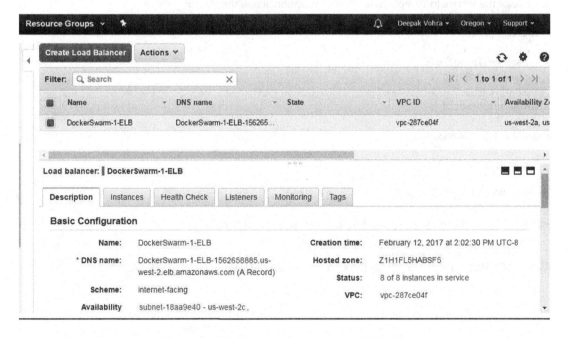

Figure 13-9. *Docker Swarm load balancer*

Access the service at <DNS>:<LoadBalancerPort> in a web browser, as shown in Figure 13-10; the load balancer port is set to 8080, the port at which the service is exposed.

Figure 13-10. *Accessing the service in a browser*

Similarly for the second Docker Swarm, create a tutum/hello-world service with a published port set to 8080. Scale the service to 10 replicas for load distribution across the Swarm.

```
S docker service create \

> --name hello-world \
> --publish 8080:80 \
,> --replicas 2 \
> tutum/hello-world

woqx2ltuibv53ctmuvssrsq8j

~ $ docker service ls

ID NAME MODE REPLICAS IMAGE

woqx2ltuibv5 hello-world replicated 2/2 tutum/hello-world:latest

~ $ docker service ps hello-world
NAME IMAGE NODE DESIRED STATE CURRENT STATE ERROR PORTS
```

```
ny9ermdgb7a4 hello-world.1 tutum/hello-world:latest ip-172-31-34-223.us-east-2.compute.
internal Running Running 15 seconds ago

5w3thlgleinme hello-world.2 tutum/hello-world:latest ip-172-31-30-180.us-east-2.compute.
internal Running Running 15 seconds ago

~ $ docker service scale hello-world=10

hello-world scaled to 10
```

The service replicas are distributed across the Swarm nodes, as shown in Figure 13-11.

```
~ $ docker service ps hello-world
ID              NAME            IMAGE                       NODE
                     DESIRED STATE  CURRENT STATE              ERROR   PORTS
ny9ermdgb7a4  hello-world.1   tutum/hello-world:latest  ip-172-31-34-223.us-east
-2.compute.internal   Running         Running about a minute ago
5w3thlgl0mme  hello-world.2   tutum/hello-world:latest  ip-172-31-30-180.us-east
-2.compute.internal   Running         Running about a minute ago
1warzpstn2wk  hello-world.3   tutum/hello-world:latest  ip-172-31-8-11.us-east-2
.compute.internal     Running         Running 25 seconds ago
ff58q94ij91m  hello-world.4   tutum/hello-world:latest  ip-172-31-8-11.us-east-2
.compute.internal     Running         Running 25 seconds ago
wtjskvuwhmu4  hello-world.5   tutum/hello-world:latest  ip-172-31-30-180.us-east
-2.compute.internal   Running         Running 27 seconds ago
8vtnxa7yktxu  hello-world.6   tutum/hello-world:latest  ip-172-31-43-174.us-east
-2.compute.internal   Running         Running 26 seconds ago
0mbtqclkqwax  hello-world.7   tutum/hello-world:latest  ip-172-31-12-37.us-east-
2.compute.internal    Running         Running 26 seconds ago
twfj8nn881u7  hello-world.8   tutum/hello-world:latest  ip-172-31-7-219.us-east-
2.compute.internal    Running         Running 26 seconds ago
98sykb376wn7  hello-world.9   tutum/hello-world:latest  ip-172-31-27-178.us-east
-2.compute.internal   Running         Running 25 seconds ago
g6cyck25jd08  hello-world.10  tutum/hello-world:latest  ip-172-31-28-182.us-east
-2.compute.internal   Running         Running 26 seconds ago
~ $ ▉
```

Figure 13-11. Service replicas distributed across the Swarm

Obtain the DNS of the elastic load balancer for the second Swarm, as shown in Figure 13-12.

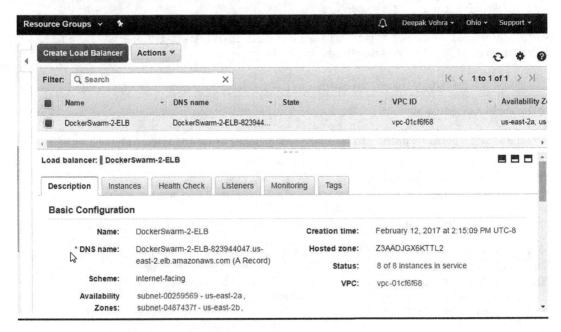

Figure 13-12. *Obtaining the DNS name for the Swarm ELB*

Access the service at `<DNS>:<LoadBalancerPort>` in a web browser, as shown in Figure 13-13.

Figure 13-13. *Accessing the service in a browser*

Creating an Amazon Route 53

Amazon Route 53 is a highly available and scalable cloud Domain Name Service (DNS) web service that connects user requests to infrastructure running on the AWS, including Amazon EC2 instances, load balancers, and Amazon S3 buckets. We already created two Docker Swarms hosting the same Docker service using the Docker AWS managed service, which automatically creates an AWS ELB for each Docker Swarm.

In this section, we create an Amazon Route 53 to route user requests to the nosqlsearch.com domain to the elastic load balancers for the two Docker Swarms. In Amazon Route 53, we create two resource record sets pointing to the two different ELBs configured for failover, with one of the ELBs being the primary resource record set and the other being the secondary resource record set.

When the nosqlsearch.com domain is opened in a web browser, the Route 53 routes the request to the primary resource record set. If the primary record set fails, Route 53 routes the user request to the secondary record set, in effect providing high availability of the Hello World Docker service hosted on the nosqlsearch.com domain. To create an AWS Route 53, select Route 53 from the AWS services, as shown in Figure 13-14.

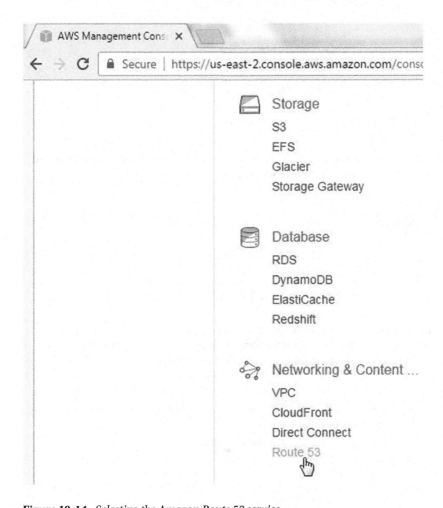

Figure 13-14. *Selecting the Amazon Route 53 service*

Creating a Hosted Zone

A hosted zone is a configuration that determines how traffic to a domain on the Internet will be routed. To create a hosted zone, open `https://console.aws.amazon.com/route53/` in a web browser and click on Create Hosted Zone in the DNS management, as shown in Figure 13-15.

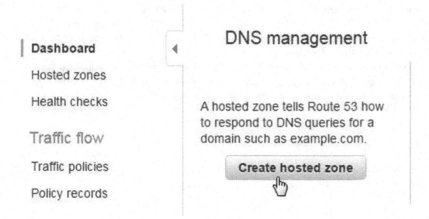

Figure 13-15. *Creating the hosted zone*

Alternatively, select Hosted Zones or open `https://console.aws.amazon.com/route53/home#hosted-zones` in a browser and click on Create Hosted Zone, as shown in Figure 13-16.

Figure 13-16. *Creating a hosted zone*

Click on Create Hosted Zone again, as shown in Figure 13-17.

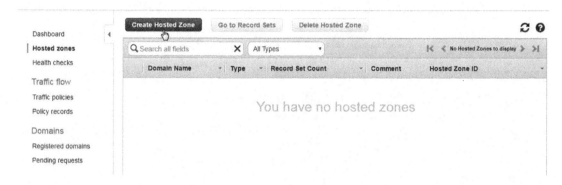

Figure 13-17. *Creating a hosted zone*

In the Create Hosted Zone dialog, specify a domain name (nosqlsearch.com). The domain name must be registered with the user. Select Public Hosted Zone for the type, as shown in Figure 13-18.

Figure 13-18. *Configuring the hosted zone*

A new public hosted zone is created, as shown in Figure 13-19. The name servers for the hosted zone (by default, there are four) are assigned.

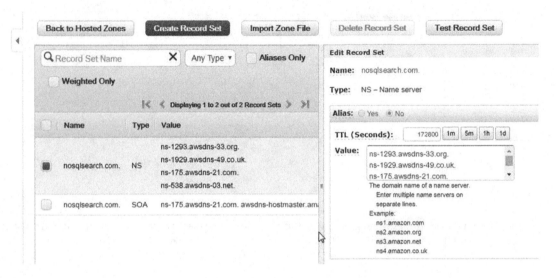

Figure 13-19. *The new public hosted zone*

Configuring Name Servers

Next, we need to configure the name servers for the domain with the domain registrar. The procedure to configure name servers is different for different domain registrars, but an option to add a zone record for a domain should be provided.

Specify the record type as Nameserver, as shown in Figure 13-20. Specify the host as @. Each zone record should point to a single name server, which may be obtained from the public hosted zone we created earlier.

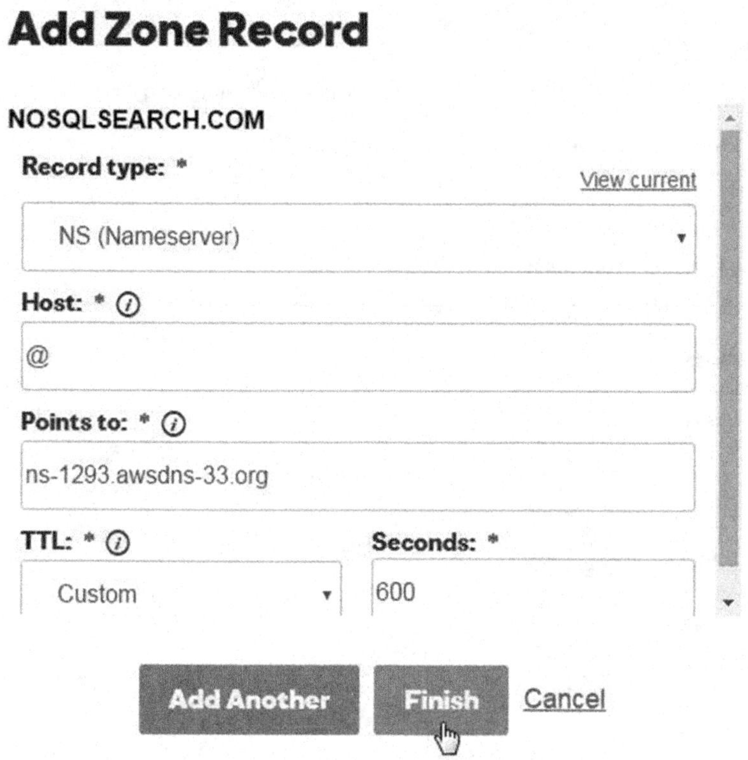

Add Zone Record

NOSQLSEARCH.COM

Record type: *   View current

    NS (Nameserver)   ▼

Host: * *(i)*

    @

Points to: * *(i)*

    ns-1293.awsdns-33.org

TTL: * *(i)*   **Seconds:** *

    Custom   ▼   600

    Add Another   **Finish**   Cancel

Figure 13-20. Adding a name server record

Add four name servers (collectively called a *delegation set*), as shown in Figure 13-21, for the domain for which a hosted zone is to be created.

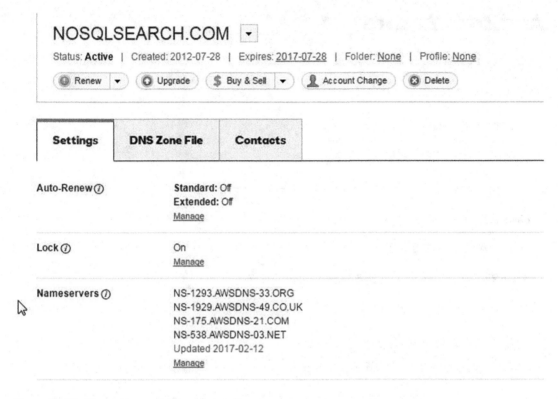

Figure 13-21. *Name servers configured on a domain*

Creating Resource Record Sets

After creating and configuring a hosted zone, create one or more resource record sets. A resource record set is a Domain Name System (DNS) configuration for routing traffic to a domain. Click on Create Record Set to create a resource record set, as shown in Figure 13-22.

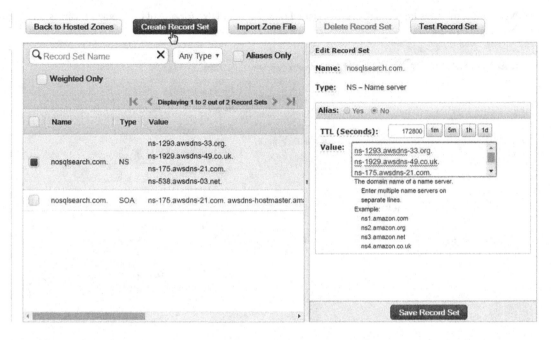

Figure 13-22. *Creating a record set*

In the Create Record Set tab, the type should be set to A –IPv4 address, as shown in Figure 13-23. The name of each record set ends with the domain name. Select Yes for Alias.

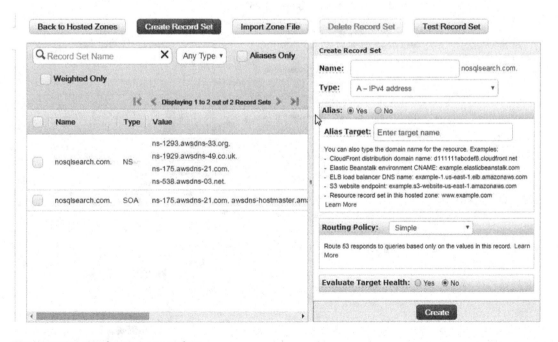

Figure 13-23. *Configuring a record set*

Next, select the alias target as the AWS Elastic Load Balancer DNS for one of the Docker Swarms, as shown in Figure 13-24.

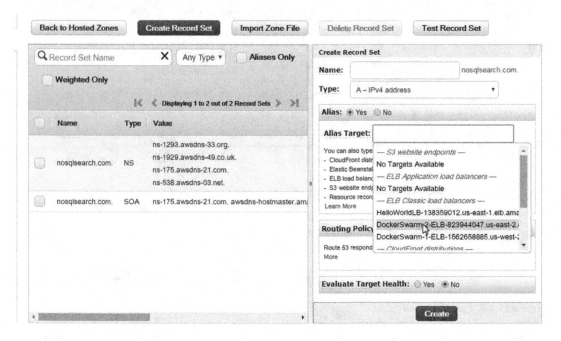

Figure 13-24. *Selecting an alias target*

Next, select the routing policy, as shown in Figure 13-25.

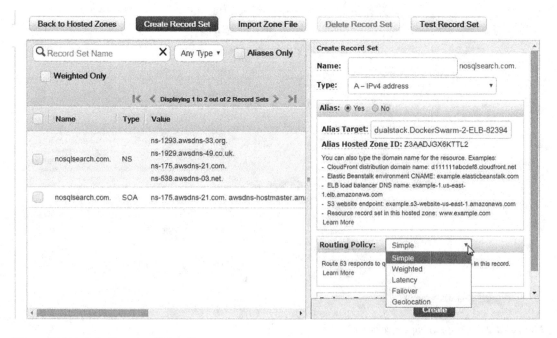

Figure 13-25. *Selecting a routing policy*

Select Failover for the routing policy. This configures DNS failover, as shown in Figure 13-26. Select Failover Record Type as Primary.

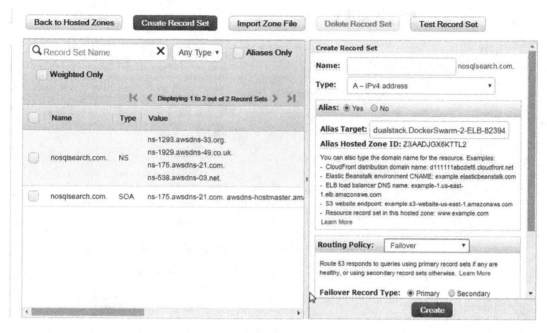

Figure 13-26. *Selecting failover record type*

For Evaluate Target Health, select Yes, as shown in Figure 13-27.

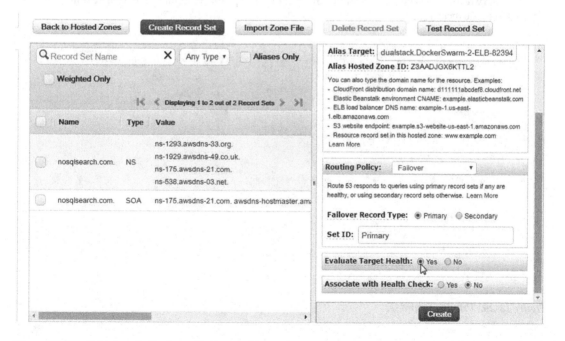

Figure 13-27. *Selecting the Evaluate Target Health option*

For Associate with Health Check, select No. Click on Create, as shown in Figure 13-28.

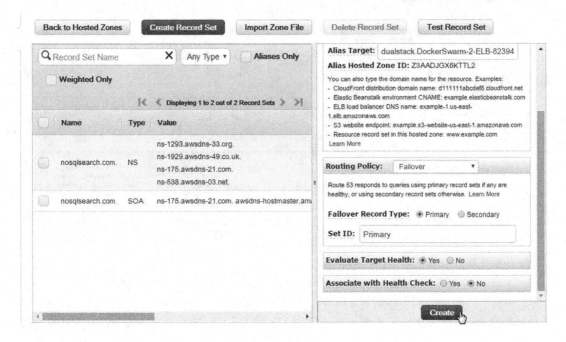

Figure 13-28. *Creating a record set*

A primary record set is created, as shown in Figure 13-29; "primary" implies that website traffic will be first routed to the record set.

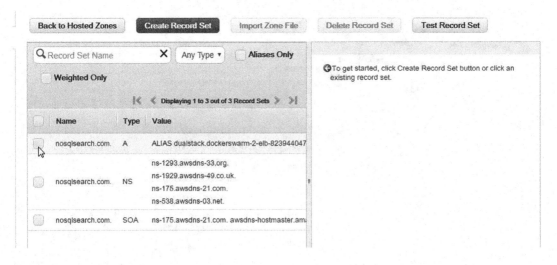

Figure 13-29. *Primary record set*

To create a secondary record set, click on Create Record Set again, as shown in Figure 13-30.

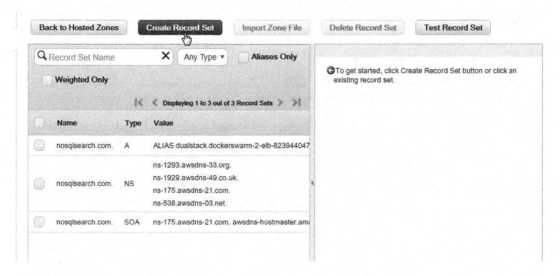

Figure 13-30. *Creating another record set*

Select the type as A –IPv4 address and choose Yes for Alias. Select Alias Target as the second ELB DNS, as shown in Figure 13-31.

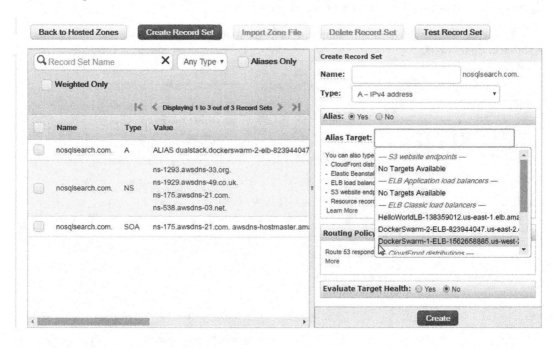

Figure 13-31. *Selecting an alias target*

Select the Failover routing policy and the secondary Failover Record Type, as shown in Figure 13-32.

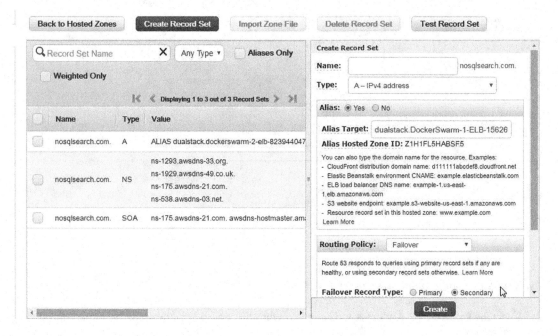

Figure 13-32. *Selecting failover record type as secondary*

Choose Yes for the Evaluate Target Health and No for the Associate with Health Check. Click on Create, as shown in Figure 13-33.

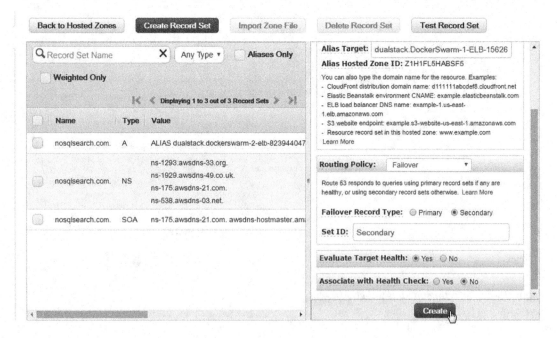

Figure 13-33. *Creating a secondary record set*

The secondary record set is created; "secondary" implies that traffic is routed to the record set if the primary record set fails, as shown in Figure 13-34. Click on Back to Hosted Zones.

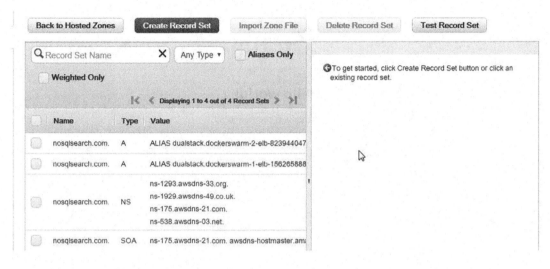

Figure 13-34. *Secondary record set is created*

The domain (`nosqlsearch.com`) is configured with four record sets, as shown in Figure 13-35.

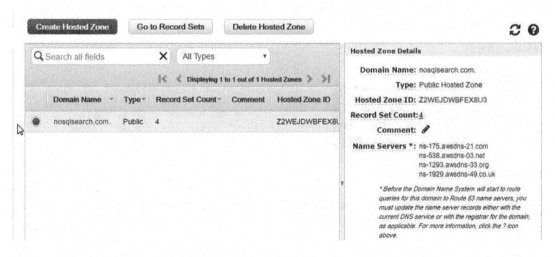

Figure 13-35. *Hosted zone created*

Testing High Availability

Next, we test the high availability we configured. Open the domain, including the service published port (`nosqlsearch.com:8080`), in a web browser, as shown in Figure 13-36. The Docker service output should be displayed.

Figure 13-36. Invoking a service in a browser

To test high availability, delete the CloudFormation stack for the Docker Swarm associated with the primary record set, as shown in Figure 13-37.

Figure 13-37. Deleting a stack

Click on Yes, Delete in the Delete Stack dialog. The stack should start to be deleted, as indicated by the DELETE_IN_PROGRESS status shown in Figure 13-38.

Stack Name	Created Time	Status	Description
DockerSwarm-2	2017-02-12 14:14:06 UTC-0800	DELETE_IN_PROGRESS	Docker for AWS 1.13.1 (ga-2)

Figure 13-38. The delete is in progress

The DNS fails over to the secondary resource record set and the domain continues to serve the Docker service, as shown in Figure 13-39.

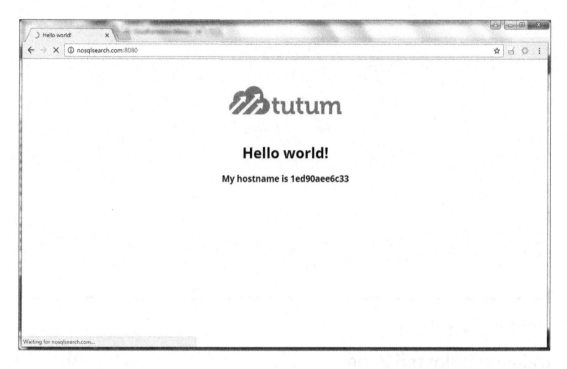

Figure 13-39. *Domain continues to serve*

The hostname in the browser could become different if the request is forwarded to a different service task replica, as shown in Figure 13-40. But the hostname could also become different regardless of whether failover has been initiated, because the ingress load balancer distributes traffic among the different service replicas.

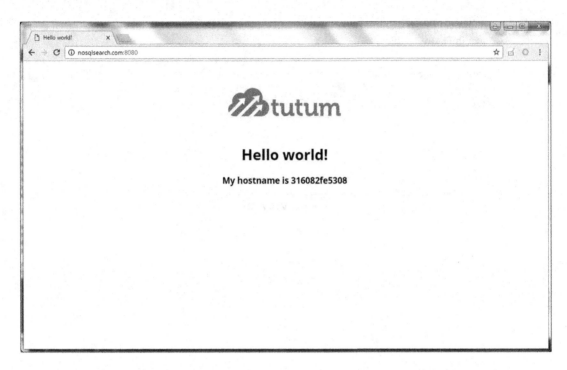

Figure 13-40. *Different hostname*

Deleting a Hosted Zone

Before a hosted zone can be deleted, all the resource record sets associated with the hosted zone must be deleted. Select the resource record sets to delete and click on Delete Record Set, as shown in Figure 13-41.

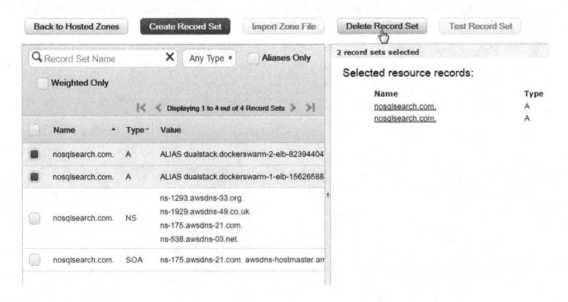

Figure 13-41. *Deleting the record sets*

Click on Confirm in the Confirm dialog, as shown in Figure 13-42.

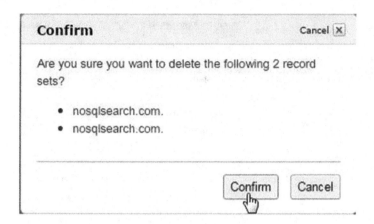

Figure 13-42. *Confirmation dialog*

Click on Back to Hosted Zones, as shown in Figure 13-43.

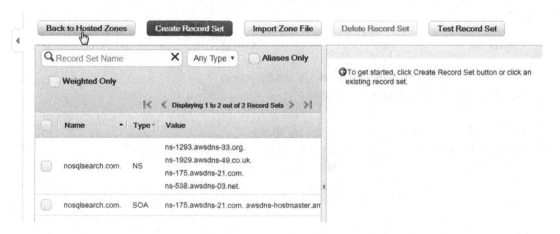

Figure 13-43. *Going back to the hosted zones*

Select the hosted zone to delete and click on Delete Hosted Zone, as shown in Figure 13-44.

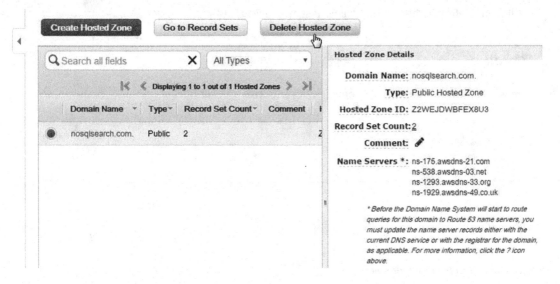

Figure 13-44. *Deleting a hosted zone*

Click on Confirm in the Confirm dialog, as shown in Figure 13-45.

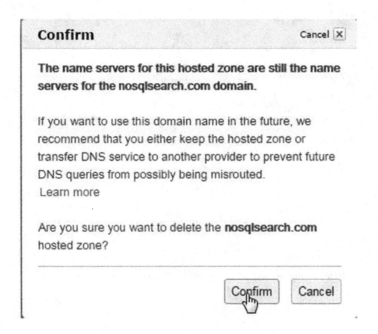

Figure 13-45. *Confirmation dialog for deleting a hosted zone*

The hosted zone is deleted.

Summary

This chapter developed a highly available website using an Amazon Route 53 hosted zone. First, we created two Docker Swarms using the Docker for AWS managed service and deployed the same Docker service on each. Each Docker Swarm service may be accessed using the AWS Elastic Load Balancer for the Docker Swarm created automatically by the Docker for AWS. The Route 53 hosted zone is to create a hosted zone for a domain to route traffic to DNSes configured in the primary/secondary failover pattern. Subsequently, we tested that if the Docker Swarm for the primary record set is shut down, the website is still available, as the hosted zone routes the traffic to the secondary ELB DNS. In the next chapter we discuss using the Docker Swarm mode in Docker Cloud.

CHAPTER 14

■ ■ ■

Using Swarm Mode in Docker Cloud

Docker for AWS is a managed service for Docker Swarm based on a custom Linux distribution, and hosted on AWS with all the benefits inherent with being integrated with the AWS Cloud platform, such as centralized logging with CloudWatch, custom debugging, auto-scaling groups, elastic load balancing, and a DynamoDB database.

The Problem

While AWS is a managed cloud platform, it is not a managed service for Docker containers, images, and services per se. Docker's builds and tests still need to be integrated.

The Solution

Docker Cloud is a managed service to test code and build Docker images and to create and manage Docker image repositories in the Docker Cloud registry. Docker Cloud also manages Docker containers, services, stacks, nodes, and node clusters. A *stack* is a collection of services and a *service* is a collection of containers. Docker Cloud is an integrated cloud service that manages builds and images, infrastructure, and nodes and apps.

Docker Cloud also introduced a Swarm mode to manage Docker Swarms. In Swarm mode, Docker Cloud is integrated with Docker for AWS. As a result, Docker Cloud Swarm mode is an integration of two managed services—Docker for AWS and Docker Cloud.

Docker Cloud provides some Docker images to interact between a Docker Swarm and a Docker host client, as discussed in Table 14-1.

Table 14-1. Docker Images for Docker Swarm

Docker Image	Description
dockercloud/client	Used on the client side to start an interactive shell to connect to a remote docker Swarm cluster using Docker ID credentials.
dockercloud/client-proxy	Used on the client side to forward local docker API calls to a remote swarm cluster by injecting Docker ID authorization information on each request.
dockercloud/server-proxy	Authenticates and authorizes incoming Docker API calls and forwards them to the local Docker engine.
dockercloud/registration	Registers a Swarm cluster to Docker Cloud and launches a server proxy.

© Deepak Vohra 2017
D. Vohra, *Docker Management Design Patterns*, https://doi.org/10.1007/978-1-4842-2973-6_14

In this chapter, we discuss the Docker Cloud Swarm mode to provision a Docker Swarm with infrastructure hosted on AWS. This chapter covers the following topics:

- Setting the environment

- Creating an IAM role

- Creating a Docker Swarm in Docker Cloud

- Connecting to the Docker Swarm from a Docker host

- Connecting to the Docker Swarm from a Swarm manager

- Bringing a Swarm into Docker Cloud

Setting the Environment

As Docker Cloud is a managed service, all that is required is an account, which may be created at `https://cloud.docker.com/`. An AWS account is also required and may be created at `https://aws.amazon.com/resources/create-account/`. Also create a key pair in the region in which the EC2 instances for the Docker Swarm will run, as shown in Figure 14-1.

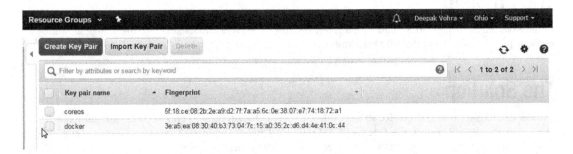

Figure 14-1.   Creating a key pair on AWS EC2

Creating an IAM Role

The Docker Cloud Swarm mode requires an AWS role with a new policy, an embedded policy for Docker for AWS. To create the IAM role, navigate to `https://console.aws.amazon.com/iam/home?#roles` in a web browser. Click on Create New Role, as shown in Figure 14-2.

Figure 14-2.   Creating a new role

Specify a role name (`dockercloud-swarm-role`), as shown in Figure 14-3, and click on Next Step.

Figure 14-3. *Specifying a role name*

The Select Role Type page is displayed, as shown in Figure 14-4. As we are linking two services—Docker Cloud and Docker for AWS—we do not need to select an AWS service role.

Figure 14-4. *Select the role type*

Select Role for Cross-Account Access, as shown in Figure 14-5, and select the sub-choice called Provide Access Between Your AWS Account and a 3rd Party AWS Account using the Select button.

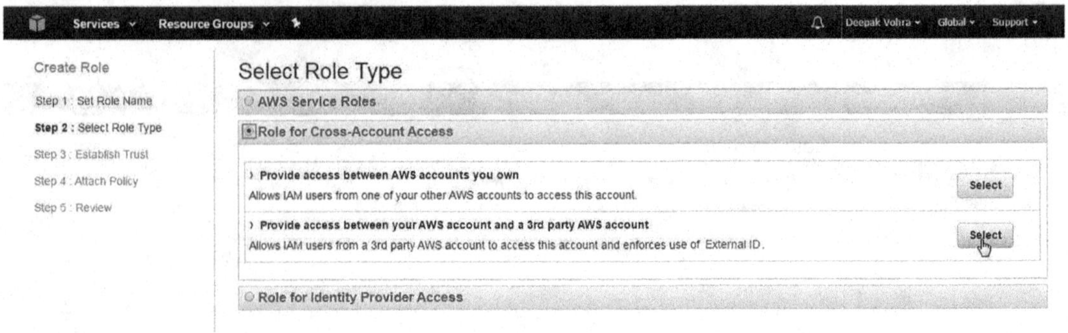

Figure 14-5. *Role for cross-account access*

Next, specify the account ID of the third party AWS account whose IAM users will access the AWS account. A third-party AWS account has been set up for the Docker Cloud service and has an account ID of 689684103426, which may be used by anyone (AWS user) linking Docker Cloud service to their AWS account. Specify the account ID as 689684103426, as shown in Figure 14-6. The external ID is a user's Docker ID for the Docker Cloud service account created at `https://cloud.docker.com/`. While the account ID will be the same (689684103426) for everyone, the external ID will be different for different users. Keep the Require MFA checkbox unchecked. Click on Next Step.

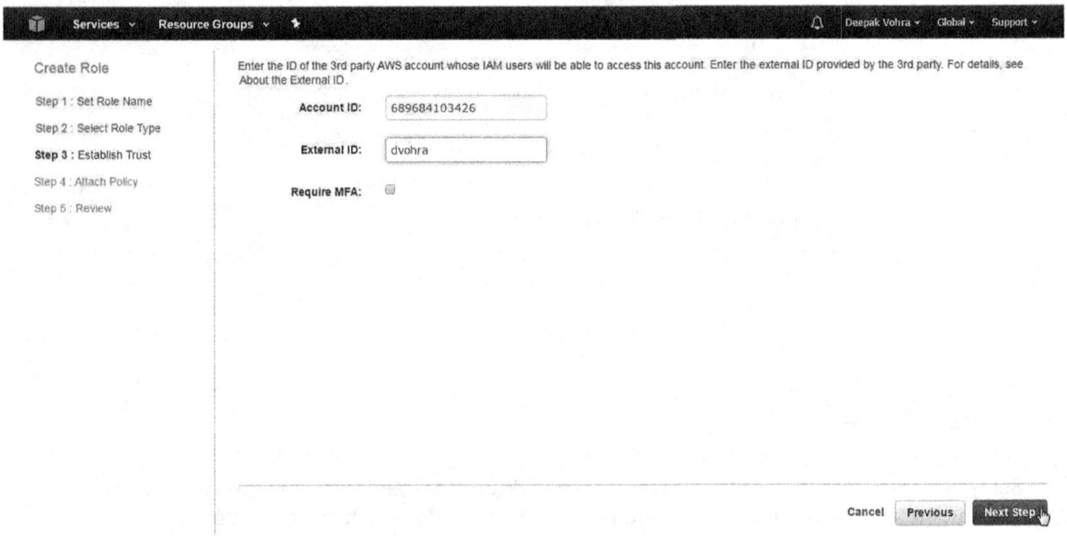

Figure 14-6. *Specifying account and external IDs*

As we are embedding a custom policy, do not select from any of the listed policies in Attach Policy. Click on Next Step, as shown in Figure 14-7.

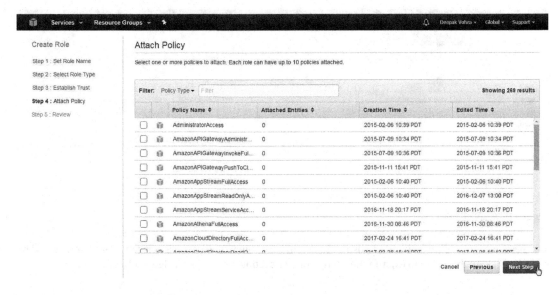

Figure 14-7. *Do not select a policy*

On the Review page, click on Create Role, as shown in Figure 14-8.

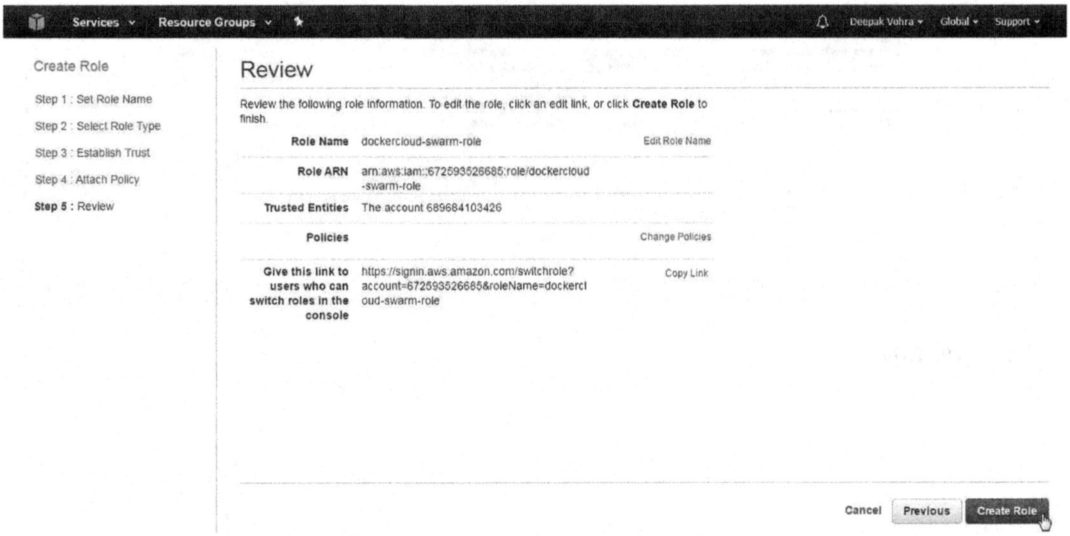

Figure 14-8. *Creating a role*

A new AWS IAM role called dockercloud-swarm-role is created, as shown in Figure 14-9. Click on the **dockercloud-swarm-role** role name.

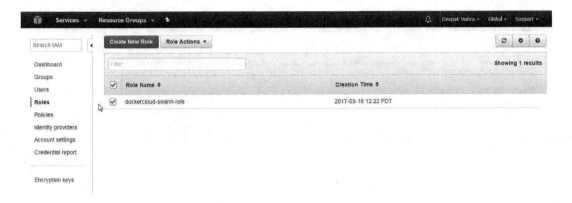

Figure 14-9. *New role*

Next, we will add an embedded (also called an inline) policy. The Permissions tab should be selected by default. Click on the v icon to expand the Inline Policies section, as shown in Figure 14-10.

Figure 14-10. *Expanding the inline policies*

To start, no inline policies are listed. Click on the Click Here link to add an inline policy, as shown in Figure 14-11.

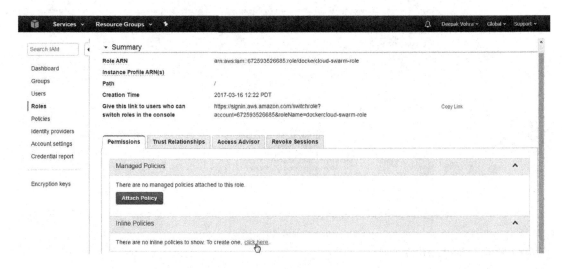

Figure 14-11. *Click on the Click Here link to add an inline policy*

In Set Permissions, select Custom Policy using the Select button, as shown in Figure 14-12.

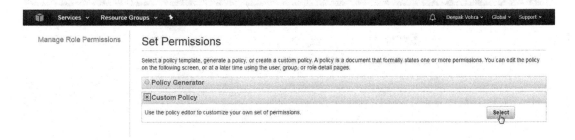

Figure 14-12. *Selecting a custom policy*

A policy document lists some permissions and the policy document for an IAM role to use Docker for AWS may be obtained from `https://docs.docker.com/docker-for-aws/iam-permissions/`. Click on Validate Policy to validate the policy, as shown in Figure 14-13.

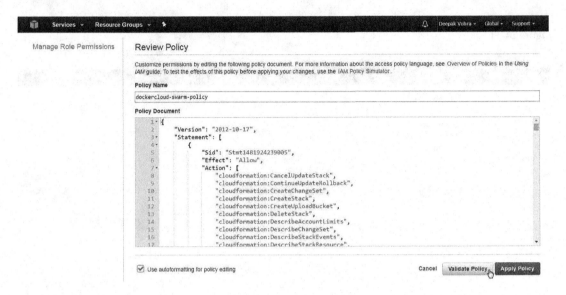

Figure 14-13. *Validating the policy*

Click on Apply Policy, as shown in Figure 14-14.

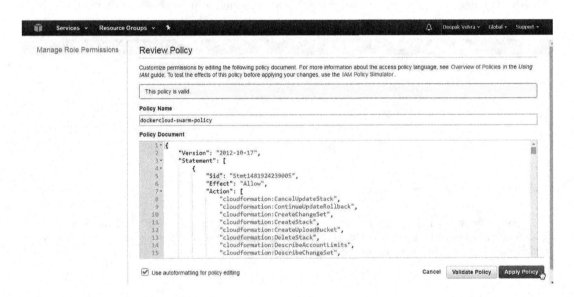

Figure 14-14. *Applying the policy*

A new inline policy is added for the `dockercloud-swarm-role` role, as shown in Figure 14-15.

Figure 14-15. *The new inline policy is added*

Copy the Role ARN String listed in Figure 14-16, as we need the ARN string to connect to the AWS Cloud provider from Docker Cloud.

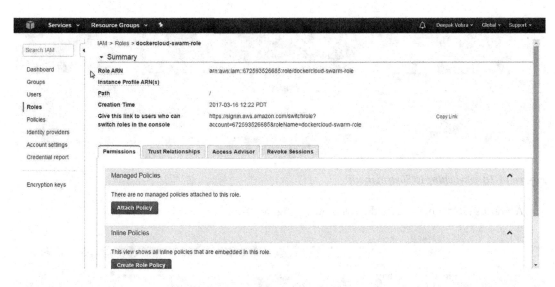

Figure 14-16. *Role ARN*

Creating a Docker Swarm in Docker Cloud

In this section, we create a Docker Swarm from the Docker Cloud service. Log in to the Docker Cloud service at https://cloud.docker.com/. The Cloud registry page should be displayed at https://cloud.docker.com/app/dvohra/dashboard/onboarding/cloud-registry. A Swarm Mode option is available in the margin and it's off by default, as shown in Figure 14-17.

Figure 14-17. *The Swarm Mode slider*

Click on the Swarm Mode slider; the Swarm mode should be enabled, as shown in Figure 14-18.

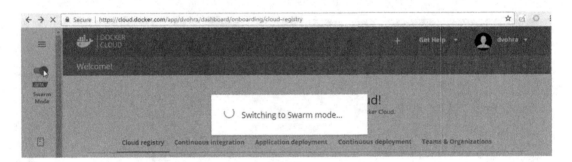

Figure 14-18. *Switching to Swarm mode*

A Swarms toolbar option is added, as shown in Figure 14-19.

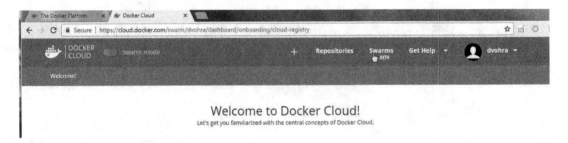

Figure 14-19. *Swarms toolbar option*

Two options are available—Bring Your Own Swarm or Create a New Swarm. Click on Create to create a new Swarm, as shown in Figure 14-20.

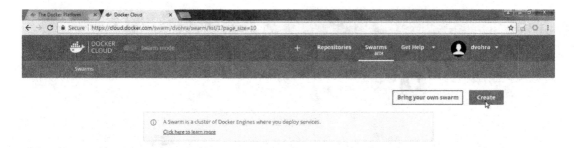

Figure 14-20. *Creating a new Swarm*

Next, we will configure the Swarm, including specifying a Swarm name, selecting a cloud provider, and selecting cloud provider options. Two Cloud service providers are supported: Amazon Web Services (AWS) and Microsoft Azure (not yet available). We use AWS in this chapter. We need to configure the cloud settings for AWS with the ARN string we copied earlier. Cloud settings may be configured with one of the two options. One option is to select Cloud Settings from the account, as shown in Figure 14-21.

Figure 14-21. *Cloud settings*

In the Cloud Settings page, click on the plug icon that says Connect Provider for the Amazon Web Services provider, as shown in Figure 14-22.

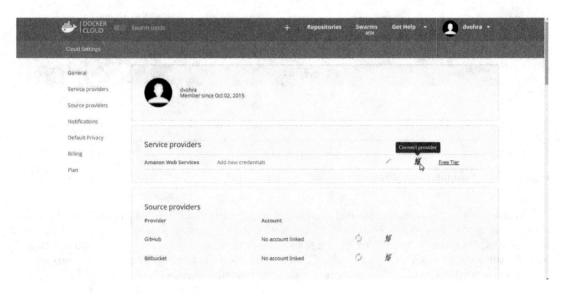

Figure 14-22. *Connecting the provider*

The Add AWS Credentials dialog is displayed, as shown in Figure 14-23.

Figure 14-23. *Adding AWS credentials*

The other option to configure the Cloud settings is to click on the Amazon Web Service Service Provider icon, as shown in Figure 14-24, which also displays the Add AWS Credentials dialog.

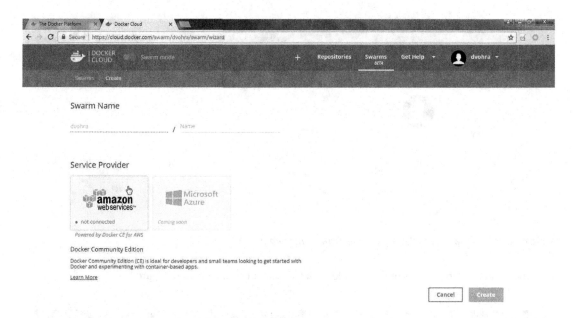

Figure 14-24. *Connecting to an Amazon web services provider*

Specify the ARN string copied earlier from the Add AWS Credentials dialog and click on Save, as shown in Figure 14-25.

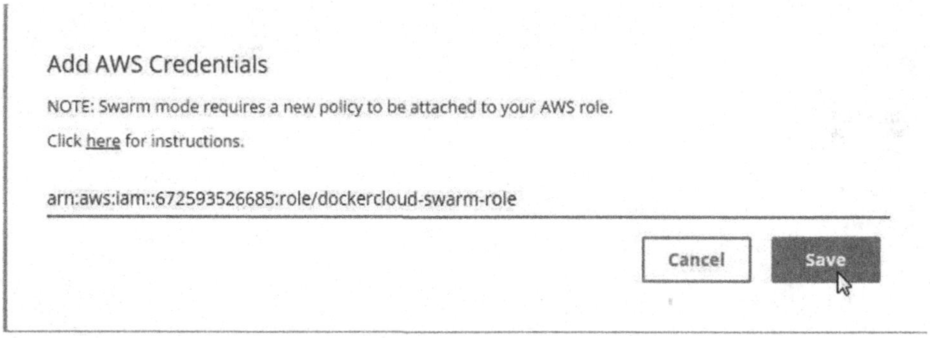

Figure 14-25. *Saving the AWS credentials*

With either option, the service provider Amazon Web Services should be connected, as indicated by the Connect Provider icon turning to Connected, as shown in Figure 14-26.

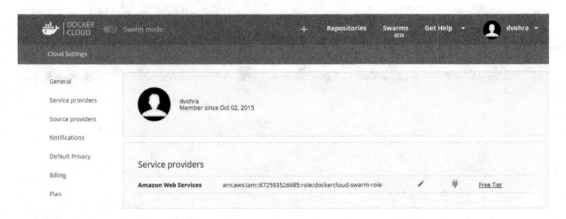

Figure 14-26. *Amazon Web Services provider in connected mode*

The Amazon Web Services option should indicate connected, as shown in Figure 14-27.

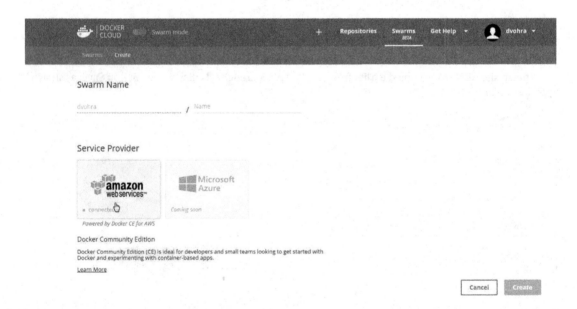

Figure 14-27. *Amazon Web Services provider connected*

Specify a Swarm name. That name should not include any spaces, capitalized letters, or special characters other than ",", "-" and "_", as shown in Figure 14-28.

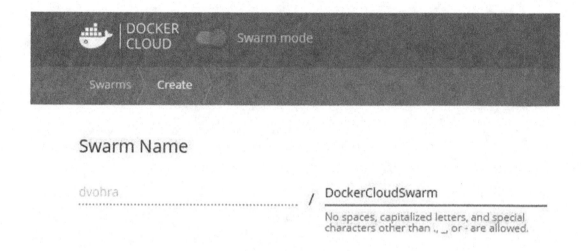

Figure 14-28. *Specifying a Swarm name*

Specify a valid Swarm name (docker-cloud-swarm), select the Amazon Web Services Service provider, which is already connected, and click on Create, as shown in Figure 14-29.

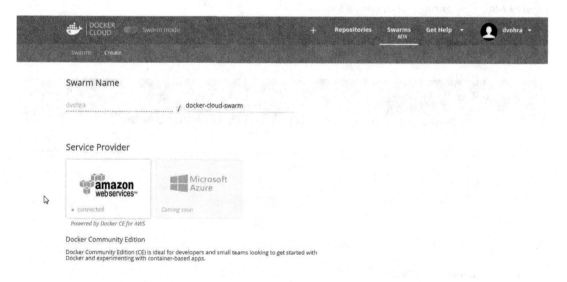

Figure 14-29. *Creating a Docker Swarm using the AWS service provider*

In the region, select a region (us-east-2), the number of Swarm managers (3), the number of Swarm workers (5), the Swarm manager instance type (t2.micro), the agent worker instance type (t2.micro), and the SSH key. Click on Create, as shown in Figure 14-30.

Region

```
us-east-2                                          ▼
```

Region where your swarm is provisioned

Swarm Size

Number of Swarm managers?   Number of Swarm worker nodes?

```
3        ▼
```
```
5        ▲▼
```

Number of swarm manager nodes needs to be an odd number   Number of swarm worker nodes (0 - 1000)

Swarm Properties

Swarm manager instance type?   Agent worker instance type?

```
t2.micro                                 ▼
```
```
t2.micro                                 ▼
```

EC2 HVM instance type (t2.micro, m3.medium, etc)   EC2 HVM instance type (t2.micro, m3.medium, etc)

Which ssh key to use?

```
docker                                   ▼
```

Name of an existing EC2 KeyPair to enable SSH access to the instance

Cancel   Create

Figure 14-30. *Configuring and creating a Swarm*

The Swarm should start to get deployed, as indicated by the DEPLOYING message shown in Figure 14-31.

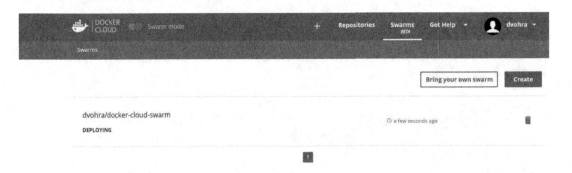

Figure 14-31. *Deploying a Swarm*

When the Swarm has been deployed, the message becomes Deployed, as shown in Figure 14-32.

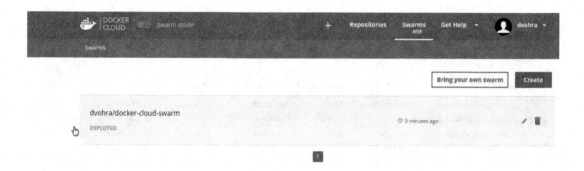

Figure 14-32. *The Swarm is now deployed*

The AWS infrastructure for the Swarm is created and configured. A CloudFormation stack is created, as shown in Figure 14-33.

Figure 14-33. *CloudFormation stack for the created Swarm*

A new proxy AWS IAM role for the Swarm is added, as shown in Figure 14-34.

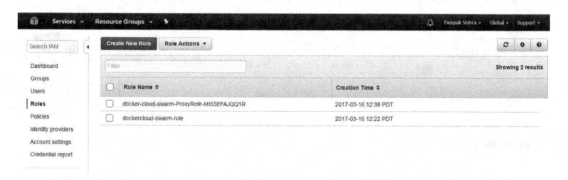

Figure 14-34. *Proxy role and Docker Cloud Swarm AWS role*

EC2 instances for the Swarm manager and worker nodes are started. Each EC2 instance is started with the proxy IAM role created automatically, as shown for a manager node in Figure 14-35.

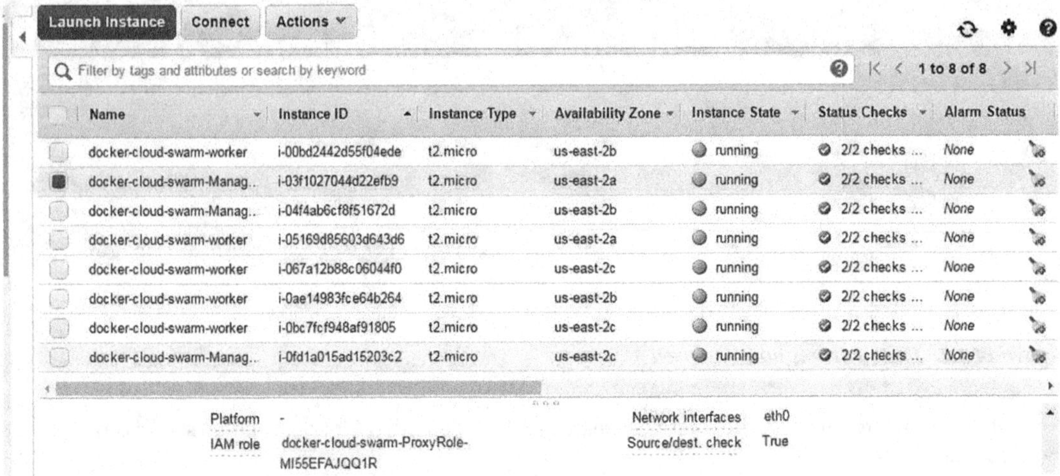

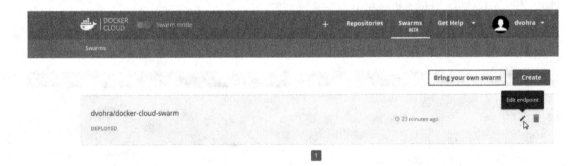

Figure 14-35. IAM role for EC2 instances

Each Docker Cloud account namespace must be associated with only one AWS IAM role. If multiple Docker Cloud accounts are to access the same AWS account, multiple roles must be created for each Docker Cloud account or Docker Cloud account namespace. Each AWS IAM role for Docker Cloud to access AWS is associated with an ARN string. The ARN string for a deployed Swarm may be edited with the Edit Endpoint link, as shown in Figure 14-36.

Figure 14-36. Edit Endpoint link

If the Swarm endpoint is to be modified, specify a new ARN string (for a different IAM role associated with a different Docker Cloud namespace) in the Edit Endpoint dialog. Click on Save, as shown in Figure 14-37.

Figure 14-37. Editing the endpoint

Next, we connect to the Docker Swarm. There are two ways to do so:

- Connect directly from any Docker host

- Obtain the public IP address of a Swarm manager from the EC2 dashboard and SSH login to the Swarm manager

We discuss each of these options.

Connecting to the Docker Swarm from a Docker Host

Click on the Docker Swarm in the Docker Cloud dashboard. The Connect To dialog should be displayed with a docker run command, as shown in Figure 14-38. Copy the docker run command.

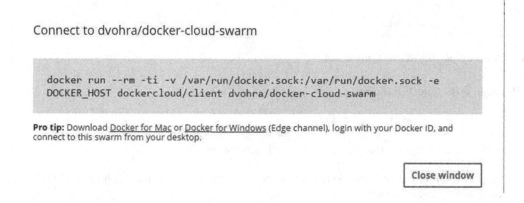

Figure 14-38. Listing and copying the docker run command to connect to the Swarm

Start an EC2 instance with CoreOS AMI, which has Docker pre-installed, as shown in Figure 14-39.

Figure 14-39. *Creating an EC2 instance with CoreOS AMI*

Obtain the public IP address of the CoreOS instance from the EC2 console, as shown in Figure 14-40.

Figure 14-40. *Displaying EC2 instance detail*

SSH login to the CoreOS instance.

```
ssh -i "coreos.pem" core@34.207.220.127
```

Run the command copied earlier to connect to the Docker Swarm.

```
docker run --rm -ti -v /var/run/docker.sock:/var/run/docker.sock -e DOCKER_HOST dockercloud/
client dvohra/docker-cloud-swarm
```

The dockercloud/client Docker image that's used to connect to Docker Cloud is downloaded. A username and password prompt should be displayed. Specify the username and password for the Docker Cloud account in which the Swarm was created.

```
Container Linux by CoreOS stable (1298.5.0)

$ docker run --rm -ti -v /var/run/docker.sock:/var/run/docker.sock -e DOCKER_HOST
dockercloud/client dvohra/docker-cloud-swarm
Unable to find image 'dockercloud/client:latest' locally
latest: Pulling from dockercloud/client
b7f33ccOb4Be: Pull complete
91b7430c5c68: Pull complete
b686674c0e39: Pull complete
l9aaa3õbba7a: Pull complete
Digest: sha2S6: 11d3cc5e1a62c7324]2a6e038]ccffi9]53tc91d0b1c69c8D1d3b68629337558a6
Status: Downloaded newer image for dockercloud/client:latest
Use your Docker ID credentials to authenticate:
Username: dvohra
Password:
```

A export command is output to connect to the Swarm. Copy the command.

```
Use your Docker ID credentials to authenticate:
Username: dvohra
Password:
=> You can now start using the swarm dvohra/docker-cloud-swarm by executing:
export DOCKER_HOST=tcp://127.0.0.1:32768
```

Run the command. The Swarm is connected to the CoreOS Docker host. List the Swarm nodes using the docker node ls command.

```
>export DOCKER_HOST=tcp://127.0.0.1:32768

>docker node ls
ID HOSTNAME STATUS AVAILABILITY MANAGER STATUS

liuomlmb6n6xtq4apxayumsx3 ip-172-31-0-251.us-east-2.cornpute.internal. Ready Active
bchea5x85m82jtzoq336trn8y ip-172-31-47-61.us-east-2.compute.internat. Ready Active
e2bl785z5pqouakdceomdpsbi ip-172-31-42-130.us-east-2.compute.internal. Ready Active
hzxb8choml.7gylaqtrjrh6phx ip-172-31-26-90.us-east-2.compute.internal. Ready Active
pcnple9l29w88ueonhdwUcoc ip-172-31-27-18.us-east-2.compute.internal. Ready Active
rupjaojommfchjgcshffdobhf * ip-172-31-10-153.us-east-2.compute.internal Ready Active Leader
uyl5xv7mhb6c8jam5ofncplyh ip-172-31-25-137.us-east-2.compute.internal. Ready Active Reachable
wi6zurda4nawf9mgku3enf6io ip-172-31-34-33.us-east-2.cornpute.internal Ready Active Reachable
```

Connecting to the Docker Swarm from a Swarm Manager

The other option is to connect to a Swarm manager using its public IP address. First, we obtain the public IP address of a Swarm manager from the EC2 console, as shown in Figure 14-41.

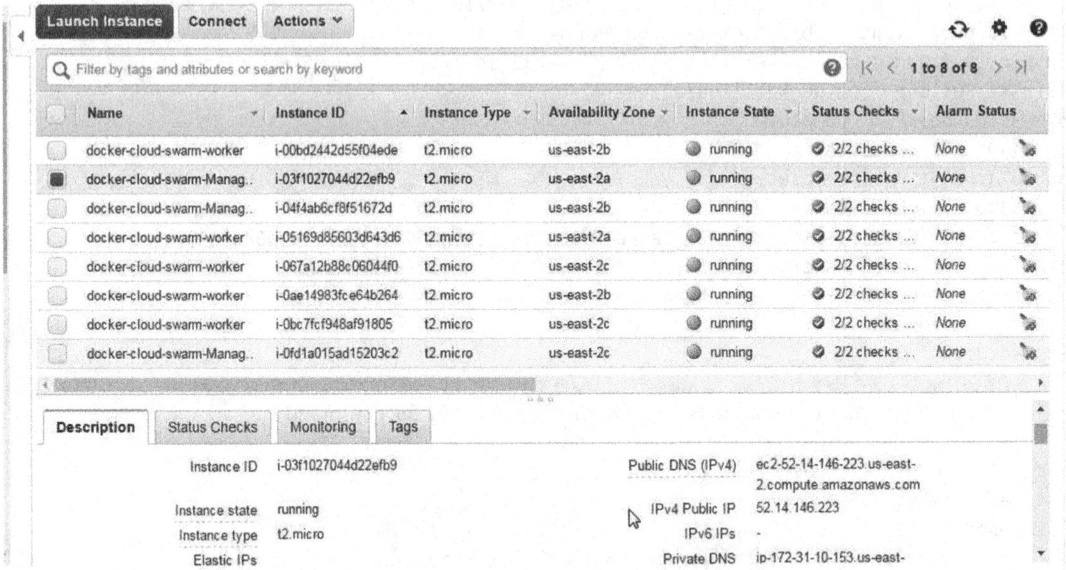

Figure 14-41. *Obtaining the public IP of a Swarm manager*

SSH login into the Swarm manager.

```
ssh -i "docker.pem" docker@52.14.146.223
```

The Swarm manager is logged in and the Swarm command prompt is displayed.

```
[root@1ocathost ~]# ssh -i "docker.pem" docker@52.14.146.223
The authenticity of host 52.14.146.223 (52.14.146.223)1 cant be established.
RSA key fingerprint is e9:7f:d2:3c:de:6d:5d:94:06:e2:09:56:b7:2a:c6:9a.
Are you sure you want to continue connecting (yes/no)? yes
Warning: Permanently added '52.14.146.223 (RSA) to the list of known hosts.
Welcome to Docker!
```

List the Swarm nodes using the docker node ls command.

```
Welcome to Docker!

~ $ docker node l.s

ID HOSTNAME STATUS

AVAILABILITY MANAGER STATUS

liuomlmb6n6xtq4apxayumsx3 ip-172-31-0-251.us-east-2.compute.internal Ready Active

bchea5x85m82jtzoq336trn8y ip-172-31-47-61.us-east-2.cornpute.internal Ready Active

e2bl785z5pqouakdceonìdpsbi ip-172-31-42-130.us-east-2.compute.internal Ready Active

hzxb8chomt7gyl.aqtrj rh6phx ip-172-31-26-90.us-east-2.compute.interna1 Ready Active

pcnple9l29w88ueenhdwflcoc ip-172-31-27-18.us-east-2.compute.internal Ready Active

rupjaejommfchjgcshffdobhf * ip-172-31-10-153.us-east-2.compute.internal. Ready Active Leader

uyl5xv7mhb6c8jain5ofncplyh ip-172-31-25-137.us-east-2.compute.internal. Ready Active Reachable

wi6zurda4nawf9mgku3enf6ie ip-172-31-34-33.us-east-2.compute.internal Ready Active Reachab1e
```

Create a service using the docker service create command and list the service with docker service ls.

```
docker service create \
  --name hello-world \
  --publish 8080:80 \
  --replicas 1 \
  tutum/hello-world
```

The hello-world service is created. A Docker Cloud server proxy service is also listed.

```
~ $ docker service create \

> --name hello-world \

> --publish 8080:80 \

> - - replicas 1 \

> tutum/hello-world

hbiejbua8u5øskabun3dzkxk4

~ $ docker service 1s

ID NAME MODE REPLICAS IMAGE

Ogzua3p56myx dockerdoud-server-proxy global 3/3 dockercioud/server-proxy:latest

hbiejbua8u5O hello-world replicated 1/1 tutum/hello-world:latest
```

293

Bringing a Swarm into Docker Cloud

Docker Cloud Swarm mode also has the provision to import an existing Swarm into Docker Cloud. The Swarm to be imported must have the following prerequisites:

- Based on Docker Engine 1.13 or later nodes
- Swarm manager incoming port 2376 unblocked

In this section, we create a Swarm and import the Swarm into Docker Cloud. First, run the docker --version command to determine if the Docker host version is 1.13 or later. One of the EC2 instances provisioned by Docker for AWS may be used to create and import a Swarm, as the Docker version on the custom Linux distribution is > Docker 1.13; the node must be made to leave the Swarm before creating a new Swarm. Using the private IP address of the EC2 instance, initiate a new Swarm.

```
docker swarm init --advertise-addr 172.31.23.196
```

Copy the docker swarm join command output to join the worker nodes.

```
~ $ docker --version

Docker version 17.03.0-ce, build 60ccb22

~ $ docker swarm init --advertise-addr 172.31.23.196

Swarm initialized: current node (ylzc3h3slx05ztbujtl3yf86p) is now a manager.

To add a worker to this swarm, run the following command:

docker swarm join \

--token SWMTKN-1-23snf1iuieafnyd1zzgf37ucwuz1.khg9atqsmysmvv6iw1.arw0-do29n83jptkkdwss5fjsd3rt \

172.31.23.196:2377

To add a manager to this swarm, run 'docker swarm join-token manager' and follow the
instructions.
```

Join a worker node on another EC2 instance with Docker 1.13 or later.

```
docker swarm join \
    --token SWMTKN-1-61gcsgkr1ildxz580ftdl3rq0s9p7h30n12byktgvbd6y3dk7r-cpes7ofdsq8abhxtznh92tjrz \
    10.0.0.176:2377
```

The worker node joins the Swarm.

A Swarm with two nodes is created, as listed in the output to the docker node ls command, which runs on the Swarm manager node.

```
~$ docker node 1s

HOSTNAME STATUS

AVAILABILITY MANAGER STATUS

trgb2t4ehs2gp3cjbrnqhs7a5 ip-172-31-6-64.us-east-2.compute.internal. Ready Active

yl.ic3h3stxo5ztbujtl3yf86p ip-172-31-23-196.us-east-2.compute.internal Ready Active Leader

~$
```

Next, import the Swarm into Docker Cloud. From the Swarm manager node, run the following command.

```
docker run -ti --rm -v /var/run/docker.sock:/var/run/docker.sock dockercloud/registration
```

Specify the Docker ID at the username prompt and the password at the password prompt.

```
~ S docker run -ti --rm -v /var/run/docker.sock:/var/run/docker.sock dockercloud/
registration
Unable to find image dockercloud/registration:latest' locally
latest: Pulling from dockercloud/registration
b7f33ccOb48e: Pull complete
b52875cf8fd4: Pull complete
23f82c866468: Pull complete
Digest: sha256: a3f39de96d2763b957e7bel22ce99b8lfbba03fbd6b2e54bd607lcafbelcabcl
Status: Downloaded newer image for dockercloud/registration:latest
Use your Docker ID credentials to authenticate:
Username: dvohra
Password:
```

Specify a cluster name for the Swarm imported into Docker Cloud, or use the default. Specify cluster as dvohra/dockercloudswarm. The Swarm is registered with Docker Cloud. As for a Swarm created in the Docker Cloud Swarm mode, the Swarm may be accessed from any Docker host for which a command is output.

```
Enter name for the new cluster [dvohra/wkhøtlq8cw5u44x22qp6r4eau]: dvohra/dockercloudswarm

You can now access this cluster using the following command in any Docker Engine

docker run -rm -ti -v /var/run/docker.sock:/var/run/docker.sock -e DOCKER HOST dockerctoud/
client dvohra/dockerctoudswarm
```

To bring the Swarm into Docker Cloud, click on the Bring Your Own Swarm button in Swarm mode, as shown in Figure 14-42.

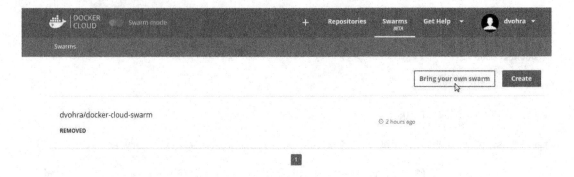

Figure 14-42. *Bring your own Swarm*

The Swarm registered with Docker Cloud is added to the Docker Cloud Swarms, as shown in Figure 14-43.

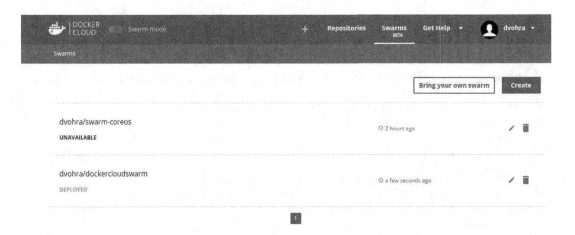

Figure 14-43. *Docker Cloud Swarms, including the imported Swarm*

Summary

This chapter introduced the Docker Cloud Swarm mode, which is a managed service for linking the Docker Cloud managed service to a AWS service provider account and provisioning a Swarm from Docker Cloud. A Swarm created on the command line can be imported into Docker Cloud. In the next chapter we discuss Docker service stacks.

CHAPTER 15

Using Service Stacks

The Docker Swarm mode is Docker-native as of Docker 1.12 and is used to create distributed and scalable services for developing Docker applications.

The Problem

While single Docker image applications are also commonly used, a vast majority of Docker enterprise applications are comprised of multiple images that have dependencies between them. Docker Compose (standalone in v1 and v2) could be used to declare dependencies between microservices using the links and depends_on options, but Compose (standalone) is archaic, other than the format for defining services, in the context of Swarm mode services.

The Solution

Docker Swarm mode has introduced service *stacks* to define a collection of services (Swarm mode services) that are automatically linked with each other to provide a logical grouping of services with dependencies between them. Stacks use stack files that are YAML files in a format very much like the docker-compose.yml format. There are a few differences such as the absence of links and depends_on options that were used to define dependencies between microservices in Docker Compose (standalone). YAML (http://www.yaml.org/) is a data serialization format commonly used for configuration files.

As of Docker v1.13, the docker stack subset of commands has been introduced to create a Docker stack. Using a *stack file* that defines multiple services, including services' configuration such as environment variables, labels, number of containers, and volumes, a single docker stack deploy command creates a service stack, as illustrated in Figure 15-1. The services are automatically linked to each other.

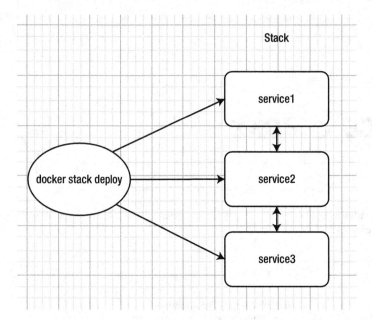

Figure 15-1. *Service stack created with the docker stack deploy command*

Docker Compose versions 3.x and later are fully Docker Swarm mode compatible, which implies that a Docker Compose v3.x docker-compose.yml file could be used as a Stack file except for a few sub-options (including build, container_name, external_links, and links) that are not supported in a stack file. Docker Compose 3.x could still be used standalone to develop non-Swarm mode services, but those microservices are not usable or scalable with the Docker Swarm mode docker service group of commands.

To use stacks to manage Swarm mode services, the following requirements must be applied.

- Docker version must be 1.13 or later

- Swarm mode must be enabled

- Stack file YAML format must be based on Docker Compose v3.x file format

To use service stacks, the Docker Compose version 3 YAML file format is used, but Docker Compose is not required to be installed.

When using Docker Swarm mode, the Docker version requirement for Swarm mode is 1.12 or later. Before developing stacks to manage Swarm mode services, verify that the Docker version is at least 1.13. The Docker version used in this chapter is 17.0x. The docker stack group of commands listed in Table 15-1 becomes available in Docker v1.13 and later.

Table 15-1. *The docker stack Commands*

Command	Description
deploy	Deploys a service stack or updates an existing stack
ls	Lists the stacks
ps	Lists the Swarm mode tasks in a stack
rm	Removes a stack
services	Lists the Swarm mode services in a stack

Run the docker --version command to list the Docker version. To list the commands for stack usage, run the docker stack command.

```
[root@localhost ~]# ssh -i "docker.pem" docker@34.205.43.53
Welcome to Docker!
~ $ docker --version
Docker version 17.06.0-ce, build 02c1d87
~ $ docker stack

Usage:    docker stack COMMAND

Manage Docker stacks

Options:
      --help    Print usage

Commands:
  deploy      Deploy a new stack or update an existing stack
  ls          List stacks
  ps          List the tasks in the stack
  rm          Remove one or more stacks
  services    List the services in the stack
```

To use stacks, the following procedure is used.

1. Install Docker version 1.13 or later (not Docker version 1.12, which is used in several of the earlier chapters).

2. Enable Swarm mode.

3. Create a Stack file using Docker Compose (version 3.x) YAML format.

4. Use the docker stack group of commands to create and manage the stack.

The chapter creates a service stack consisting of two services, one for a WordPress blog and another for a MySQL database to store the data in the WordPress blog.

Setting the Environment

We use Docker for AWS available at https://docs.docker.com/docker-for-aws/ to launch a Docker Swarm mode cluster of nodes. Docker for AWS uses the AWS CloudFormation template to create a Docker Swarm mode cluster. Click on the Deploy Docker Community Edition (stable), shown in Figure 15-2, to launch a Create CloudFormation Stack wizard to create a Docker Swarm mode cluster.

Deploy Docker Community Edition [CE] for AWS [stable]	Deploy Docker Community Edition [CE] for AWS [edge]	Deploy Docker Community Edition [CE] for AWS [test]

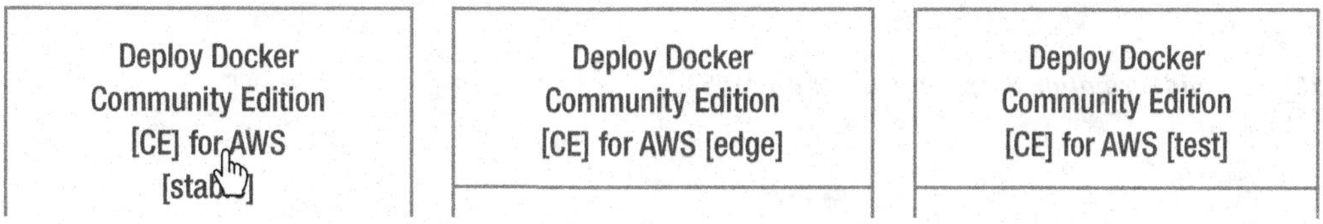

Figure 15-2. *Deploying the Docker Community Edition for AWS (stable)*

299

Configure a Swarm using the Create Stack wizard as discussed in Chapter 3. You can specify the number of swarm managers to be 1, 3, or 5 and the number of Swarm worker nodes to be 1-1000. We used one Swarm manager node and two Swarm worker nodes, as shown in Figure 15-3.

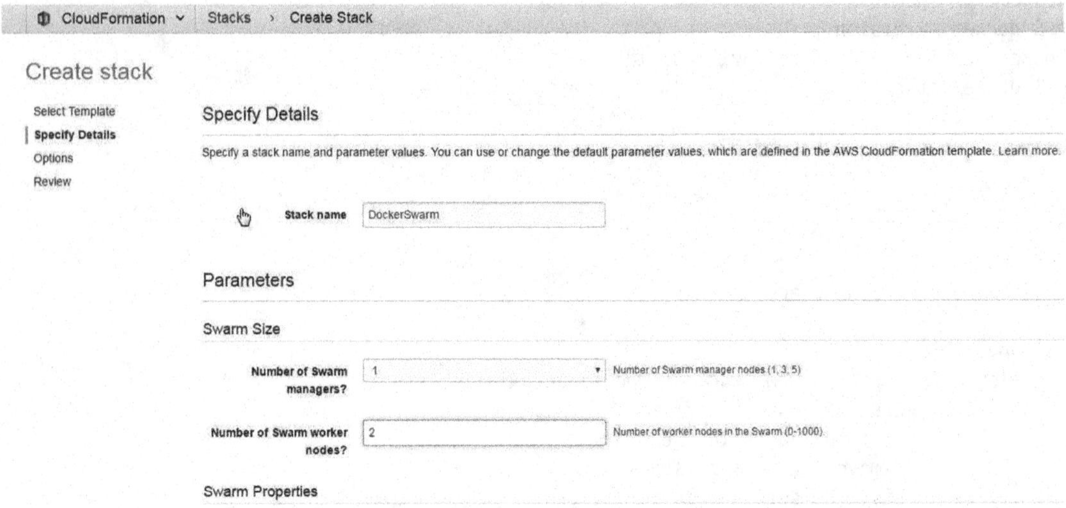

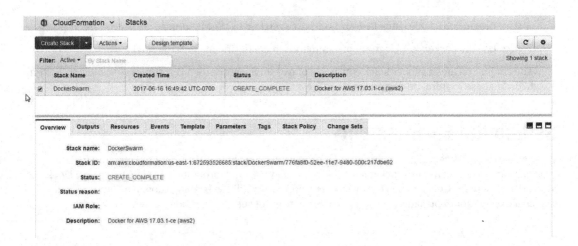

Figure 15-3. *Configuring a CloudFormation stack*

The CloudFormation stack is created, as shown in Figure 15-4.

Figure 15-4. *CloudFormation Stack for Docker on AWS*

Three EC2 instances—one for Docker Swarm manager node and two for the Swarm worker nodes—are launched, as shown in Figure 15-5. The Linux distribution used by the CloudFormation stack is Moby Linux, as shown in Figure 15-5.

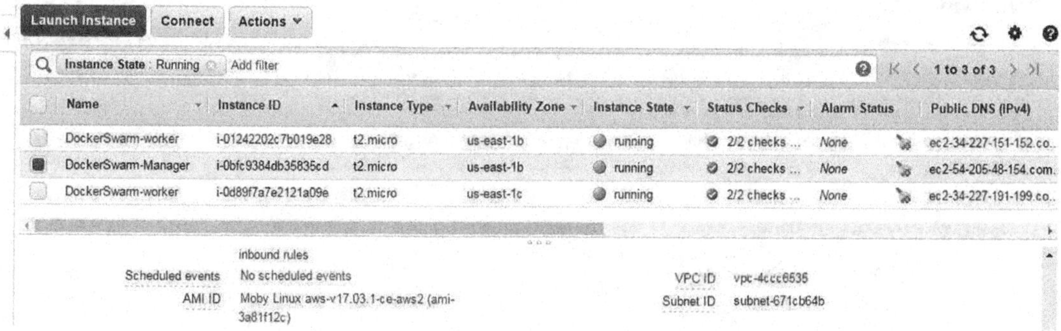

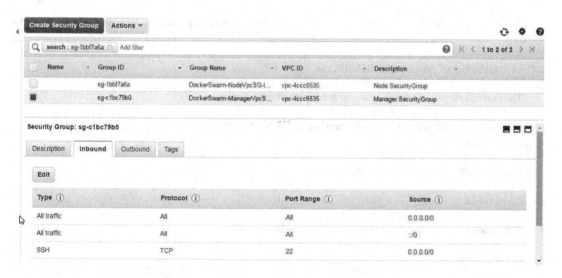

Figure 15-5. *The Moby Linux AMI used for Docker on AWS*

Before being able to use Docker on AWS, enable all inbound/outbound traffic between the EC2 instances in the security groups used by the EC2 instances. This is shown for the security group for Swarm manager node instance inbound rules in Figure 15-6.

Figure 15-6. *The security group inbound rules are enabled for all traffic*

SSH login into the Swarm manager EC2 instance and obtain the public IP address from the AWS management console, as shown in Figure 15-7.

Figure 15-7. *Public IP address*

Using the key pair used to create the CloudFormation stack SSH login into the Swarm manager instance.

```
ssh -i "docker.pem" docker@54.205.48.154
```

The command prompt for the Swarm manager node is displayed.

```
[root@localhost ~]# ssh -i "docker.pem" docker@54.205.48.154
Welcome to Docker!
```

List the nodes in the Swarm mode.

```
docker node ls
```

Three nodes, one manager and two workers, are listed.

```
~ $ docker node ls
ID                           HOSTNAME                      STATUS  AVAILABILITY  MANAGER
                                                                                 STATUS
bf4ifhh86sivqp03ofzhk6c46    ip-172-31-21-175.ec2.internal Ready   Active
ozdhl0jtnricny1y95xbnhwtq    ip-172-31-37-108.ec2.internal Ready   Active
ud2js50r4livrqf3f4l30fv9r *  ip-172-31-19-138.ec2.internal Ready   Active        Leader
```

Test the Swarm mode by creating and listing a Hello World service.

```
docker service create --replicas 2 --name helloworld alpine ping docker.com
```

```
docker service ls
```

The docker service commands output indicates a Docker Swarm service, so it's created and listed.

```
~ $ docker service create --replicas 2 --name helloworld alpine ping docker.com
q05fef2a7cf98cv4r2ziyccnv

~ $ docker service ls
ID              NAME          MODE          REPLICAS      IMAGE           PORTS
q05fef2a7cf9    helloworld    replicated    2/2           alpine:latest
~ $
```

Configuring a Service Stack

To create a service stack consisting of two services, one for a WordPress blog and another for MySQL database, create a stack file using the Docker Compose version 3 YAML format (https://docs.docker.com/compose/compose-file/). Create a docker-cloud.yml stack file (the filename is arbitrary) to specify two services (web and mysql) using Docker images wordpress and mysql respectively. Set the environment variables for the Docker images. The only environment variable required to be set is MYSQL_ROOT_PASSWORD for the mysql Docker image. The WORDPRESS_DB_PASSWORD environment variable for the wordpress Docker image defaults to the MYSQL_ROOT_PASSWORD, but may also be set explicitly to the same value as the MYSQL_ROOT_PASSWORD. Some of the other environment variables used by the wordpress Docker image are listed in Table 15-2.

Table 15-2. *Environment Variables for the Docker Image WordPress*

Environment Variable	Description	Default Value
WORDPRESS_DB_HOST	The linked database host, which is assumed to be MySQL database by default.	The IP and port of the linked mysql Docker container
WORDPRESS_DB_USER	The database user.	root
WORDPRESS_DB_PASSWORD	The database password.	MYSQL_ROOT_PASSWORD
WORDPRESS_DB_NAME	The database name. The database is created if it does not already exist.	wordpress
WORDPRESS_TABLE_PREFIX	Table prefix.	""

If we were to create a WordPress blog using the wordpress and mysql images with the docker run command, we would create Docker containers for each of the Docker images separately and link the containers using the -link option. If we were to use Docker Compose (standalone), we would need to add a links or depends_on sub-option in the Docker Compose file.

303

Next, specify the Docker images and environment variables to the stack file for creating a service stack. To use the Docker Compose YAML file format for Swarm mode stacks, specify the version in the stack file as 3 or a later version such as 3.1. The docker-cloud.yml file is listed:

```
version: '3'
services:
 web:
  image: wordpress
  links:
   - mysql
  environment:
   - WORDPRESS_DB_PASSWORD="mysql"
  ports:
   - "8080:80"
 mysql:
  image: mysql:latest
  environment:
   - MYSQL_ROOT_PASSWORD="mysql"
   - MYSQL_DATABASE="mysqldb"
```

The ports mapping of 8080:80 maps the WordPress Docker container port 80 to the host port 8080. Any stack file options, such as links that are included in the preceding listing that are not supported by docker stack deploy, are ignored when creating a stack. Store the preceding listing as docker-cloud.yml in the Swarm manager EC2 instance. Listing the files in Swarm manager should list the docker-cloud.yml file.

```
~ $ ls -l
total 4
-rwxr-x---   1 docker   docker         265 Jun 17 00:07 docker-cloud.yml
```

Having configured a stack file with two services, next we will create a service stack.

Creating a Stack

The docker stack deploy command is used to create and deploy a stack. It has the following syntax.

```
docker stack deploy [OPTIONS] STACK
```

The supported options are discussed in Table 15-3.

Table 15-3. *Options for the docker stack deploy Command*

Option	Description	Default Value
--bundle-file	Path to a Distributed Application Bundle file. An application bundle is created from a Docker Compose file just as a Docker image is created from a Dockerfile. An application bundle may be used to create stacks. Application bundles are an experimental feature at the time the chapter was developed and are not discussed in this chapter.	
--compose-file, -c	Path to stack file.	
--with-registry-auth	Whether to send registry authentication information to Swarm agents.	False

Using the stack file docker-cloud.yml, create a Docker stack called mysql with the docker stack deploy command.

```
docker stack deploy --compose-file docker-cloud.yml mysql
```

A Docker stack is created and the links option, which is not supported in Swarm mode, is ignored. Two Swarm services—mysql_mysql and mysql_web—are created in addition to a network mysql_default.

```
~ $ docker stack deploy --compose-file docker-cloud.yml mysql
Ignoring unsupported options: links

Creating network mysql_default
Creating service mysql_mysql
Creating service mysql_web
```

Listing Stacks

List the stacks with the following command.

```
docker stack ls
```

The mysql stack is listed. The number of services in the stack also are listed.

```
~ $ docker stack ls
NAME    SERVICES
mysql   2
```

Listing Services

List the services in the mysql stack using the docker stack services command, which has the following syntax.

```
docker stack services [OPTIONS] STACK
```

The supported options are listed in Table 15-4.

Table 15-4. *Options for the docker stack services Command*

Option	Description	Default Value
--filter, -f	Filters output based on filters (or conditions) provided	
--quiet, -q	Whether to display only the IDs of the services	false

To list all services, run the following command.

```
docker stack services  mysql
```

The two services—mysql_mysql and mysql_web—are listed.

```
~ $ docker stack services  mysql
ID              NAME          MODE         REPLICAS   IMAGE
ixvOykhuo14c   mysql_mysql   replicated   1/1        mysql:latest
vl7ph81hfxan   mysql_web     replicated   1/1        wordpress:latest
```

To filter the services, add the --filter option. To filter multiple services, add multiple --filter options, as shown in the following command.

```
docker stack services --filter name=mysql_web --filter name=mysql_mysql  mysql
```

The filtered stack services are listed. As both services are specified using –filter, both services are listed.

```
~ $ docker stack services --filter name=mysql_web --filter name=mysql_mysql mysql
l
ID              NAME          MODE         REPLICAS   IMAGE
ixvOykhuo14c   mysql_mysql   replicated   1/1        mysql:latest
vl7ph81hfxan   mysql_web     replicated   1/1        wordpress:latest
```

The services created by a stack are Swarm services and may also be listed using the following command.

```
docker service ls
```

The same two services are listed.

```
~ $ docker service ls
ID              NAME           MODE         REPLICAS  IMAGE
ixv0ykhuo14c    mysql_mysql    replicated   1/1       mysql:latest
sl2jmsat30ex    helloworld     replicated   2/2       alpine:latest
vl7ph81hfxan    mysql_web      replicated   1/1       wordpress:latest
```

Listing Docker Containers

The docker stack ps command is used to list the Docker containers in a stack and has the following syntax; output the command usage with the --help option.

```
~ $ docker stack ps --help
Usage:    docker stack ps [OPTIONS] STACK
List the tasks in the stack
Options:
  -f, --filter filter    Filter output based on conditions provided
      --help             Print usage
      --no-resolve       Do not map IDs to Names
      --no-trunc         Do not truncate output
```

To list all Docker containers in the mysql stack, run the following command.

```
docker stack ps mysql
```

By default, one replica is created for each service, so one Docker container for each service in the stack is listed. Both Docker containers are running on a Swarm worker node.

```
~ $ docker stack ps mysql
ID              NAME              IMAGE             NODE
DESIRED STATE   CURRENT STATE             ERROR   PORTS
n9oqwaikd61g    mysql_web.1       wordpress:latest  ip-172-31-37-108.ec2.internal
Running         Running 3 minutes ago
infzi7kxg9g9    mysql_mysql.1     mysql:latest      ip-172-31-37-108.ec2.internal
Running         Running 3 minutes ago
```

Using the −f option to filter the Docker containers to list only the mysql_web.1 container.

```
~ $ docker stack ps -f name=mysql_web.1 mysql
ID              NAME            IMAGE             NODE
DESIRED STATE   CURRENT STATE           ERROR   PORTS
n9oqwaikd61g    mysql_web.1     wordpress:latest  ip-172-31-37-108.ec2.internal
Running         Running 9 minutes ago
```

List all the running containers by setting the `desired-state` filter to running.

```
~ $ docker stack ps -f desired-state=running mysql
ID              NAME            IMAGE              NODE
DESIRED STATE   CURRENT STATE           ERROR   PORTS
n9oqwaikd61g    mysql_web.1     wordpress:latest   ip-172-31-37-108.ec2.internal
Running         Running 10 minutes ago
infzi7kxg9g9    mysql_mysql.1   mysql:latest       ip-172-31-37-108.ec2.internal
Running         Running 10 minutes ago
```

Using the Service Stack

Next, we use the stack to create a WordPress blog. The stack service called web may be accessed on port 8080 on the Swarm manager host. Obtain the public DNS of the Swarm manager node EC2 instance, as shown in Figure 15-8.

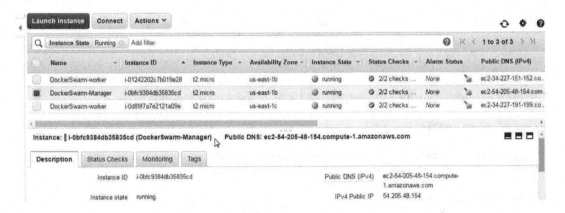

Figure 15-8. *Public DNS of Swarm manager*

Open the `<public dns>:8080` URL in a browser. The `<public dns>:8080/wp-admin/install.php` URL is displayed to start the WordPress installation. Select Continue. Specify a subtitle, username, password, e-mail, and whether to discourage search engines from indexing the website. Then click on Install WordPress, as shown in Figure 15-9.

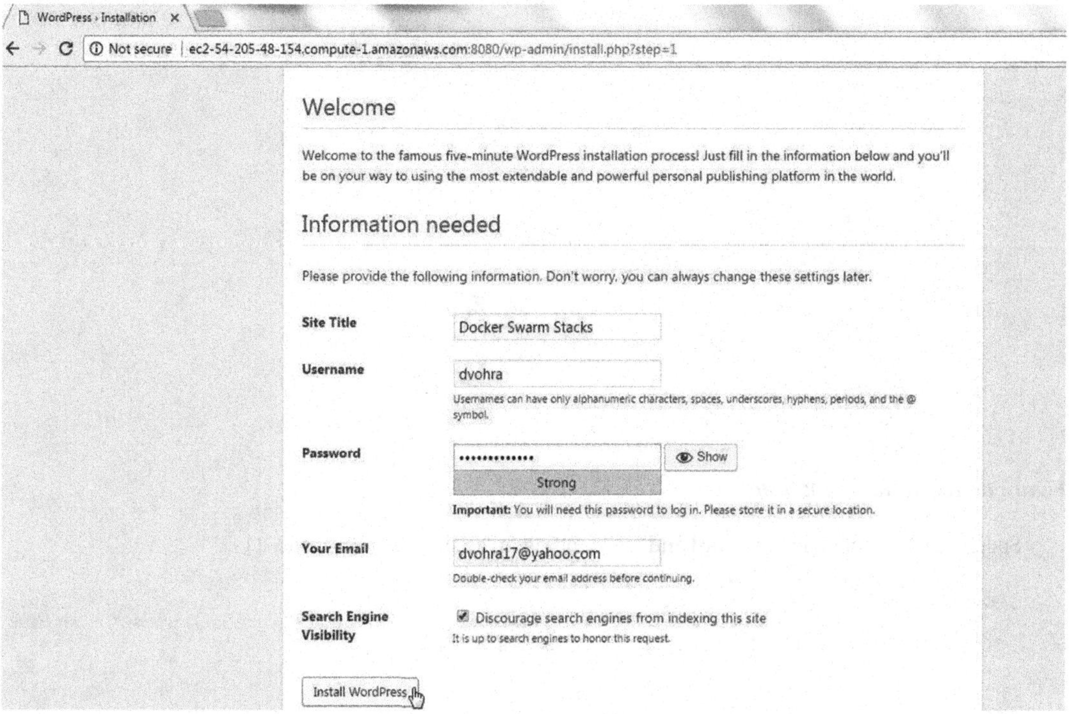

Figure 15-9. Installing WordPress

WordPress is installed, as shown in Figure 15-10. Click on Log In.

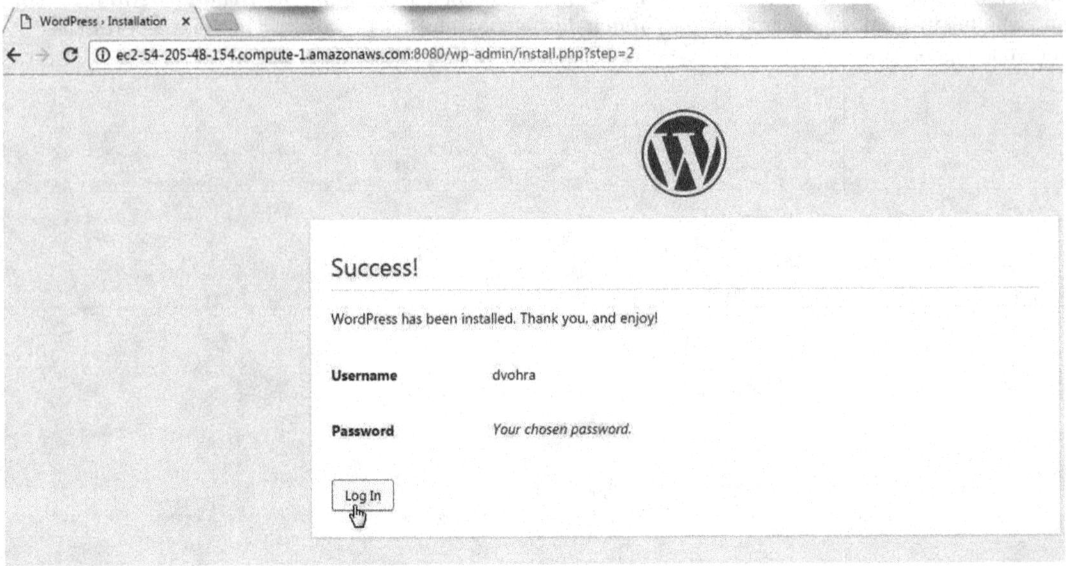

Figure 15-10. *WordPress is installed*

Specify a username and password and click on Log In, as shown in Figure 15-11.

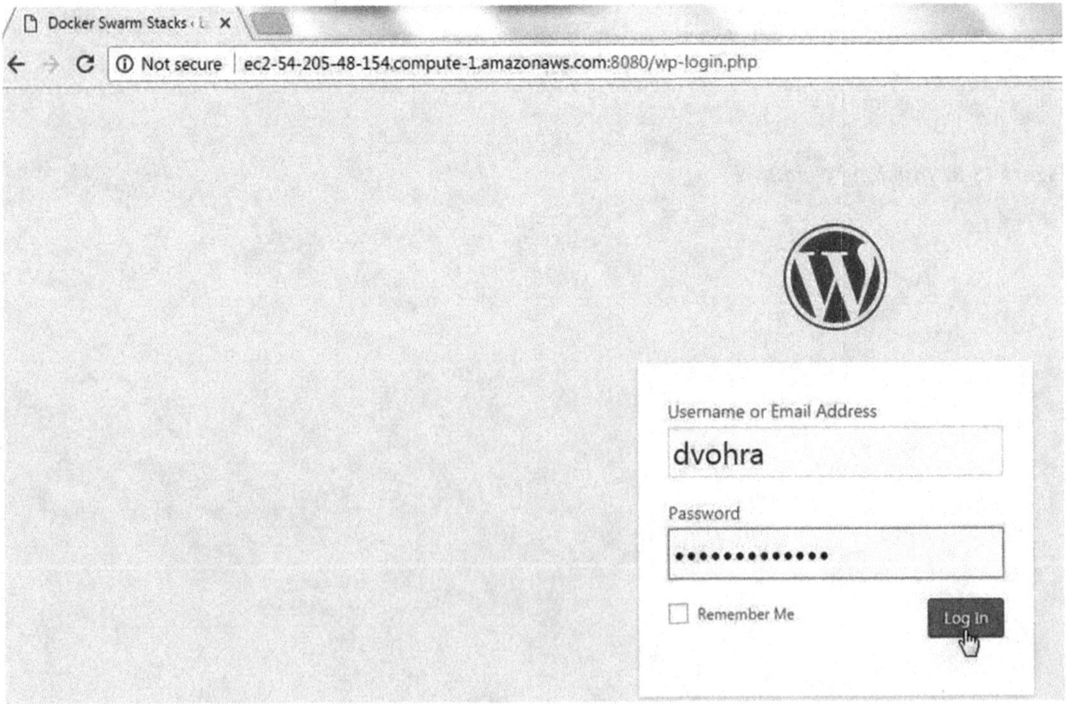

Figure 15-11. *Logging in*

The WordPress blog dashboard is displayed, as shown in Figure 15-12.

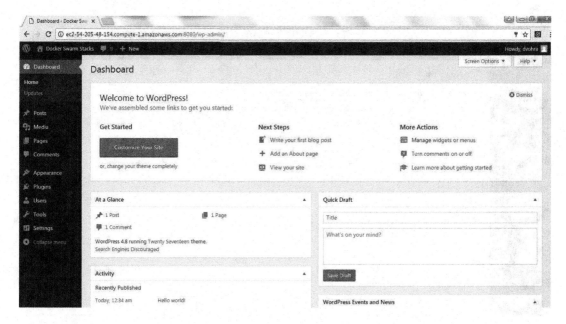

Figure 15-12. *The WordPress dashboard*

To add a new post, select Posts and click on Add New, as shown in Figure 15-13.

Figure 15-13. *Adding a new post*

In the Add New Post dialog, specify a title and add a blog entry. Click on Publish, as shown in Figure 15-14.

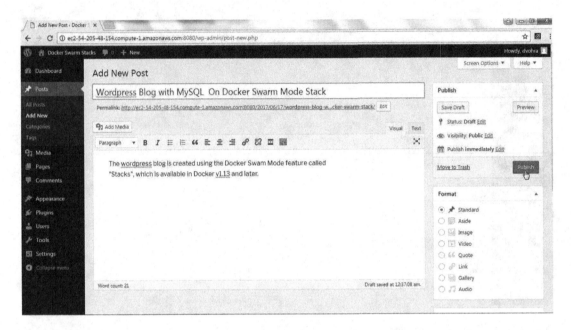

Figure 15-14. *Publishing a new post*

The new post is added. Click on View Post, as shown in Figure 15-15, to display the post.

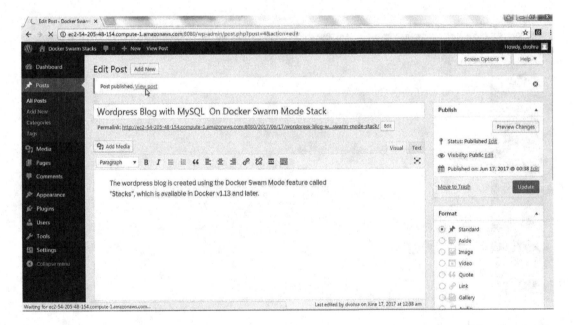

Figure 15-15. *Viewing the new post*

The blog post is displayed, as shown in Figure 15-16.

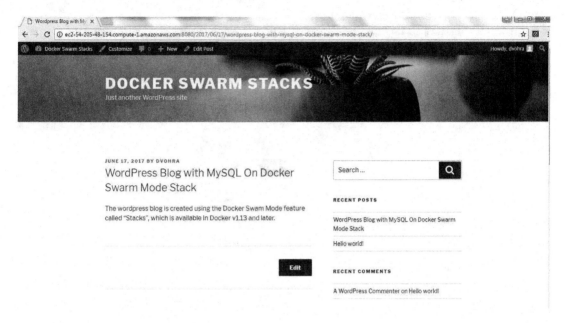

Figure 15-16. *Displaying a blog post*

Scroll down and add a comment, as shown in Figure 15-17.

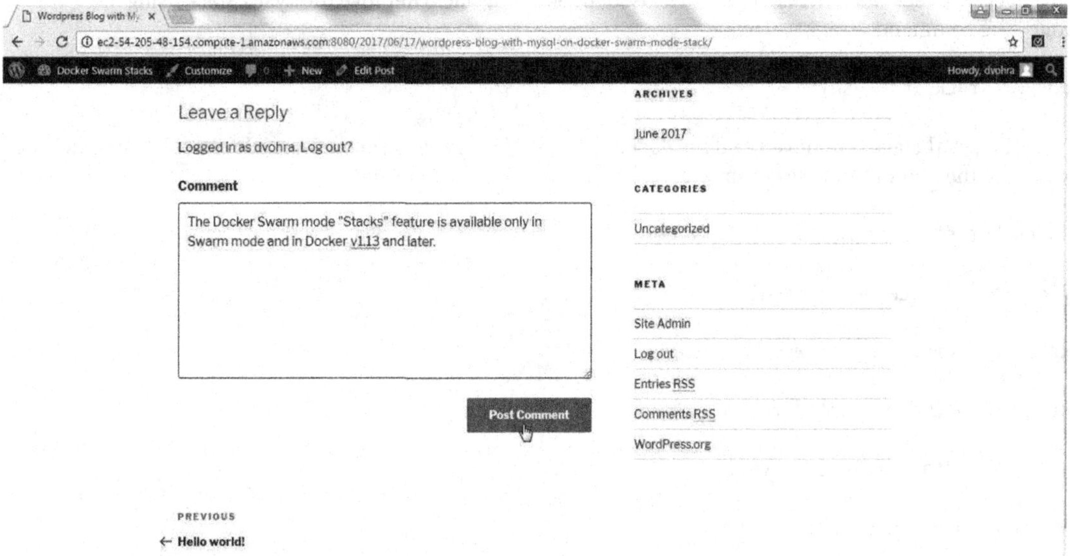

Figure 15-17. *Adding a comment*

The comment is added, as shown in Figure 15-18.

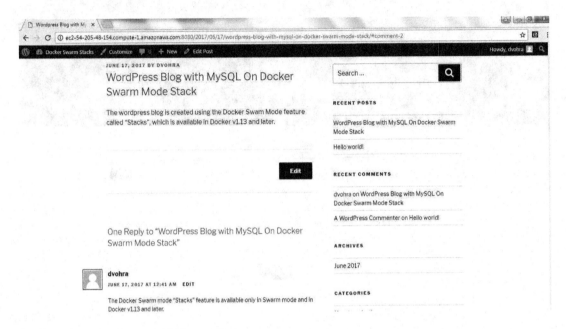

Figure 15-18. *The comment has been added*

Removing a Stack

The `docker stack rm STACK` command is used to remove a stack. Remove the `mysql` stack using the following command.

```
docker stack rm  mysql
```

The `mysql` stack is removed and the `docker stack service mysql` command does not list the stack, as shown in the output from the command.

```
~$ docker stack rm mysql

Removing service mysql_mysql

Removing service mysql_web

Removing network mysql_default

~$ docker stack services mysql

Nothing found in stack: mysql
```

Summary

This chapter introduced stacks, a Docker-native feature added in Docker 1.13. A stack is a collection of related services and is created using a stack file, which is defined in YAML format similar to the Docker Compose v3.x YAML syntax. This chapter concludes this book about Docker management design patterns. As new features are added to Docker, other design patterns may be used for developing Docker-native applications.

Index

■ V, W, X, Y, Z

Get the eBook for only $5!

Why limit yourself?

With most of our titles available in both PDF and ePUB format, you can access your content wherever and however you wish—on your PC, phone, tablet, or reader.

Since you've purchased this print book, we are happy to offer you the eBook for just $5.

To learn more, go to http://www.apress.com/companion or contact support@apress.com.

Apress®

All Apress eBooks are subject to copyright. All rights are reserved by the Publisher, whether the whole or part of the material is concerned, specifically the rights of translation, reprinting, reuse of illustrations, recitation, broadcasting, reproduction on microfilms or in any other physical way, and transmission or information storage and retrieval, electronic adaptation, computer software, or by similar or dissimilar methodology now known or hereafter developed. Exempted from this legal reservation are brief excerpts in connection with reviews or scholarly analysis or material supplied specifically for the purpose of being entered and executed on a computer system, for exclusive use by the purchaser of the work. Duplication of this publication or parts thereof is permitted only under the provisions of the Copyright Law of the Publisher's location, in its current version, and permission for use must always be obtained from Springer. Permissions for use may be obtained through RightsLink at the Copyright Clearance Center. Violations are liable to prosecution under the respective Copyright Law.

Printed in the United States
By Bookmasters